Incarceration JA:
A self-reflective analysis of my life

Stephen Graham was born in London, England and still lives in London. His days of crime and violence are long behind him. Today, Stephen is a multidisciplinary, educational service provider. He truly is a man of many talents. He has a degree in Sports Medicine, which he obtained in 2011, and is a qualified musculoskeletal rehabilitator, personal trainer, and filmmaker. Prior to this work, he published three books, two of which he wrote whilst facing time behind bars. Stephen also works with young people and families and offers various services within the global community.

This book was not written with the intent to glorify violence, but rather to explain the deep impact that trauma and unresolved issues can have on the psyche. It gives insight into how misdirected energy sends out a low-level vibration, wherein can be found great pain and sorrow. Not just for oneself, but also for anyone with whom one may come into contact. Unlike matter, yet through matter, energy transfers even faster; people it is time to heal.

Other titles by Stephen Graham

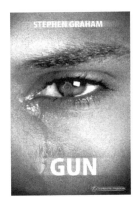

I'm a Gun

When a gun suddenly decides to share its story, it's time to listen. The use of street grammar and slangs sets the scene in this metaphorically written crime novel based on the life of Blacka, and the violent streets of London. The death of a love one stares Blacka, a young black male further down the criminal pathway, where violent crimes and terror are the norm.

Compatible Minds

This story tells the tale of destiny, determination, and the true meaning of love as an empowering force. Yolanda the up and coming barrister meets the love of her life, Donell. The story unfolds, in the depiction of deep and powerful love affair, between two people, who by faith stumbled across one another's paths.

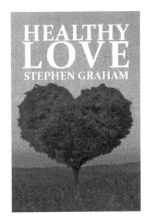

Healthy Love

Healthy Love is a compilation of poems that will take you the reader on a journey, one that will stare at you. Reflecting love and life; feeding you the mirror images of its attributions. Whilst giving meaning to circumstances and situations as the mind intakes nothing less than the powers of healthy love.

Incarceration JA:

A self-reflective analysis of my life

stephephengrahamprojects.com

First Edition

Book design by Damian Ryan
Photography by Damion Anniekie
Editorial by Khoisan Mensa

Acknowledgement

Firstly, I'd like to say my children have been an unshakable rock in my life, love you guys always and forever. Their mothers are truly appreciated; life has taught us many valuable lessons.

To all of my family and friends who helped me to unlock my past -you guys know who you are- and helped fill in gaps regarding situations, times and occurrences, I am truly thankful for your support. Your contributions did not go unnoticed.

I'd like to send a special thank you to Damian Ryan for all his support over the years; his belief and contributions, and our many ventures together are priceless. I would also like to thank Katie Harris, Ms Smikle, Michelle Grant, and Michael Gordon for contributions at different stages of the book. Thank you to Tiana Scott for helping to formulate the title. I give a massive thank you to Khoisan Mensa too, for the final proofreading and editing of this book.

Last but not least, I'd like to thank and show my appreciation to you the reader, may the words within these pages touch your heart, while enlightening you to the reality and circumstances that so many are faced with on various levels. Truth alone, inasmuch as true awareness and acceptance has the power to reshape our society, but it must first start within one's very own mind.

Dedication

To the memories of my loving mother, Janita Bathsheba Samuels,
sister, Lavinia (Pudding) Simone Palmer,
and my daughter, Abikara Shemay Janita Bathsheba Graham.
I feel your presence and support from the realm of the ancestors.

Contents

I've come face to face with death. Only God knows why I'm alive today. I believe everything happens for a reason and all my experiences have shaped me to be the man I am today.

Picture taken in General Penitentiary, Kingston Jamaica, 2005

Chapter 1:
Mixed Emotions

Whenever the thought of a hammock came to mind, I always visualised sunshine, sea and sand, beautiful trees that bear fruits and tropical weather; sipping Bacardi, Rum, Ice Tea or in my case Ital Juice. Back in those days scissors, comb and I were not friends, my dreadlocks were my companion; I was a strong believer in the Rastafarian way of life. Not that my perception of the importance of connecting with nature has changed that much, but that's another story. Such blissful images regarding hammocks were crushed the previous night when I entered prison. Daylight didn't seem like daylight, especially when the brightness of the sun shone through a little grille vent that made the worst substitute for a window. Awoken by the sun piercing into my eyes, a new day had begun, and I told myself countless days to go. My hammock was high above the ground, tied at one end to the small grille vent at the back of the cell, through which hardly any breeze entered the sweatbox of a cell, to which I was confined. The other end of the hammock was tied to the grille bars just above the cell door. It surely wasn't a picture of paradise, seashells and sand. It was a total nightmare. Before I could finish thinking about this disastrous new environment that would be my place of abode for a very long time, a voice broke my concentration "Foreigner" I heard another say, "Money yout." In the back of my mind, I wondered if he thought I had money because I was wearing Nike Air Max, designer jeans and a Fubu top when I arrived in hell, the evening before my unforgettable first day in Spanish Town District Prison; now known as St Catherine Adult Correctional Centre.

Honestly, from my point of view, only the ignorant inmates perceived life in that manner, believing that when you're from abroad you're rich. It's just a shame that there are so many of them in prison. Quickly putting that thought to one side, I looked down from my hammock. "Wah gwaan foreigner, yuh sleep well?" one of my cellmates, who introduced himself as Matterhorn asked. Matterhorn came across as a true Rasta, very chilled in character; he was dark, slim and had long locks.

"So weh yuh seh money, yuh get good sleep don't? No chink nah bite yuh inna dis cell, no chink nah deh." Said the other cellmate Alton. "Inna da right cell yuh drop my yout, seen money."

Alton was the opposite of Matterhorn, he had broad shoulders and was quite muscular, and he wore his hair very low. He had trouble written all over his face. I just knew we would never get along; he saw me as a gold mine and I saw him as problematic.

"Mi sleep good still yuh kno." I responded to them both. At that time in my life I had a strong Jamaican accent, for I had resided in Jamaica from 1991 to 1994, and most of my key associates on my return to the UK were Yardies. I kept close links with my mother's native country, but it was now 1999, and I was beginning to experience a piece of the Island in the Sun that would change my life forever.

From my hammock, I looked at my third cellmate who also wore dreadlocks. His action was a repeat of the evening before; he just nodded at me and resumed drawing. It didn't take me long to acknowledge this short, slim Rasta youth was humble and talented, not to mention the most dangerous one in the cell. Everything about his aura said he wasn't to be messed with. He was an inmate who had come to grips with his sentence. He was serving what I would have served if my case hadn't been dropped to manslaughter.

Lying back in my hammock I began thinking again. Thoughts of my daughter and son back in England, their mother, my family, my situation, everything meaningful to me ran through my mind. As I lay there, just mind travelling, I found myself back at the scene. Replaying the whole incident in my mind, I was bothered by one thought. Making sense of everything that happened from the moment I had taken another human's life, to the time I was arrested. All that had occurred in that brief moment in time was going to reflect on my life until I had mental closure regarding the whole situation, and what really led me to return to the murder scene after getting clean away. From one thing to another, my mind journeyed. To be honest, at that time, anger consumed me, and my brain was working overtime, which made me a bit of a loose cannon in the Lion's den. Ignorance had the better of me and to add fuel to the fire, knowingly and willingly, I allowed anger and frustration to nurture me, which like oil and water, was a terrible mix. Looking back at myself then, there was no substance of stability within me; I was mentally and emotionally unbalanced. I knew not what my future held. My life was in limbo. Twenty-five to life minimum ran through my mind constantly, tormented by thoughts of never seeing road again. One would have to have been in my predicament, to truly understand what I felt. I had given myself to my frustration allowing it to take control. I fuelled it with thoughts of the complete nightmare that had taken place and the months spent locked up in various police stations after my arrest, before being sent to Spanish Town prison and placed on Gibraltar Block, more commonly known as Remand Block, also abbreviated and referred to as GB3 and 4.

The funny but yet not so humorous thought was, where were such reflections of distress, horror and terror when I had gotten away with previous crimes? Looking back on myself today, I realise it took a serious knock back in my life for me to begin to reflect; on the other hand, who heard or understood my cry for help? Sadly, this is common in society, resulting in deeper, devastating outcomes. Not everyone survives or has a second chance to reanalyse their lives, or reflect on the life they've lived. Yet at the same time, understanding what led me down this dark path would be key to the non-judgemental mind. You see, there are many factors that taunt a child, causing someone like myself to do the things we do. Interrelating with the reader, my personal experience may just give you a greater insight into the life of someone around yourself who may be going through his or her own trauma and drama. Believe me, by judging and/or accusing, while not understanding the root of their problem, is more destructive than good. It is important to understand where so-called troubled children are coming from; you just may be able to save one if you answer their cry. You may just save a life. Unfortunately, no one saved me, well not in this realm anyway. My beloved once told me that my ancestors were fighting for me. Being the man I am today, awoken after attaining a level of self-consciousness and direction, I totally agree. To the realm of the ancestors, I give thanks.

I had never reflected on life as much as I did whilst incarcerated. Believe me when I say I reflected on everything, the good, the bad, and the unknown. It's amazing when you have more time on your hands than you wish. When your movement is restricted because you're banged up most of the day, the mind will really travel both in the realm attached to physical experiences and in the realm of fear, dreams and desires. Trust me, despite the number of books you can get your hands on to read and the electrical appliances that are there in your midst, or the amount of whatever it is you're smoking, the mind will travel endlessly when you're constantly face to face with the cell bars.

I couldn't believe what was happening to me, my children back in England were ripped out of my life. I just knew it would be a very long time until I saw them again, and that tormented me in ways I cannot express. As everything sunk in, my emotions changed, in fact they fluctuated, affecting the beating of my heart. Drowning in my anger, my emotions generated cramps in my inward parts that weren't out of fearfulness but out of sorrow, pain and longing. Mentally it was going to be rough, I just knew, because the way visitation worked on the Island in the Sun meant things weren't going to be any easier emotionally for me anytime soon. The Jamaican prison system and their policy, which applied to institutions such as Spanish Town and General Penitentiary, meant children under a certain age weren't allowed in the prison compound. What made it worse was that I didn't know where I stood concerning my case at that time, I was still on remand for murder, and had no clarity. The uncertainty made my blood boil; my future was non-existent. I couldn't set my mind towards anything but anger, anger fuelled me; all I wanted to know was where I stood. An unsettled mind is a dangerous mind, one's actions are unpredictable and so was I.

Saved again from my thoughts by the sound of keys rattling, one of my cellmates said to me, "Fly up, my yout, grab yuh piss-gal and come down."

I didn't look to see who it was calling to me, I just responded, "Mi no piss last night, mi bokkle empty."

"My yout, my yout, look hear nah."

I looked down and saw it was the artist looking up at me. "Yes iyah," I responded.

"Jump down my yout, an mek him show yuh di runnins," he was looking at and talking about Matterhorn. "Jus follow him seen."

"Yeh man." I responded.

What the artist was showing me was logical. Whether or not I had urinated that night in my bottle, it made sense to go and see where I'd have to throw it out in the future. After all, it was my first day in unfamiliar territory, knowing the rules that aided survival on the battlefield was important.

When looking back I wonder why I didn't urinate at all from the early evening to the following morning, which isn't natural, was it fear, anger, physical and/or mental discomfort. Or had it anything to do with the fact that I didn't drink any water the evening I came in. Unlike a machine, the human body has a way of shutting down certain functions in times of distress.

In the old Jamaican prisons like St Catherine Adult Correctional Centre and General Penitentiary, now referred to as Tower Street Adult Correctional Centre, there are no toilet facilities in the cells, so inmates use a plastic two litre fizzy bottle or the five-litre jug to urinate in. This was done by cutting a hole around the top of the bottle, big enough for the individual's hand to go into the bottle. This made it easy to wash it out with a piece of sponge and cheap prison issued washing powder, or crushed bathing soap mixed with water in a small plastic bottle which was commonly referred to as gal-soap.

The fact that we kept these plastic bottles to urinate in for a while, inmates took pride in keeping them clean. Me personally, I changed my bottle from time to time, but that wasn't on a monthly basis. These plastic bottles were considered a man's piss-gal; the institutionalised had terms for everything.

A Walkman was known as a walk-gal, the gym was called Kim, tin mackerel referred to as dutty-gal; not to mention, no two men in prison were ever located (enclosed in a cell) at any time, it was always three or more to a cell unless you had a cell for yourself. It was a clear sign that the general population wanted to be considered homophobic, which was a word many would use. However, with terms like piss-gal, walk-gal, dutty-gal and Kim, realistically it didn't sound female friendly to my ears, in fact it sounded a bit sexist and discriminative to me, which is why throughout my sentence, I didn't speak the prison lingo.

If you're wondering how and where under lock do inmates do *number two,* as there are no toilet facilities in the cells, then that's a whole different story with rules and regulations to that too.

Using the cell gate, I came down from my hammock and stood there with my cellmates as we waited for the warder to come and open the padlock. The cells were opened manually; there were no electrical door systems in place, none whatsoever. As I stood there, fear ran through my mind, from the crown of my head to the tip of my toes, adrenaline made its presence known as I felt it flowing in my bloodstream. It was my first morning in prison, for I had reached Prison Oval Rock the previous day just before the second and last lockdown. I thought about the inmate who had given me the knife mark across my chest whilst in Runaway Bay police station. Him and some of the other inmates that were at St Ann circuit court had also come up in the prison truck. My heart thumped within my chest, I was scared, I didn't know anyone from road on the block that I was on, and this made me extremely wary, and reluctant to step out of my cell. As the warder stood before my cell and opened the padlock, my adrenaline caused my heart to beat rapidly. I had already experienced in jail how easy it was for inmates to get weapons if they knew the right people. I couldn't help but wonder if he, or any of the guys I had fought with in St Ann, had friends on the block, not to mention if they ganged up on me all tooled up, I wouldn't stand a chance. Gripping hold of my fear, I geared myself for the worst and was prepared to die fighting; yet in the same breath I stepped out my cell without fear. Looking back at that incident and various others in my life, I truly accept that even when I'm fearful I'm equally as vigorous, the strength that can arise from a fearful mind once one's thoughts are put into perspective, are highly powerful. Nothing happened that day between him and me. In fact, nothing happened between us for a long time. It seemed he had no real friends on the block, in fact, neither of them did. Nevertheless, I always had him in mind. He had marked my flesh. In my eyes, he desired my life, even if he was hyped or forced to do what he had done, in my mind, he was a marked man. You see, when you have nothing and no-one but your anger as a companion, human life becomes of very little value, and the thought of revenge that ticks continuously in one's mind is sweeter than the thought of freedom. Well at least that's how I felt back then, but then we know where my mind was in those days. I wasn't always using my foresight in the best and most positive way; although there were times in the past when my ability to think and play chess moves was truly different and impactful, allowing me to do and act in ways that I prefer not to explain.

What I witnessed later that morning clarified what I already knew. Just in front of the outside toilets, a man accidentally bounced another inmate, who was also queuing to empty his piss-bottle. A tiny bit splashed out onto another inmate's leg. From the hips of inmates came out 'three-star ratchets' (knives), 'Jammers' (prison made shanks) and ice picks, a stabbing spree was about to begin. Warders quickly intervened and no one was seriously harmed. By this time, I had stepped back and was watching everything and everyone, with one thought in mind and that was that I must get myself a weapon if I was going to survive my prison sentence.

I had followed Matterhorn back to the block and waited for him as he put his piss-bottle back in the cell, then we began to talk. When I think about it, Matterhorn was kind of cool. We got talking and he began filling me in with all the information I needed to know about prison. While we were talking, the orderlies returned with breakfast, consisting of bread and tea, or should I say dough and black water. One would think being on an island like Jamaica where good Caribbean food is the pride of the people, the prison system wouldn't be too far off from good traditional cooking, I mean well prepared and spicy, believe me it was far from it. At times, we would have the privilege of milk in our tea. On certain days, we would get egg, or poorly made cornmeal porridge with our three slices of bread. On special days, with tea, we would get hard food and Mackerel, or sometimes instead, it was liver or kidney, none of which was cooked fit for human consumption.

I had received my tea and bread in my plastic cup and container. Prison prohibits iron and glass instruments. The only glass allowed was mirrors, and if an inmate was caught with a broken mirror, it was confiscated. I'm sure I don't need to explain why. To be honest, I don't even know if mirrors were legal. Quite a few inmates had them though, but then with the right links in prison, what could an inmate *not* get? All metal cutlery was illegal and against prison rules, but that didn't mean an inmate wouldn't have them in his possession, it just meant that if you had cutlery or anything illegal, hide it and only use it during lockdown or risk the chance of being caught.

After washing my cup and container at the outside sink and replacing them in the cell, I walked back towards the exit of the building. The clear blue skies captured my eyes. As I looked down again and stepped outside, I remember myself looking at the old beat down sink and shaking my head. I just couldn't believe this was going to be my life for a long time. For a second my heart sunk, a lifeless feeling came over me. It's literally impossible to describe how I really felt, but dead inside is a good way to start. I envied the birds, wishing I could just fly away and escape the reality that tormented me.

The hygiene facilities on the block were a joke; everything was outside, meaning each inmate had to fill and store water to drink while under lock. Imagine, only one single sink for over a hundred inmates, so inmates had to wait their turn to wash out their eating utensils every time. The waiting game could be problematic, especially if someone decided that they weren't going to wait and were under the illusion they were made out of iron, thinking they're the man of steel and wanting to prove something, or worst-case scenario, just woke up angry and ignorant which was quite common, all hell could break loose.

There was also a small pipe used to wash out our piss-bottles, and a standing pipe right at the back of the block next to the fence that separated Remand and Death Row block, which was used as a shower. The queue at that shower pipe was also a location for the display of ghetto superheroes and local hotheads, whose acting roles definitely weren't going to win them a Grammy any time soon. The set up was ridiculous; the institution's design kept people agitated, not rehabilitated. Considering that the basic necessities of life were only supplied within limits, how could one truly believe that they could just do their time and go home, in a system literally designed to make one as uncomfortable as possible. Not that it made a difference. The shower stand at the back of the block could also have been used to fill one's plastic drinking bottle. However, if the person under the shower made you wait, not feeling the need to stand aside for you, even if he was soaping his body and therefore didn't need the pipe at that moment, then there would again be the potential for a physical altercation. The set up was, and is, totally destructive and psychologically distressing, not to mention depressing.

Unfortunately, ignorance rules, and within the few seconds of me looking up again into the clear skies hoping the nightmare would end, loud voices followed by a scream snapped me back to reality. I saw blood dripping from between someone's fingers as he held his stomach, shouting in rage as he cursed and swore. I remember him saying, "Pussy, watch, bet mi kill yuh pussy." Standing there, I just stared and watched, as he came running in my direction. My first instinct was to move out of his way as he ran into the block, his T-shirt covered with blood. In no time, he returned. High on adrenaline, dripping blood with each step, this dark, tall, slim inmate ran out of the building; one could only imagine what was going through his mind. At the very first sight of his weapon, warders rushed towards him and began to beat him relentlessly with their batons. In his hand was a long rusty prison made jammer, wrapped with thin strips of old clothing for a handle. That morning both inmates were beaten by warders, and the stabbed inmate was taken to the prison hospital. Nothing made me surer at that point that I needed a weapon of my own.

That night before I slept, thoughts of my loved ones came constantly to mind as I thought about my situation, while dreading what tomorrow would bring.

The following morning started with what would be a part of my daily routine for an unknown period of time as I went and emptied my piss-bottle, then waited for my three slices of bread and black water. It was my second day in prison and the tension in the atmosphere on the block could have been cut with a knife. Throughout both times we were let out of our cells I kept myself to myself. It was the ending of the second and final lockdown. Angry and depressed is an understatement regarding how I really felt. It wasn't fear of people that gripped me, at that point and time in my life, how I saw it in my mind was that the answer to the problem pertaining to prisoners was plain and simple, all I needed was a weapon. A weapon was the answer on a physical level, but inside I felt something gripping at me, pulling me to further destruction, I didn't need spiritual intuition or any intuition to know it was my surroundings that weighed heavily on my soul. The vibration I was in the midst of was extremely low, engulfed in negative energy, daylight seemed like darkness, I felt like I was sucked into a black hole, a place where brightness never shone. I remember stepping into my cell and climbing into my hammock before looking down at my cellmates and shaking my head. The thought of being in a cell the size of a box room with three other grown men, cramped in this hot and sweaty little place I'd been confined in. Not to mention, the scent of human body heat, which literally could be felt rising from the ground and bouncing off the walls. It just frustrated and angered me; I just couldn't believe this was going to be my place of abode for a very long time; I felt rotten. In my anger I just laid still, like a corpse, I lay frozen, thinking deeply until I fell asleep.

Chapter 2:
Trials & Tribulations

Thoughts about the many months I spent in various police stations in St Ann, back in late 1998, before being shipped off early 1999 to Spanish Town prison, were visual. In police lock up, otherwise known as Jailhouse, new inmates that had no respected connections on the inside, or weren't known or respected themselves on the streets, always faced a challenge, their will and fate was always tested. The successful ones were those that had the heart of a warrior and would rather die than be treated as less than a man. On more than one occasion, I can recall an inmate that had died defending himself. It was an individual's determination to fight back, which earned him his respect.

Certain unsuccessful inmates became modern day slaves, taking turns with the bucket carriers, relocated into the grounser (scum) cell, and stripped of their money; which I thought was quite silly, because if a man is now considered an outcast, why take anything from him? Double standards were the norm regarding jailhouse rules, which made it that much more dangerous and confusing, as there were no set principles.

During the months spent in various police stations in St Ann, I witnessed unbelievable cruelty take place with some new inmates, their first night behind bars would undoubtedly affect them psychologically forever.

Inmates were beaten, and the unfortunate ones were told to sleep on the grille. I mean literally, an inmate was forced to sleep standing up, holding onto the cell bars. There, that individual would spend the whole night. If anyone indulging in this foolish behaviour heard the slightest noise of the grille shaking, or if he fell onto the inmates sleeping on the floor (that's if he was capable of sleeping up there to begin with), it would result in a continuous beating until a police officer came and intervened. Unless alternatively, someone like myself told the inmates to stop beating on him. To be honest, there were very few of us spread out along the block that showed such compassion. I guess the excitement and joy of 'entertainment' caused many to indulge in this foolish behaviour.

Thinking about what others went through, led me to think about my own experience in jail. Twice, I had my own faith seriously tested, but for different reasons. According to the word on the streets, a hit was on my life due to the youth who had lost his by my hands, as well as some other things that had taken place in the parish of St Ann during the years I spent living in the countryside. As a foreigner, I had made quite a reputation for myself on the Island in the Sun.

On one occasion, a police officer removed me from the cell I was in and transferred me to the cell next door. I knew something was going to happen and was prepared. It wasn't just intuition, body language speaks volumes, and their control dials were turned to max. Two edgy looking youths in the cell rushed me, and by the grace of God, I only received a dull mark across my chest, which was the result of an attack gone wrong with a jailhouse made weapon. In my heart I knew if they weren't wary of me due to my reputation at that time, they could have done me serious damage, even taken my life. Half-heartedness and lack of conviction in their actions, gave me the split second I needed to react. The same night they transferred me back to my original cell, before certain high-ranking officers came back to work their morning shifts. This left me and still has me believing that specific police, not all, but some wanted me dead.

One thing I do know is if it had been a successful hit, I wouldn't have been the first inmate to be set up by police and killed in custody.

The build-up leading to the second attempt on my life was overshadowed by what seemed to be an in-house war, when really it was a direct hit, an attempt to rob me of my physical existence on this earth. I remember for days, tension on the block rose due to foolishness, which at first seemed like vibes between two cells. A youth from one cell was transferred to my cell for his supposed safety. Hours later that individual and an inmate from my cell began arguing due to something said from another cell. As I stood up between them to make peace, I was stabbed in my lower back with a blunt but rusty piece of iron. Thank God it hadn't been properly sharpened. I was able to turn on it, giving me the opportunity to fight for my life. The fight didn't last long, as the other inmates broke it up very quickly once they saw I got the better of the inmate. I was taken to St Ann's Bay hospital under police guard where I received an injection in my bottom and had my wound dressed. Later that evening, they returned me to my cell. By the time I returned from hospital, the inmate who had tried to kill me had been transferred from Runaway Bay police station and taken elsewhere. Within the week, I was taken back to the hospital, after other inmates and I created a scene on the block demanding the police attend to my wound, which had begun oozing pus and discoloured blood. At the hospital, I received a further two injections, one in my arm and again another in my bottom, and they redressed my wound too.

Within the first month of being in the police station, the British Embassy had paid me a visit. My family in England had contacted the British Embassy notifying them of my circumstance. Prisoners Abroad, an organisation established to support British inmates incarcerated on foreign soil, were also notified, and I believe this was done through the Embassy.

As a British inmate, I received roughly forty to forty-five pounds every time the British Embassy made their visit, thanks to Prisoners Abroad. That supportive income was one visit I always looked forward to getting every six to eight weeks. Not to mention that I'd receive money from my family back in England through the Embassy, so I was capable of eating well. To be honest, no matter how much one has behind bars, it can never take away the cry for freedom. I felt like a caged animal, a well fed one.

In those early days, I learnt quickly that I couldn't depend on certain family members in Jamaica, not that they were obligated to support me; it was my situation, my problem. No one had sent me to St Ann, nor implied that I should leave Kingston and go to country; my travel and actions were all my own choices. Could I be angry with them for not coming to see me regularly in jail? Of course not, even though in my ignorance at times I was. However, the truth is, I had created my own bed and now had to sleep in it, so I looked forward to seeing the Embassy, and if or whenever I saw anyone, it was cool.

Supposedly, the jail forbids one from having money in one's possession, so to make their corrupt selves look good, every time the Embassy visited, the police made me sign the money into a red book. This book logged all possessions belonging to criminals, as they would call us. This really didn't make much sense. On days when others or myself signed for money, whether it was a police officer, cleaner woman, or someone's family member who was willing to shop for us, they not only gave the officer on duty whatever we had asked them to buy, but also the change. This could be hundreds if anyone had signed out for a nanny (500J$), or even two nannies; the officer would then hand us our belongings as well as the money. To be honest, there was no logic to their rules, but then again, they say rules were made to be broken, and the line drawn between inmates, police and prison officers were made by the individuals, or should I say, made up as they went along.

The system was corrupt, the police were more crooked than we inmates were, but when you're getting what you want, at the end of the day there's no complaining, you just need to get on with it. It's only when they start messing with you that shit gets ugly, and things became pretty ugly for me.

Having certain police officers disliking you from your youthful days, threatening to kill or lock you up, doesn't win you any favours. In fact, it can make your life a misery once you're in their house, which is what a few officers didn't just *intend to do* but did to me.

On various occasions in jail, the cunning and deceitfulness displayed by members of the Jamaican police force prevailed. Physically and psychologically, they made my life hard, especially Runaway Bay police staff. They usually had two main theories for why my money could not be found as I went from station to station during my jail time in St Ann. Their excuses were that I spent all that I had, while they themselves signed it out, or that they couldn't find my name on the register.

Unforgettable was the day I returned from a court appearance; the judge had told me that he was going to remand me for a further four months until next circuit court. I remember thinking I'm heading off to prison now where I'll be held on remand and every penny counts. Looking back on it now, that day was the beginning of my long-suffering. They say God gives no man more than he can bear, I believe in that saying, but what I didn't know was that I had the mental strength to endure such hardship; I learnt this with time. According to an officer at the desk the day I was leaving the police station, I had already signed for my money. To make it worse, a few of my underpants, tops, a pair of jeans and trainers had disappeared from my bag. The reason for me travelling light from Kingston was that I only intended to spend a few days, if necessary, in St Ann to sort out my son's documents and passport, neither of which I got to do. Seeing my travelling bag almost empty, instantly I lost my temper and began to create a scene at the main desk, not that it got me anywhere, the prison truck was leaving, what could I do. I had been ordered to run my remand in prison. I was heading there without any money, a few underpants, one T-shirt, a pair of flip-flops, a pair of Bally shoes in a bag, the clothes on my back and a pair of Nike sneakers on my feet. I just knew times were going to be hard, and began preparing myself mentally, but the suffering and pain I incurred in my early days whilst on remand in prison I wouldn't wish on my worst enemy. What seemed dull now darkened, suddenly darkness overshadowed me, life's test is different for everyone, no two men's road to light and happiness is the same. I know that now.

As stated earlier, the travel from Kingston up to St Ann was to look for my son. If it were not for the fact that at that appointed time, I saw the journey necessary to make, I wouldn't have gone there. That parish and I seemed to have a bad connection, at least at that time I believed so. The countless things that occurred in St Ann are enough to write a book in itself. On numerous occasions, I've come face to face with death. Only God knows why I'm alive today. It was one parish wherein I believed I had no luck. Then on the flip side, I believe everything happens for a reason and all my experiences have shaped me to be the man I am today. Now, looking back at myself as a youth in Jamaica, knowing the energy projected via the frame of mind I was in, and that for every action is a reaction, can I honestly say St Ann has had a negative impact on my life? In all reality, no I can't. My actions in St Ann manifested the drama that came time after time. Although so many bad things occurred with me there, this parish that can be found on the north coast of the island has brought forth the likes of Bob Marley and Marcus Garvey, as my beloved so pleasantly reminded me, so surely it can't be the parish to blame for all of my misfortunes. Undoubtedly, St Ann itself is blessed, and having self-reflected on my actions as a youth, I created problems for myself, some of which followed me for many years and contributed to my incarceration.

I was now in prison with less than nothing to maintain myself but my dignity, and to be honest, to many, that didn't mean shit. I had limited clothing with me. I literally had nothing. The basic necessities a man needs to maintain hygiene were now low in supplies and I was praying for a miracle visit. Instead of a miracle, I received a curse. Within days of my arrival at Spanish Town District Prison, a bad-minded inmate stabbed something through the bubble of my Nike Air sneakers and slashed the side of both feet. How I felt mentally at that time, if I had a weapon and knew who did it, I would have killed him or them without a second thought. To me, the worst thing a man can ever do is to mess around with someone who's filled with anger and confined to unfamiliar surroundings. I felt like a cat trapped in a corner ready to attack, and believe me, controlled fear is a powerful tool; it strikes hard, hits fast, and shows no remorse.

What I predicted came true. My worst nightmare became a reality. Within the first week of my arrival at St Catherine Adult Correctional Centre, Alton and I had a fight under lock. It shouldn't even be considered a fight. Alton had pulled out a knife and then punched me in my face. God knows tears came to my eyes; and rage engulfed me. Until then, I didn't know that a million and one thoughts could run through the human mind in a split second. I stared at the knife in his hand; I wanted to kill him. I looked at my cellmates who were just staring. I was trying to read their facial expressions. They gave no indication of being for him or against me, which made me more on edge. I didn't know anyone on my block at that time, and that made it worse.

Something inside me just clicked, and I went for him. The whole event occurred in a moment. Matterhorn jumped between us, and the artist held him. The artist told me to go back up into my hammock. That night I was unable to sleep, all I could think about was taking Alton's life.

Looking back on it, God knows best. If they hadn't intervened, the situation could have gone either way. He could have killed or seriously wounded me, but if death weren't my companion and I was lucky to disarm him, whether wounded or not, one thing I know is, I would have been facing another murder charge. At that time in my life, I was consumed with anger and accompanied by rage and doubt. With such mental uncertainties regarding how I felt about life, it's not even questionable. At that time, I would have killed him with no second thought of tomorrow's consequences.

Even though I would reflect upon and miss my life and family on the outside. To understand my thought pattern back then, one would have had to be living in my skin; or have experienced physical and emotional drama to the point of physiological trauma like what I was going through, to comprehend my feelings. I was a loose cannon.

Alton had accused me of dripping urine down from my bottle, which hung high next to the hammock and directly above where Alton lay. Whether it was Alton's own urine or mine, which had stained his sheet during the darkness of the night, either way, this was the excuse Alton used to initiate an altercation.

That night I lay in my hammock, fuelled with anger and unable to sleep as I thought about Alton lying there unharmed in the midst of the dream world; torturing myself as I slightly turned my head to see below me, capturing his feet in my peripheral vision. Wishing for a weapon, driving myself insane, I wanted to kill. What made it worse, causing my blood to boil, were thoughts of a previous incident, awakening a trigger in me. Sleep was unimaginable for me. There was no way to find peace of mind at that time, as my mind travelled back to myself being locked up in Runaway Bay police station in St Ann. I had stabbed an inmate, which led to him throwing a bucket of human urine into my cell. The interrelationship between the current and past situation were not too far apart. Very different circumstances, but when anger sets in, all manner of things run through one's mind, especially things that share a form of similarity no matter how small, this I call the trigger; willed by an emotional experience. One thing I know is, when anger sets in, everything seems interrelated. By the mere fact that the circumstances had some relation to urine and a knife, they were interrelated to me, very interrelated. As I lay there with my eyes closed, I burst out laughing, waking up my cellmate who asked me why I was laughing so loud. After telling him nothing, just reminiscing on the past, he went back to sleep. I believe Alton was awake but didn't want to talk with me. Reliving the memory of the altercation with some Montego Bay youths and myself in St Ann had caused me to laugh, in a weird but cruel way the memory felt good. I guess it was because I knew what I was capable of.

The thought of the past ran through my mind like rivers of water, memories of my encounter with those Mo Bay guys were crystal clear. We had been arguing for days over foolishness. They were supposed to be related to some big drug man's family, honestly, I don't know if they were and at that time didn't care. I was under lock and they were on the passage talking breeze amongst themselves. A man's thought and heart is unseen unless he reveals it, which I didn't. I did the unexpected. I made peace with them, luring them in. Like a fool, one of them came close to my cell grille. Instantaneously I grabbed him, pulled out my sharpened toothbrush and poked him in his chest. Reacting, he held the arm that I used to grab him and stepped backwards, jarring my shoulder joint on the grille in the process. Again, it was another reckless move. Realistically, I should have bided my time and hoped to get him on the passage one day, but that was my irrational mind working. The youth looked down at his chest. Blood trickled down his naked upper body. He cursed and cursed while I smiled fiendishly at him, with one intention in my mind. Surely, he could read my mind now and knew my heart, the look in my eyes said I wanted him dead. Grabbing the nearest thing to him, he picked up the piss-bucket. My smile disappeared instantly. I knew what was coming. I jumped behind my cellmates and held up a piece of clothing to cover my face. He ducked my cell with the bucket soaking up nearly everything. The police came on the block, put them in their cell and then let us out to clean up our own. I didn't wait for the police to leave the passage before I

32

returned a dose of urine drenching their cell. I told the police if they didn't move him and his friends, I was going to kill them any chance I got and they were saying similar things. Looking back on it now, knowing how certain police in Runaway Bay station didn't like me, I'm surprised I wasn't beaten for it that day. Instead, they moved the guys to another station. Recalling the whole incident up in my hammock, every little detail had me wishing, thinking about committing murder as I thought about what had just happened to me. To be honest I was so angry I don't remember if I even slept that night.

What I do know is that the next morning to my surprise, as our cell door opened, a stranger walked over to Alton as we all stepped out. The two of them began arguing because of what happened with me during the night. All of a sudden, the man hit Alton on his head with a brick and the two of them started fighting. Alton received a buss-head, and his scalp tore open. A quick reaction from prisoners and warders, and the fight ended. Deep down in my heart I rejoiced at the retribution, however slightly disappointed that he wasn't killed. Looking back on it now, I see life in a totally different way. Back then, I was blinded by anger, hatred and revenge. Having changed my outlook on life, I only hope that like me, Alton is no longer a troubled individual.

The man who had fought my war that morning was known as Foreigner. He had explained to the warders why he did it, and showed them my face. I had a coco (bump/bruise) to the corner of my eye, so the warders moved Alton and put him on a different block. I thanked Foreigner for what he had done for me. I had made a friend, but still I chose to remain a loner. At that period of my incarceration, my heart just wouldn't allow me to connect or trust anyone, I was filled with anger and just wanted to be alone.

Believe me when I say, what happened between Alton and I, was just the beginning of my problems. At that time, I was considered a broke foreigner or deportee as some prisoners would call me, and because of my circumstances, trouble followed me. In Jamaica, money buys friends in prison, and because I had none, I found that many people on the block would take sides with other inmates against me, or anyone else who was broke like me, and not getting their regular long bag. Even when the individual was wrong, it was the 'licky licky' (greedy tendencies) mentality and strategy to befriend an inmate and gain a reward. It's unbelievable to witness how weak the human mind can become and display itself when under pressure. The things some people do, yet they still have the audacity to call themselves 'bad man' and 'big man' in prison, it's just unreal. Realistically, it's not that confusing if an individual allows himself to become institutionalised, for he then becomes a part of the bullshit, and therefore no longer aware of what's right from wrong, or the reality of life and the outside world.

In regards to myself, my body had been confined, but my mind, *never*. In spite of my anger within, deep down I couldn't change. My personality displayed my character, it was my identity, I was whom I would always be, and therefore refused to take anything from strangers.

When you lack basic necessities in prison, life can become extremely hard and mentally challenging. You either hold your suffering or become a beggar, which is the easiest and fastest way to grouns (become looked down upon). Alternatively, an inmate can become someone's puppet and I refused to be a yes man to anyone or see life through another man's eyes. Because of my mentality and my circumstances, my first five months on Remand Block were hell. For some reason or the other, I had not seen the British Embassy, upon which, at that time I depended. It began to seem like even they were letting me down. I argued and fought constantly due to allegations made against me, which led to me being transferred from cell to cell. I moved around like an alley cat. Even an alley cat can find peace, but myself, I found none. These allegations ranged from such petty, stupid things, for example, I snore too loudly, I don't bathe, to I'm unhygienic and smell; all of which looking back on it, I now find funny. When I think about it, some inmates just wanted a bit of the action, entertainment led by childish behaviours helped pass time in a place where there is not much to do. The reality of the situation was, they were making *my life* uncomfortable.

Despite the bullshit allegations made up because I had nothing to offer, everyone on the block in their hearts knew that I always kept my 'prison issue' (free sanitary products) before I began to get visits and was in the position to give away my monthly prison issue. It consisted of one toilet roll, two red soaps and a cup of fab (prison washing power). Throughout my period of suffering, I refused to sell my prison issue for my nose. During those times, I had eased up on smoking. I refused to sell myself short or beg. I can proudly say, though at that time I had nothing, I kept myself clean, showered daily, and whenever I was down to my last soap or piece, my three slices of bread became my insurance. I would exchange it with an inmate, telling him to take my bread for two to three days, sometimes a week straight and give me his prison issue. I figured I could easily go without bread in the morning and just drink the tea, because I knew before lockdown we would get fed, and then be fed again just before second lockdown.

At that time in my life, I had dreadlocks. I was a sure follower of the Rastafarian faith. Before I came to prison, I was an Italist; flesh and blood would not pass my lips. However, when suffering became unbearable, and with so many reasons not to befriend anyone, I preferred to return to eating flesh and define my body. I had strong emotions and was unwilling to fight against my views. Had I done so, I would not only have been sucking up to someone else, but also fighting my very own principles and that which I perceived to be right, and I couldn't do this.

In those days, there was a tall slim Rasta man on the block who was known by the name Nia. I find it pretty hard to forget how much he added to my pain. At the very same time that I was going from cell to cell due to fighting and the allegations that were drawn against me, he used to throw his word after me because I was eating meat off the 'tray' (prison food), "Rastaman no eat meat, fire bon a false dread!" he would say. During those moments it hurt me, I'd be in denial if I said it didn't, maybe deep down I expected better of him, but then expectations of others can also be our downfall. Nevertheless, the fact remains that he was getting regular visits and I wasn't. I used to tell myself, if he was so righteous, then when he used to cook his own food, not that I would have ate from him anyway, but why didn't he offer, try help out a fellow brother in need. No, not Nia, he would play Garnett Silk or Bob Marley and bon fire on the whole block, especially me. I remember he too drew an allegation against me saying I smelled, which was funny because most of the guys that he would deal with would shower about two to three times a week, using terms like, "Man nah sleep wid no gal so man nah fresh every day, man no stink." To be honest, the scent of BO was extremely high on some inmates, and yet I'd see him and them together, I'm sure he never once told them how badly they stank.

Those early months into my time on Remand Block, without doubt, anger had clouded my judgement. I wasn't thinking clearly or straight, and I would push away anyone who tried to get close to me. My actions caused me to inflict more pain on myself than I needed to, but then again it won me respect as the months went on. Therefore, there was logic to my madness. Inmates began to nod their heads to me, I would nod back, but I hardly ever spoke. I was consumed with anger; it was eating me up. The more I thought about my surroundings and all that I was missing, my children, the life I had, the progressive things I was doing in the community, the more it angered me. For I had begun to ease off the streets back in London before being locked up, I had my own little clothing business which I predicted would grow, and the way things were going, it would have. I had the communities' support, from South Kilburn all the way to Church Road and Stonebridge. Northwest wasn't so divided in the 90's, and then there was international support. A French company were interested in my designs, and I had grown the business so that black bookshops were stocking my clothes. Out of my profits, I had given away just over a hundred of my T-shirts and some sleeveless bomber jackets when I went to South Africa, along with other stuff that I could afford to buy from my legal hustle, believe me, things were going well. Then there was also the music side of my business; but all those dreams died when I was locked up. To be honest, I don't really know what angered me more back then; could it have been the fact that I was unable to see what would have become of my ventures, or the fact that all the positive that I was trying to do came to nought. The more I thought, the more I became angry. Street life is crazy like that, one minute you're feeling great, the next you can hit rock bottom and have to climb back up again. The reality is not everyone has the ability, strength or chance to. That's the plain truth. RIP all my friends, which are way too many to count; lost to the streets or the prison system doing life, some serving life without parole, others receiving sentences amounting to more years than they have life left in them. This is the reality of the streets. Soldiers gone but not forgotten, all defeated by the illusive game we were playing, this I've come to understand.

Chapter 3:
Adaptation & Change

My life had become one big routine with constant reprogramming. Although my actions of being a loner and standing up for myself began to win me respect, it also made me experience so many different cells on the one block. Arguing and fighting constantly, I wasn't going to take anything lying down, it just wasn't my character. I had nothing to give, so then leave me the hell alone I thought, and stood for what I believed in. For every cell I transferred into, the rules and regulations of how it functioned were different. Some cells were washed out more frequently than others, some never washed out at all during the time I was located therein. In some cells people lived as one, in others, like cat and dog. Some inmates allowed number two in their cell. This was otherwise known in the Jamaican prison system as *ride*, because the way in which it was carried out it was similar to being on a motorbike, in a squat position. In other cells, to do a number two was prohibited; you better hold that until morning or be ready to die fighting or kill to do it. Then there is the hygiene situation, some inmates were on top of their game washing out their cells regularly, re-papering the walls or just painting it and having no paper at all, believe me the latter is the best thing one can do; and then you got the filthy ones, and those were the ones I hated more than anything. As for the cells where inmates didn't give a shit about their walls, damn, the germs that multiplied in and on them. There was a change of mindset every time to adjust to my surroundings. Whether it was regarding where I lay my head, or just how I dealt with others. Things changed, changing constantly and frequently, especially because I wasn't taking crap from anyone.

Even in my anger, I knew I had to stay psychologically above the pitfalls of the system, meaning adapt, yet disengage from my situation; and believe me the Jamaican prison system is unpredictable. Therefore, the mind needs to adjust and adapt at the blink of the eye. Some would call it survival mode, but to stay on top of things, one had to do more than just survive. I could never accept prison lingo, but I became comfortable with the order, which goes against human nature and the brain's wiring regarding freedom of movement. Yet for the sake of one's sanity, any other choice but acceptance of the situation, and to rise above it, could be detrimental. It's not hard to understand how replication can become habitual, even in the worst of situations. You see, to make the best of a bad situation one needs to accept, let go and allow the mind to be free, truly free, yet ground oneself in the process. While all this adaptation and letting go is occurring in a single stage, it's also paving the way for a new beginning. But that depends on the individual. Looking back at what I was going through, it was the preparation period for a new chapter in my life. It was not only preparing me for my current situation behind bars, but for the outside world. Not that I knew freedom would one day come my way, as I was still facing a murder charge at that time, but God knew better. Now I'm not saying that one needs to go to prison to learn, although individuals like Mandela and Brother Malcolm did, and came out to do extraordinary things. I'm not comparing myself to them; our relation is the reflection time, you see, that's the key. The importance of self-reflection is seriously consequential for growth and development. Unfortunately, we are never taught of our greatness within and society is so speedily paced, extremely fast going. If one is never taught to look within, then we will go even faster in the wrong direction to achieve what we think we need, when in reality, one only needs to step back and take a moment to reflect from within. To be honest to myself, because of my stubborn ways I couldn't see myself reflecting to the level I needed to whilst on road, but hopefully you the reader, will comprehend the importance of such actions. So, you see, for me prison was necessary, it was my training ground. I was very hard-headed and needed that experience. I've come to that realisation. I know I'm not the only one that feels this way; there are those who've been incarcerated and totally changed their thought patterns, and are doing well in society. If asked, they would say their greatness is their alignment with self. For those still incarcerated that can relate, looking forward to, or hoping to be free to manifest themselves on a higher frequency, no longer psychologically trapped; free souls destined to fulfil earth's journey in this time, I wish them all the best. Personally, without actually knowing it at the time, my soul refused to procrastinate with my destiny for another cycle. I came to the realisation that I was no longer willing to be my greatest and only obstacle. I had to escape the confinement of a physical and spiritual illusion, emotionally being broken down and rebuilding myself, life is a continuous journey of learning. Now I understand why my life was like this, and so will you as I continue to share my experiences.

Like everyone else excluding those who lived and worked on the orderlies block (inmates that work), we were let of our cell twice a day, once in the morning and again in the afternoon, depending if a search was taking place on one of the blocks. Warders had a regular habit of carrying out random searches, looking for drugs, mobile phones and weapons.

Most illegal items were kept in a Chappy (a hole in the wall or floor) and if found, depending on the inmate, he may have gotten beaten, had time added on to his sentence, or even both; but then there was also the possibility that no charges or punishment may follow. In prison, there are different levels to respect, this can also be said for the outside world too, whether we're referring to the street or social status. One really must ask, is it respect, or is it based on opportunity or fear? The notion of fear isn't always about the threat of physical harm to an individual; it can go beyond this to intimidation through exposure. *Secrets are powerful weapons.*

Depending on the inmate and warder relationship, or should I say the respect, *opportunity* or *fear* would reflect in the outcome when contraband was found. Regarding prison, this form of respect could be attained in many ways, personal, road, jailhouse, financial, blackmail or a combination of the latter. The reality is, personal positions can create favouritism and at the same time prevent situations too. Like the world itself, jailhouse is corrupt and doesn't abide by the very laws it sets out. Hypocritical systems.

In those days there was an extreme level of conditioning within the prison, especially on my block GB 3 and 4; inmates could be quite immature to be honest the mentality was crazy. If a man dropped a clothing item or anything on the ground outside, or in the passage way on the block by accident it was considered that garment, food or drink container had 'bow' (was no good) and you know what that meant, don't pick it up or you're gone with it. People looked down on you for the silliest of things. It was so easy to end up in confrontation over what seemed so irrelevant, but when the mind is conditioned to accept an illusion, it then becomes a dangerous reality, and if so many are wired in the same manner, this illusion grows and the false reality seems the norm. Not until that chain of thought is broken can things truly change. The sad thing back then was, so many weren't in the frame of mind to break loose and this mentality caused verbal abuse, bullying, fights and even the loss of life, all because of practises sown to reap havoc. Who implanted this destructive seed I used to ask myself, witnessing what others went through, and at times, being on the receiving end of false judgement, but my character back then was very stubborn, to a point, it was my strength to resist and my resistance undoubtedly created changes over time.

By this time, my beautiful white Bally shoes were filthy and utterly destroyed, but in my state of poverty, there was no way I was throwing them away. I kept them, using them as sliders. I had no time for pride. The sneakers, destroyed by an unknown inmate or inmates, had come in handy. I was now wearing them, they felt extremely uncomfortable, but life gave me no option. The few underpants I had needed changing, they were discoloured and the elastic around the waist of some weren't as fitting as I would have desired, but when constant washing of any garment occurs, reformation is naturally going to occur. I had now only one pair of jeans and the same Fubu top I wore when I entered the prison. My t-shirt had disappeared. Nobody seemed to know where it went. I had left it on the fence to dry and someone must have taken it. I guess to be either spiteful or just for a laugh. But what's a joke to someone is death to somebody else; I don't have to explain further what was going through my mind. The anger I felt was indescribable, but I held it down. I was trying my best to get control of my emotions, still fuelled by my lost livelihood and circumstances. Not knowing what was to be, was worse than being sentenced. Nothing was a certainty. I was living in limbo; more like hell. Temptation and torment, not just through the things I was going through, but also the evil thoughts that ran through my mind regarding other inmates, or the thought of just befriending someone to gain reward or access to a phone, but my stubbornness would never allow me to. When I think of it, it may not have been my stubbornness at all, but more my self-respect. I may not have been the perfect child growing up, but an opportunist I was never. Call that pride, I call it dignity. As my mother would say, "Even a thief has dignity."

The state of suffering I was facing, kept me in no position to throw anything away, nor take anything for granted. The memories of my tribulation ignite my strength today. The sneakers and Bally shoes I had broken down the back of and wore as sliders, came in extremely handy, because I learnt in jail that most of those plastic flip-flops, despite what make they were, whether name brand or not, didn't last long if you only had one pair. Flip-flops tended to fall apart quicker if you had to wear them in the showers and then walk around in them. In prison showering barefoot is not advised, you can never be too careful of what germs you may pick up in the worst-case scenario; it's just not advisable.

Understanding the situation I was up against, and the level of suffering and poverty I faced, paints a clearer picture as to why some inmates would take side against me. In their eyes, I was just a broke foreigner or deportee, as some would call me from time to time, a nobody with nothing to offer. But as I stated earlier, I fought for my respect and would stand my ground no matter what. It was hard, extremely hard, more mentally than physically, in the sense that I had never experienced the level of pain that accompanied my thoughts. My mind would work overtime; constant thoughts meant non-stop internal conflict. That's a lot of weight to carry, enough to sink any man into the ground, but due to my mindset, I wasn't willing to go down like that. At that time I didn't see how strong I was, I just knew I had to survive. Embodied with so much anger, I felt and questioned myself concerning the reason for my suffering, whether it was a beating for my wrongs in the past, or just bad luck, but one thing I knew was that I wasn't giving up; nor turning to no-one on the block, I was going to make it through. I was unsure of how, but I had to. I still had a suitcase in Kingston with clothes and a pair of trainers in it, but that's a whole other story. Imagine knowing you have clothes just up the road that are unreachable. What that can do to the mind, what manner of thoughts will one think? This was my situation, tormented in so many ways.

Prison itself was infested with germs, and the amount of flies around the food dump was disgusting. Hygiene was not compatible with the life I knew on the outside, but the outside at that point in my life no longer existed or was of concern. Reality calls for adaptation, and adapt I did, if I was thinking of surviving mentally that was. Not to say I totally gave up on the outside world, but my rational thought made it very clear that the outside world wasn't coming to me anytime soon.

In prison, you find numerous insects and I'm not talking about just outside the building. It wouldn't be too bad if it was, at least I could sleep peacefully at night. To be honest, not every cell suffers from the same problem. Different cells, different pests. You got roaches, spiders, working and biting ants, bloodsucking chink (bedbug) and of course, you can't have tropical heat, water pipes and filth and not expect to have loads of mosquitoes. Excluding the mosquitoes, I must state, depending on how you maintain your cell, you can keep the growth of these insects down. Then, if the cell next to yours or the cell next to that isn't as hygienic as your own, members of his little breeding nest will send themselves an invite.

Then you have the cell walls. Some of them were so disgusting, if they weren't plastered with fresh pictures or painted, which kept down the growth of parasitic insects that feed on human blood, it wasn't advisable to lean against them. I saw various inmates with what they call liver spot; to me it looked like some kind of a discoloured skin disease. According to prisoners, they say they caught it from the cell wall; whether it was true or not, I wasn't looking to catch it and I didn't.

Sleeping at night, if you had chink in your cell, was a challenge. I remember experiencing what I thought was my first encounter with them, at that time I didn't know anything about these bloodsucking insects; I'm trying not to cringe as I express my emotions. If it were a challenge, I'd fail gladly.

I recall being woken from sleep feeling and thinking mosquitoes were biting me. I would slide myself up and turn my head to see the clear skies as I looked out of my hammock through the vent, a little small grille on the back wall. It was something I did regularly from the first night I entered prison and would continue to do throughout my sentence, if ever I were up in a hammock. Looking for the moon, observing the skies at night and just thinking about life could be very calming, especially as the block was usually quiet at that time.

In those early days I knew nothing about what a chink was, prior to my incarceration I had no knowledge of these dirty little bloodsuckers; nasty parasitic insects. I had never experienced their bite in my life, so I didn't know what to expect; it was all a new experience to me. Lying there, I was thinking, how the hell are mosquitoes finding their way up my jeans, onto my lower legs and up on my thighs? My back likewise was burning and itching, my hand also, but that drew no suspicion that I was getting my blood sucked by these unfamiliar insects. I remember rolling my jeans leg up and scratching vigorously; it was really itching, and doing the same with my upper thigh, putting my hand down my pants. Repeating this to my back and thinking damn, I hate this feeling. I can't recall why, but I remember touching my face for whatever reason and rubbing my nose thinking to myself, what's that smell? What I didn't know was I had killed a few as they were sucking my blood. Only God knows how many people these filthy insects had sucked before withdrawing blood from me. It was when I put my hand up towards the grille bars, I saw bloodstains on my finger. I then realised it was the scent of blood, but then, where did the blood come from and why did it smell so bad? Speaking to a cellmate the next morning about my experience, he told me I had been bitten by chink. He gave me the rundown on these pests of nature, explaining you hardly see them in the day, but they come out at night like vampires. He blamed other cells, even telling me how they air out the sponges that they sleep on and had washed their hammock only recently when the last man left. To me, it was neither here nor there. All I knew was, I wasn't escaping the reality of what I faced at night as long as I was in that cell, and my mind needed to accept that and to know that whatever little I could do to help myself, I would. Other than that, I just had to ride it out. That was my first experience, and I knew it wasn't going be the last time I'd encounter those blood driven insects. In all truth, that cell was my home, and I had no control over the cell door. It was where I was ordered to lay my head. The truth is I was in another man's house. The only thing I had control over was my mind and even that at times, I had no control over when my head got hot, but I was trying, trying not to be a victim of my own circumstances and anger, which isn't easy, especially when your emotions are all messed up. When I began to analyse my emotions, my surroundings, and most importantly, started to accept, I realised that the greatest obstacle in my life whether incarcerated or free, was me. I learnt over time that the true power wasn't in the realisation, but the acceptance of the reality. There lays true strength in one whom is able to overcome and be free, even when physically bound and I found this, turning weakness into strength.

Depending on the cell an individual was located in, the order was set and varied. Some inmates permitted others to do a number two in their cell, while some saw it as a violation. For the lucky inmate, he would squat over a plastic bag lined with layers of pages from a newspaper to prevent any leakage in case it was runny and just to hold the scent in. He would release his waste, tie the plastic bag and put it to one side, ready to throw away first thing in the morning as the cell opened. The prison term for defecating in a bag was known as cargo. The not so lucky inmate would face serious emotional, psychological and physical discomfort. Emotional and psychological because no man wants to soil themselves or have their dignity taken away. For me, what bothered me was the thought of hearing another human cry, sometimes screams from discomfort, pain, cold sweat causing bodily dysfunction affecting the neurological system and other systems of the body. The way their body reacted; you would think that inmate had gone for a run. Sometimes other inmates would laugh. In my mind I'd think, you evil bastard, but for some it was just entertainment. The following day the same inmates who were laughing would talk to the same man who was screaming or crying the night before. It was kind of crazy like that on the block. Worst-case scenario, an inmate would be submitted to the hospital wing if he had held it too long. Depending on the time when he first felt like he wanted to defecate, it could stem from just after second lock, say late afternoon until early hours of the morning. I remember seeing cold sweat pouring off an individual whom warders rescued; I can never forget the look on his face. The thought of hearing a grown arse man cry because he wasn't allowed to do a *number two* in his cell at first saddened me. I felt sick to my stomach. Sometimes I would speak out but to be honest, after a while I got used to it. When I think about it, it's even more distressing that another human's pain became of no interest, or of little importance. I would wonder to myself, at what point did I lose compassion. Maybe I just knew psychologically that it was unrealistic to take on such energies and so I locked myself off from what was going on. Trust me, Remand Block in those days was crazy, and the more I thought about getting to grips with my emotions, the uncontrollable environment became of little interest to me. Trust me, I didn't like my surroundings from the beginning, so distancing myself felt like a blessing not a curse, although it made my life harder in more ways than one.

Prison is unpredictable. One day all is well and the next, all hell can break loose. With such instability, one's mind needs to be adaptable and ready for change at the blink of an eye. I remember my first experience of a hunger strike. I was new to prison yet understood straight from the get go, this wasn't going to be the last strike I would be a part of. Inmates decided they weren't going to eat the food issued by the system, I was told this was occurring throughout the whole prison; and I was told by my cellmates not to take food off the tray when it came if I valued my life. Not that they would have killed me, but others would; I was in no rush to test the waters, nor create enemies. I might have been a bit of a loose cannon, dealing with my own anger, but not suicidal. There were limits to how far I was willing to stand up for my own. Not going against the order at that time wasn't because I was scared, but more about being smart. Although I had nothing, no food prepared, so of course, I wanted my entitlement, but I valued my life more and the risk versus reward wasn't worth dying for, especially when it was a whole prison thing. However, years later I found myself in the position where I could stand up for all those like myself back then who weren't getting visits, who had nothing, but that I won't go into now. If I remember correctly, what caused the hunger strike was the fact that inmates weren't satisfied with the daily diet that was provided. It may have had something to do with the food being prepared with the copper pots they were using. It was an entire prison operation and everyone had to participate, as the orders were coming from the top.

Those who had received food visits prior to the strike, or had money, were in a better position than people like myself, we had to prepare ourselves for the worst. They could eat, whether they shared food or bought food from one another, but individuals who had no friends or like myself, who wouldn't take from people even when offered, knew there would be rough days ahead. To be totally honest, I could have had a packet of biscuits going under lock, but I refused it. I had told the inmate thanks but no thanks. It was a weird moment, because as much as I knew I needed it, there was a deep feeling inside me fighting against it. What made it worse was, I didn't know how long this strike was for, but my stubbornness was never going to allow me to ask, beg or take; that was just my character. I remember filling up my water bottles thinking this is my meal and I'm going to sleep as much as I can. There is nothing worse than being confined to a cramped up little room with nothing to eat. Worst of all, none of my cellmates at that time had sufficient food nor smoke so they were as miserable as hell, it was torture. Trying to sleep, all I could hear was murmuring and cussing. It was late evening at this time; I had slept, drank water, and slept again. I had no more sleep in me; my belly had begun speaking to me, I could literally hear the water moving around. Hunger was killing me. I had to soldier it out. The following day the orderlies bought the food to the block but no one took it. I watched as the hot black water and bread went back to the kitchen. My belly was rolling over and over, trust me I wasn't the only one. Observing others, they were feeling it too. However, this was more than just a strike; it was a test of will, not really for those who had food, or who were sharing or buying, but for us who had none. We were much stronger than they were. I knew it but when I think about it, I wonder how many saw it like that. Truly, the collective with *nothing* to eat had the real endurance and were the true backbone behind the strike.

It was the second 'fly up' (opening of cells) and the strike had ended, a day and a half of no food just water. For many it sounds easy, even myself who knew about fasting and spiritual cleansing back then as a Rastaman, I understood about the health benefits from abstaining from eating at times. But that day and a half felt hard to accomplish, if it weren't for personal experience, I wouldn't have understood the deeper aspects of it. The real challenge was the manner in which it was done. There is a difference between choosing and having a choice made for you. When actions stem from circumstances that are out of one's control, a completely different mindset is established, affecting people in various ways. It can either make you or break you as many like to say. With all the reflecting and thinking I was doing over these months, the anger, the rage, all of which I was starting to channel and challenge, I recognised this was both making and breaking me or better worded, breaking and rebuilding me. I was in training. Being behind bars was restructuring my own perception, self-worth and love. Like a tree planted by rivers of water, this understanding grew and blossomed more and more as time went by. I understood more about my strengths, well some were actually weaknesses; for example, I thought being quick to wrath was a mixture of bravery and fearlessness, when in reality it was actually my downfall. Some of what I thought were weaknesses were actually my strengths. Over the months I had begun to truly see and acknowledge my likes and dislikes about myself. I hadn't come to grips with them, as true change never occurs overnight, but I was more self-aware, and that was a positive start. It's amazing that on the outside I didn't know, see or consider any of this; guess I didn't really have or give enough time to myself. It's just sad that I had to go to prison to learn.

After the strike, in the same period of the second fly up, inmates received the order to smash all padlocks used to lock their cell doors. Perfectly planned, this was done at the end of our last lockdown. Not having enough locks on site to replace every cell, warders chained the main gate and allowed us to run free on our blocks for the night. This took place on more than one block. That night was crazy, inmates were going up and down the landings, funny enough no war broke out as far as I can remember; everyone was having a nice time. As for me, my belly was full. I had eaten off the tray and gone straight up to chill in my hammock until the next day. I had survived my first prison strike and to think it was only the beginning of the things I was about to see and participate in.

During my early period at St Catherine Adult Correctional Centre, the system had brought about a change in its institutions. Inmates were no longer going to cook the prisoner's diet. The government had given the contract to Kara. Who Kara was or what it meant, up until today I have no idea. Inmates and warders were calling the company that prepared and brought our food by that name and so did I. The introduction of Kara wasn't of concern to me personally, I really didn't care who cooked the food, but for some inmates it was a detrimental blow to their daily diet. As prisoners were the chefs and the warders assigned to kitchen duties had inmates they were cool with, some but not all inmates were allowed to purchase food and would then cook for themselves and others. But with the new contract given to Kara, uncooked food items were no longer coming into the kitchen and therefore, those prisoners had to look to other means. As for me, I couldn't even afford sugar at that time, so Kara or no Kara, it had no impact. When looking back at it, it's amazing how content I was. Having nothing, and no means of getting anything because I was too stubborn and proud to ask or take, I just became content to wait. Night and day, I'd hope to see the British Embassy or members of the family that I was staying with before being locked up, but I saw neither. I was more disappointed in not seeing the British Embassy's representative to be honest, as I had counted on them for support. Deep down I kept the hope alive, frustrated at times, but I knew I was a citizen of the United Kingdom; they had an obligation to visit me and check on my wellbeing. I knew when that day came, I planned to take full advantage of it, sending back letters and information as well as hoping I'd receive that money they used to give me when I was in the police stations down in St Ann.

Chapter 4:
British Embassy

Almost half a year into my remand at St Catherine Adult Correctional Centre, there I was waiting with a few other inmates to see the British Embassy employee. Out of curiosity, I asked the other inmates where they were located. They told me South Block. I remember wondering why I was the only foreigner at the back of the prison whilst they were on a block that seemed to be a prison all to itself. Not that it wasn't a dangerous block. I knew that a few of the top prisoners were located there, but it was right at the front of the prison where inmates were first checked in, and not part of what was considered the main prison population, also known as the 'collection of bodies' as warders would say, and inmates reiterated so freely. It was common slang; we were regarded as bodies, not inmates. There were no prison numbers issued; one wasn't always referred to by name. Individuals were more called 'inmate', unless a warder took a liking to them, or had some level of respect. The truth of the matter is we were just bodies in their eyes.

Excitement mixed with anger, I was frustrated that it had taken so long, yet happy to see a friendly face. I sat before a short, slim, white lady who greeted me with smiles. Initially she asked me a few questions regarding my health and confirmation of my identity, after telling her, I couldn't help but ask why no one from the British Embassy had come to visit me for months, nor before I came to prison. The lady sitting before me was not the same woman whom had visited me when I was down in St Ann. The Embassy person explained that I would have missed that visit in St Ann due to the time that I had left the police station. No longer smiling, with a straight face and honest look in her eyes she made it clear that she had come to the prison on more than one occasion, not to see all British inmates, but to see me personally and was told I was refusing to see her. Her response sent my blood boiling instantaneously; I kept calm, but I recall looking at the warder standing in the room, and wanting to kill him. I was so angry. I explained that I was never told she had come, and that when I asked if they could contact the British Embassy, they would say the British Embassy is coming soon. We both know there and then that there was a problem, but I could see by the look on her face that she didn't want to address it. She, like I myself, knew the system was corrupt. She explained in a professional manner that now she'd seen me, there would be no problems in seeing me in the near future. She looked at the green suit warder who looked away. She gave me letters that she had from my family, also toiletries and told me she had twice the money as normal for me and would put it on the book. In front of the warder, I openly stated that I would never get to spend that money, and told her what happened in the station down at Runaway Bay. She said the warder would assist me. I had no trust in him but then knew she had signposted this warder of higher rank to make sure I was ok. Green suit warders were higher in rank than warders who wore grey and blue uniforms. Then you had green suits who had strips on their shoulders they were even higher in rank than normal green suits. The officer that signed to make sure I received my money had two strips on his shoulder. I explained to her I needed a pair of sliders, clothes, and snacks, and asked if she could take most of the money and get these items for me when she came back, she agreed. Mixed emotions ran through my mind as a warder escorted me back to my cell. He was pretty cool still, telling me to keep my head up and that he didn't know I was a foreigner, due to the way I spoke, he thought I was a Jamaican.

That night, I lay reading the letters repeatedly, especially the one from my sister-in-law, and smiling to myself, and then getting angry as I recalled the embassy woman's words regarding me not wanting to see the embassy. It was mentally painful. I was fuming, yet filled with hope. I knew I was loved and missed, and as much as it made me happy, it made me sad too. The greatest thing was that the embassy came through, as I knew they would. I was just glad that the long anticipation came to pass, I knew then I had not been forgotten. Within a fortnight she returned, so I knew it was a special visit and not to see all British inmates. She gave me two bags of food items, a pair of sliders, underpants, shorts and a few T-shirts. I thanked her and her smile alone let me know she knew I was more than grateful. The change left from the money she had spent, she would put in the book for me.

Chapter 5:
Momentary Joy

The morning after the visit from the embassy, one of my cellmates who observed me reading the evening before, spoke to me regarding my letters. We held a conversation, which was something I hardly ever did, especially not about my personal life or anything pertaining to me, but we did. I even told him about the little money I had on the prison book, which was known as the rit, and that she would bring me more things when she came back. He told me to buy items in prison, that it was much cheaper, not that I didn't know this, but I wasn't the man to mix, I preferred not to. Thinking about what my cellmate said, I asked the warder who escorted me back to the block the day before, if he would take me to front office, he told me he would do later and he did. That lockdown, I had a brand-new pair of sliders, two underpants put to one side, a few biscuits and a little something to drink. I still kept my mashed-up trainers and Bally shoes to walk in, and my rubber sliders that I showered in were in good nick. There was no way I was throwing anything away. I just knew now I had a new pair of name brand sliders tucked away for a rainy day. Having food to eat under lock other than Kara felt weird. To explain how I felt after months of not being able to have these luxuries, it felt strange yet glorious. I remember looking at empty biscuit rappers next to the bag of munchies I had and smiling within. I gave my cellmates a pack of biscuits and had bought smoke for them, but they knew that it didn't mean we were friends now, they knew I loved my own company and was comfortable like that. But for that moment, we ate biscuits and exchanged a few words. Over weeks their respect for me would grow, I had never taken anything from them before, and when my money ran out and they offered, I still wouldn't. I was good, this do for self attitude was my character and wasn't about to change.

When deprived of necessities, or something one is so used to, and then opportunity presents itself and it comes to you through whatever situation, it brings about a crazy happiness. That's how I felt momentarily, being in the position to buy what my heart desired. I was really excited about munching biscuits and drinking Lasco.

Chapter 6:
Familiar Faces

My first year in Spanish Town I found extremely challenging, not to mention my first six months; that was rough beyond measure, and materially, I literally went down to nothing. I was unwilling to communicate properly with inmates, not to take it away from some of them because some did try, but I just refused. It meant that it was quite impossible to ask a favour from anyone who was getting visits to pass on a message to the outside world, as I didn't want to relate with anyone like that. From time to time, I thought about writing a few numbers down and asking an inmate, who had access to a phone, to call my people, but as usual, something inside me just wouldn't let me. Whether it was my anger, pride, ego, or just too much hurt, I went deep into myself and refused to come out, something forbade me. In the craziest of ways, it made me not only come across as a strong character, it made me feel strong and thinking about it now, it still does today.

During the first year of my incarceration, my family in Kingston 8 had visited me twice in jail, not counting Max's visits. I had only met this side of my mother's family a year earlier in 1997. Desiring to chill out from the usual places in St Ann, Spanish Town and Kingston, I chose to reside on their ends. Max wasn't blood family, but I considered him as one. Max was a 'road darg' (real one) from Whitehall, who was residing at Manning's Hill. I had met Max through my family who lived in that area and we became close like brothers. It was because of Max, my cousin Jaro visited me, whilst I was on Remand Block in my first year. That upset my spirit deeply, because Jaro and I were very close, and it took Max for her to come and check me. When she did visit, she did not return with the things I had asked her to bring. Because it was her I had originally made contact with from that set of family in Kingston 8, and being a woman that understood street life because of whom she was, her affiliation to a specific area in West Kingston, and the generals that she associated with, I would have expected better, but it was a lesson learnt.

I can never forget, it was about six to seven months into my remand time at Spanish Town prison, and I saw familiar faces step onto the block. It was the same friend that made my family come to check me. Max was right before my eyes. With him was Chuku (R.I.P), another roadman from the ends. Both of them were roughly the same height, just over six-foot and quite well built. As I looked at Max and Chuku, I felt good to see familiar faces, but instantly the realisation of why Max hadn't checked me in jail or visited me caused me to feel it for him. Prison was nowhere pleasant and I wouldn't wish it on my enemy, much less my friend, but here he was in front of me. So many thoughts ran through my mind seeing him again. After a few visits to me in St Ann, I never saw him again, and thought that he, like certain others up at Kingston 8, had turned their backs on me. I was angry with myself for so many reasons, including the fact that the family that I was familiar with over the years from 1991 to 1994, especially some friends whom I considered closer than family during that period, had no idea I was in the country, not to mention in prison. This upset me severely. It felt like I had left the old for the new. Everyone knows you can't disrespect foundation although that was never my intention. Indeed, it was a sad reality check. I wanted a different experience of Jam-Down, that's why I went amongst new people and believe me, I was living one. I was thrown down into the pits of hell, with only myself to draw me out. I knew deep down my old peers would have had my back, but it was a valuable experience well learned.

In the yard Max and I began to reason, he didn't have to tell me why I hadn't seen him, it was obvious he had been locked up, but he told me nevertheless. Not only was he locked up, but on the run for a hot minute. I had no need to tell him my circumstance; he could see that for himself. My red jeans and red Fubu top had turned pink due to the amount of times I had washed them with prison fab, which contained a high level of bleach. As for the sneakers, they were indescribable. I explained I had sliders to shower in and a spare pair in my cell. I recall Max laughing and calling me mad man. We both laughed and spoke for a bit before I followed him to his cell where he gave me two new pairs of underpants, toiletries and some food. As I stated earlier, the only reason why my cousin checked me was because Max had sent word to her via another man from the ends that also knew me and knew how I treated everyone the first time I visited.

Max and Chuku weren't held on remand for long. A few months if that, then one day they went to court and later that day the word came back that Chuku had beat the case, but Max was sentenced for armed robbery and illegal possession of a firearm. He was shipped out to General penitentiary. I had found myself alone again on the block. I wasn't fighting anymore; people weren't playing with me. I think they understood I wasn't having it, or taking it lying down. Nevertheless, I found myself alone again, comforting myself with the thought that my family in England would come to Jamaica and look for me. I knew they loved me. I knew my children and their mother loved me. I had friends in the UK I knew missed me, but with all those thoughts running through my mind, I was trying to run from the truth which was, I was missing Max and Chuku, that was the plain reality of the situation. I had come out of my cocoon for a moment and transformed, laughing and joking day after day, only to return to my dark shell. Only someone who has been in a really bad place in their life and experienced some sort of comfort along the trod, then lost it, can truly comprehend. It's not a feeling I wish anyone to experience, but it's a powerful and sensitive emotion that should not be overlooked. Lesser experiences have contributed to depression; I saw this occur time after time with prisoners, depressed but never diagnosed with depression. Sadly, this is a fact; inmates have taken their own lives because they felt sad and alone. But for others, loneliness accompanied by each experience, can make you very strong psychologically, finding a will that exists beyond the physical, can even become your companion. In spite of losing my friends, I had and have a frame of mind that was easily adaptable.

For me, as much as there is sorrow in being alone, I find pleasure in it too, and so I did.

Chapter 7:
Friendships Developing

As I came near to the end of my first year on Remand Block, I was doing some serious self-reflecting, challenging my anger and questioning myself. I was trying harder to refrain from thoughts that were non-productive and non-beneficial. Believe me it's not easy. In my mind there was still a lot of blame directed at others for all that had gone wrong in my life as a youth and my circumstances. Trust, I wasn't getting over it quickly. It took time; I acknowledged the realisation, but the acceptance was a challenge. Coming to grips with so many issues wasn't easy. Unfortunately, these couldn't be resolved in a day or weeks, oh no, it took years to truly accept and understand. Honestly, some things I'm still fighting with even today. Not that I'm pardoning or dismissing all who have wronged me, nor underestimating the negative impact of a broken home, disoriented family, abuse or being tormented, all of which can affect the mind of a young child. Even in such bad situations, there are still always choices to make. I began to see these choices, and seeing them brought a next level of anger out of me, and I constantly battled with my emotions. I was challenging my choices prior to my incarceration. This had me fighting my anger and myself, based on the feelings that I carried for others deep within. What I came to realise was, my real anger was towards me for not making other choices, and for why I didn't make them. What stopped me from making them, and if I didn't know I had them, then why did it happen? You see, I was fighting self and believe me, the fight wasn't pretty at all. While going through this internal war that lasted for years, I was still a loner, and wouldn't take anything from anyone, until I met Puppa. Puppa was a slim, happy faced youth, but a serious youth at the same time. He was the first person I really opened up to on the block aside from Max and Chuku, but they were friends of mine from road.

It was about the tenth month into my remand in Spanish Town, maybe a little bit more, when I met Puppa. He and I clicked; we lived like brothers. National (R.I.P), who is now deceased, was another inmate that I had begun to open up to. National was built like a truck, a true warrior; him and I knew one another from jail, from my first circuit court appearance in St Ann. Between us, respect was there, but I wasn't allowing myself to mingle at that time, I was too closed off in my own realm of thought, and did not want to share my world with anyone. There were also a few other inmates that I grew to have an understanding with. We were all located on the same block. One was called Puerto Rican, and the other Moses. Both were from the USA, charged with murder, and serving life sentences. I met them when I first went to Remand Block, they understood me; understood that I didn't what any friends, so they gave me my space and respect at the same time.

My first year in prison was coming up fast, I recall this moment because Puppa and I were not only linking at that time but also now sharing a cell with another inmate named Scoffla, from Capture Land in Spanish Town. I was located with two genuine brothers. I remember us talking about my first year being around the corner and the two of them telling me how much of a soldier I was. It was that same day, Puppa had literally begged me to let him give me a pair of sliders he had, but me being the way I was, I refused to take them. My shower sliders had busted and I was now using my spare for both washing and wearing on a daily basis. I had finally thrown away my sneakers and Bally shoes. They had served me well.

"Israel, if yuh no wah da sliders, mek mi tell mi family fi bring mi a new pair an mi jus gi yuh dem," he said to me.

"Jus cool, every ting criss."

"Wha happen to yuh Isreal, yuh ah man link yuh kno."

At that time, I had received the name Israel in prison because I was always reading the Bible, and when anyone would ask me if I was a Christian, I would tell him no, I was a descendent of the biblical nation of Israel. I must state, it was the reading of the Bible, especially the Old Testament, through which I began to find my source of comfort.

"Jus cool Puppa, man rate yuh, yuh no see not even my yout dem over ship mi nah tek nuttin from ah jus call, straight link, man people soon forward, an den a bare tings."

"So mi, Scoffla and National ah no yuh friend?"

"Wha yuh mean?" I replied.

"Den mek mi get de sliders gi yuh. Yo Israel, yuh see when mi food bag cum, if yuh nah eat, nobody nah eat, mi nah gi nobody no food." I laughed. "God kno Israel, no body nah get no food." Puppa went on to say.

Every Wednesday without fail, Puppa was one of the very few people on the block who would get a long bag containing all different kinds of biscuits, bun, cheese, drinks, you name it, and a big basin of rice and peas with different meat every time. Puppa was one of those good-hearted people, conscious of his position in life and very aware of his surroundings. He knew he was fortunate and was never boastful with it. Instead, he shared his meal with others, especially with those who he classified as friends, and the less fortunate ones. It was the kind of person he was. I suppose that's why I found myself reasoning a lot with him until we became as close as we became.

"Gi de man dem food man," I laughed, "Wha kind of food yuh ah get?" I asked.

"Chicken." He replied.

"Alright, gi mi ah likkle," I responded. He smiled.

So many occurrences took place in prison especially in the earlier days. I kind of find it hard to remember exactly what happened, what led to it, or maybe unconsciously I chose to block those memories out. I can definitely say that in my personal life and experiences growing up, there are things that happened I just couldn't remember. But there are some experiences I will never forget and never want to, specific occurrences that will never fade and I thank God for that. Puppa is a part of those undying memories; he was the first inmate that had won my trust. The first inmate that I ever took anything from, whom I did not know from road, and no matter where in the world he is, he will always be in my heart and have my blessing.

Chapter 8:
Prison Politics

The basic rules in prison were, there were no rules. The underpinning factor was all boundaries are broken in some way or another, that's the bottom line. The guidelines set in place were never kept, and that went for warders *and* inmates. The politics within the Jamaican prison system ran deep, you never knew if you faced a stream, river, ocean or a storm. Sinking physically or psychologically can happen at any given moment due to actions or reactions caused by anything, placing one's life either at risk, causing confusion, or on the flip side, gaining and benefiting from a situation you just never knew. I think about inmates like Puerto Rican, Moses, and so many others; Spanish Town prison was crazy. When I think about it, these two guys were both charged for murder and sentenced, yet they were still located on Remand Block, which was supposed to be for inmates awaiting sentencing, and they weren't the only lifers there. You had inmates on the block sentenced to more years than they had left in them, unless they were Enoch or Noah, then they may have the opportunity to see road again. However, if you weren't living to the ages of these biblical characters, then locating them with people awaiting sentencing or the possibility of freedom was literally endangering lives. When I think about Remand Block, a wire fence separated Remand Block and Death Row from one another. No walls, just a wire fence; now how dangerous is that? Death Row is a block that houses inmates sentenced to death. The only thing keeping them alive was the fact that hanging was abolished. "Thanks to the British." was a term some inmates would use. Whether or not I agree with their statement, considering history, well that's another story. Then you have Boys Town, Boys Town is block for those regarded as batty boys. Although according to what I've heard, not everybody located on Boys Town was really homosexual. Some, according to inmates, requested a transfer there due to owing other inmates money and being unable to pay; they fled there to save their lives. Some would transfer during the riots, or whatever circumstance. But hey, at the end of the day, what do I know? As long as people allowed me to live my life while I was incarcerated, and didn't bring their argument to me nor cross my path, I didn't give a shit what they did with their lives. That's how I felt in prison, and I still feel the same way today. Not to stray from expressing and giving insight into the crazy way in which the system runs however, while on the topic of batty boys, there were two individuals in Spanish Town located on Boys Town who had the privilege of walking amongst the general population, and to my knowledge, weren't looked upon as outcasts. One went by the name of Zulu, and the other Natty. Zulu's appearance was wild. He made his own outfits, I don't know if he got his name because of the colourful prison made slippers and pieces of clothing he wore, or if he had that name from before. What I do know, is that his tall slim frame, crazy dress code and funny talk made him stand out. As for Natty, he was pretty stocky and moved quite humbly.

From what I heard, Zulu had spent clear over 25 years in prison, and when the time had come for them to let him go, he took one step outside of the prison and asked them to let him back in. According to inmates, he must have had nowhere to go. From my point of view, if what inmates say about Zulu is true, Jamaica's government, like any other government in the world that haven't or don't set up programmes for offenders, will only reap more devastating outcomes, such as reoffending, or in Zulu's case social depression. Personally, I believe that Zulu was beyond institutionalised. For the fact that the thought of the outside world frightened him, he definitely needed help, psychological help. Therefore, the rehabilitation system had failed, but then to be honest, there was no real rehabilitation process geared for long or short sentenced inmates to help them psychologically prepare for life beyond the walls of confinement. There were one or two odd courses and a limited amount of work, nothing really major to create real change. It's no secret why crime is on the increase, when nothing is set in place to reduce it. The only sad thing is, my parent's beautiful paradise of an island is under attack and they don't even know it.

Any human being, once his or her time is soon up and they're to return to society, should be offered counselling as a standard procedure, and then it's up to the individual to take it or not. But hey, that's my point of view. Who the fuck am I? As for Natty, in 2005, he helped to organise the prison football tournament and every block in Spanish Town prison took part in this tournament apart from Boys Town where he was located, again what can I say? The fact is I just don't get involved in prison politics.

Spanish Town prison was disorganised, likewise Tower Street Adult Correctional Centre. An inmate serving six months could be placed in a cell with men doing life, or serving a sentence for murder, and a rapist could be pushed into the same cell. A petty thief shoved in a cell with three murderers, all serving life with nothing to lose. Now that's some crazy shit. When you think about it, life doesn't have much value in a Jamaican institution. They have a motto in prison which any old prisoner on road who has this book in his hand will know and that's 'once you enter through the prison gate, the authorities receive a body and not a person'. Meaning death can come at any time.

As for the dude whose jail made shank marked my chest at Runaway Bay police station, the one I was wary of the first morning after landing in Spanish Town prison, wondering if he had friends on the block and it turned out that he didn't, he found batty boy block the safest place to be. Unfortunately, for him it wasn't that safe at all. He had transferred there to escape any retaliation from my friends and I. Word has it that he was sexually abused over there. Why and how it happened is unknown, but it was definitely an incident he found hard to live with. In fact, he tried to commit suicide because of it.

Things were changing in prison; nothing with or around me would ever be the same again. I had begun making regular walks to New Hall a.k.a Ship. The Ship is the largest block in Spanish Town prison. Although South Block also had three floors and was a well-respected block, New Hall was long in length and housed more inmates. It was also notorious for the multiple murders that took place within its walls and therefore, New Hall was also called Slaughterhouse. I had found out that a friend of mine from the streets of Kingston, named Buju was located in this notorious block. He would make it his obligation to look out for me. To him and his friends over there, I needed a friend, no matter what I said. If it were not for Puerto Rican who took me over to New Hall to take care of some important business, I wouldn't have known my friend was over there. For that, I will always be grateful to my bro Puerto Rican from the boogie down Bronx. Puerto Rican had introduced me to Speci who had taken care of business for me. One thing led to another and Speci and I became very good friends. He had also introduced me to a Ras called Screw, who introduced me to a Ras name G-Go, whom I later found out due to reasoning with him that we were family.

Puerto Rican was, and even today is as far as I know, well respected. Not in the sense of being violent in prison, it was for the way in which he conducted himself. While incarcerated, Puerto Rican had turned Christian and had become a leading figure in the prison church. Puerto Rican and a well-respected inmate from East Kingston known as Buck-Wheel (R.I.P) and three other inmates, educated themselves highly in prison and received certification for it. An outside organisation set these examinations, which drew media attention to the prison, having the only true positive effect that I can recall throughout the years I spent locked up on the island. Buck-Wheel inspired me during my incarceration. Not because of the reputation that was connected to his past life, but because of the transformation of who he was becoming. Mentally it touched me, stimulated and triggered a change in me, you see I was going through my own wars at that time and seeing someone else coming from a similar background, being strong willed, determined and showing change, was what I needed. I told him on various occasions he inspired me, most of the time he would just smile. It's so interesting to think about the character and the person he was, and the person he was becoming. Everybody in prison knew if they got on the wrong side of him, what he was capable of doing, but the way in which he dealt with everybody, everyone knew his mind and eyes were open towards better things and thoughts of life. He was a man who had been there and done it all. He spent time on death row and won his appeal, which allowed him to relocate amongst the general population, making the best out of a bad situation. When I had reached prison in 1999, Buck-Wheel had already come off death row and was located at South Block where he, Sexy Paul, and a few others set the order. Buck-Wheel was one of those humble guys, who always came across mellow. He was nothing fearful to look at, in fact quite the opposite, he was neither thick nor slim, just averagely built and gave off good energy. It could be said that his reputation and energy didn't align, which in itself testifies that one doesn't have to walk around as a bully or troublemaker just because people fear you.

It was way into my first year before I visited South Block in the sense of checking anyone. I was linking with New Hall mainly. Apart from the few friends on Remand Block, I felt safe in the Ship. For many, those waters weren't to be stepped in lest you drown, but I was good with the captains, so boarding that voyage brought no fear. Not only with my friends was I good over there, but I began linking with others too. Many people just took a liking to me. I was receiving more than giving because at that time, I didn't have much, but the level of respect was crazy. I can only describe it as genuine respect because I had nothing to really offer, yet received calls, munchies, anything really and many of these individuals were from all over the island. Sometimes I wouldn't return to my block until lockdown time. You see, I built, and would continue to build my own respect in prison. It wasn't based on friends, family or anything other than people seeing me for me. They saw a man who could hold his own, and handle his own. Some inmates at the Ship would tell me I was a blessed youth; I had a good energy and they just loved how I carried myself. The truth is, over the years this was expressed to me on numerous occasions and at many locations throughout the system. During the days of my growing connections on New Hall, aka Ship, in the year 2000, I'd make the odd trip to South Block and I got to know Buck-Wheel a little better. Never once did I bring it to his attention that my mother was from Franklin Town or mention that I had any connection to his area. At the end of the day I was just living. I was never a man to push myself on to people. I told myself if we were to hold a deep conversation, or for some reason the topic came up, I would tell him, which it did. A year later, after I was sentenced and moved to General penitentiary, more commonly known as GP, I then told him exactly with whom I was connected. In fact, he saw it for himself. When I think about it, Buck-Wheel and I really became close years later in 2005 to be precise, after all hell broke loose whilst we were in GP. It led to all foreigners and certain top Jamaican inmates being shipped out to Horizon Adult Remand Centre and then transferred to St Catherine Adult Correctional Centre where I ended up again. I was back where I started, but this time, located on South Block, before being shipped out to Tamarind Farm, one of Jamaica's open prisons. The sequence of events and politics of prison running's surrounding this crazy incident that took place on the grounds of Tower Street Adult Correctional Centre better known as GP, I will explain in more detail later in the book.

Accepting mistakes is never an easy thing to do despite what anyone says. But the real challenge is correcting them. I believe my surroundings caused me to open my eyes to the faults of man, and willed me to want to do right. I can't speak for every prison in the world, but from what I experienced inside various Jamaican institutions, the level of humanity is very low, and for most inmates, self-esteem is at rock bottom. Despite the poor level of educational facilities offered to rehabilitate inmates, prison warders were less clued to their role of responsibility than the inmates were to theirs. I am speaking in terms of code of conduct and practice. The behaviour of the majority of the officers had a negative impact on the inmates. It's quite impossible to demand correct behaviour if you yourself aren't walking in an upright code of conduct. Daily, I watched inmates' and warders' patterns of behaviour; to me, they were one and the same. Warders and soldiers would bring whatever problems they had outside of the prison walls and take it out on inmates, instead of being professional and leaving it at home, or wherever it stemmed from. And if it wasn't road problems, then a lot of those warders and soldiers needed anger management counselling, or are just not psychologically fit to work in the field they have chosen. Regarding soldiers, they are trained to kill period, so it's understandable when they are less tolerant. However, if they're in the prison to carry out a job, knowing fully well, it's not just for a day or two, it's up to the government or someone with power to send those selected to counselling prior to starting, or use whatever means necessary to make sure they're fit to work with the vulnerable. As for warders, there're no excuses, they weren't trained to kill and defend the country. They were trained to serve the prison system and carry out justice, not to intimidate and inflict more pain on already traumatised people who act out based on their own life experiences, where's the rehabilitation in that? Who really saw the bigger picture? I believe that inmates and authorities were very similar in their behaviour; everyone seemed to love throwing their stresses on one another.

There is also the topic of bribes. If the Jamaican government were paying the prison officials enough money, they wouldn't need to borrow or play double standards to survive. Speaking from experience, I loaned prison officials money on more than one occasion and through another inmate's hands, have sent warders to buy me illegal substances. Me personally, I never liked the idea of prison officials doing me direct favours, you never know when they would switch on you and send a colleague for whatever it was they had brought you. I always played it safe. In admitting that I had illegal things brought in for me, I'm saying I had to survive; but what I refused to do was to think like I was institutionalised because I was penalised. This I refused to do; I simply rode the waves. Mentally I became a wind surfer. As time went on, I stood out in a way that won me both respect from inmates and warders alike. My actions were changing through my observation of everything taking place around me, yet at the same time, my actions were also changing and capturing others.

Chapter 9:
Energetically Charged

It was every three to four months myself, along with the other circuit inmates, were taken from Spanish Town prison to the parish of St Ann to face Jamaica's kangaroo court system. Some were tried and either sentenced or set free. Then you had those like me, whose trial seemed as if it would never end. I had been returning to St Ann for circuit court for just over a year when the most amazing emotional experience hit me, awakening and fulfilling a dormant and empty energy within me. I truly came to life. I had never experienced what it felt like to really yearn for someone, and then receive what I had so longed for and missed. It was an awakening to understand what it really felt like to have that sensational need met. As a youth, I had longed to see my biological father, but recall seeing him and not feeling that void filled. Maybe because I was a mature man when he walked back into my life, as much as I respected him, the need wasn't there as much. Maybe I just didn't need him again. Whatever the reason, there was no comparison to the energetic feeling of strength and comfort I felt when I encountered my loved ones. I believe the build-up to seeing them also heightened my emotions. I knew from my friend back in the UK whom I would contact when over at New Hall, that my family were coming to visit me soon, but I hadn't anticipated that the time had come. I can never forget being locked up in Ocho Rios police station awaiting my court appearance when I heard a police officer call my name as he came down the passageway, "Stephen, Stephen, visit!" he shouted. To tell the truth I didn't make anything of it, it hadn't crossed my mind that it was for me. I knew my family was coming to Jamaica, but when you're so used to not having or getting visits, your awareness to receive just isn't that quick. It was when I heard the main gate open and he called my name again "Stephen," and then said, "Israeli." I got up off my bunk and walked to the grille.

Our faces met at the cell front.

"Come, visit," he said.

"For me?" I replied stupidly.

He looked at me. "Wha yuh kno wah visit?" he asked as he opened the door to the cell. At that time, I was experiencing mixed feelings. I desired a visit so much, I was excited, yet I couldn't express how excited I was due to me being *so* not used to getting visits. Something was telling me it's not my visit. What made it worse was, it wasn't visiting time, or the correct day that visits occur, so I was sceptical and straight up confused. Nevertheless, I walked behind the police officer and followed him to the main gate. I stood there between the left and right gates that separated the section of the jail and waited. Watching him walk off, I was anticipating yet confused as to who it could be. He had been gone about two or three minutes and I can recall myself growing wary. It felt at that time like an hour, maybe an hour and a half. I began to wonder if he had made a mistake and anger hastily became my companion as I became frustrated. All of a sudden, my little sister Minnie, and my children's mother Lele came from around the corner accompanied by the police officer, they walked towards me, towards the grille gate where I stood waiting. To describe how I felt at that time would be impossible. There is no word in the English vocabulary that could define my emotions. The energy that rose within me lit me up from within. At the same time, I was in that much shock I couldn't cry. Anger fled like an unwanted fly hovering in my presence, I just smiled.

Word for word, I'm unable to remember how we began conversing, my emotions were so high, but my little sister's embrace was unforgettable. The love, sadness and joy, her emotions oozed from her body and I felt everything, she kissed me on my cheek and told me she loved me, it felt great to hear, it felt even greater to see her. I felt her love and longing for me to be free. Not that such thoughts were possible, nor was it impossible but right then all I wanted to do was to live in the moment and nothing less, enjoy what was before me, allowing no sorrow to rob me of this temporary bliss. As for Lele, her touch, scent, emotions not to mention the warmth of the sweetness of her lips as we kissed sent tingles down my spine, her warm embrace moved me from within, I couldn't believe it, yet at the same time I was truly cherishing this blessing, I was actually kissing my children's mother. Lele and I in that brief period were in our own bubble as we kissed, engulfed in that moment. It was then I knew what it was like to yearn for someone, as we held one another. I didn't know how empty I felt, how much I really longed for and missed her until then. Prior to seeing her, I knew I loved and missed her, but what I felt, it was just such an amazing experience of natural chemistry; an energetic burst of life ran through my veins and into my heart. We stood there and talked. Realistically, they did more of the talking, as I stared at them both, especially Lele. There they were, I just couldn't believe, they were standing there right before my very eyes. I remember them telling me I looked slim, and asking me, how I am. I also recall them telling me to remain strong. Observing them, I noticed they both tried to hold and maintain a brave face. I guess they both felt they had to be brave and not cry, lest it reflected on me and weakened my spirit. At that moment, I honoured them for it. I made no mention of it to them that I could see how much it was killing them, instead I channelled every bit of the energy and strength that they displayed before me, and used it to empower my own will to survive whatever it was I might undergo in the future.

We talked for a while covering topics on the family, my children and whatever information they could give me about my case and where I stood. I remember asking them if I was going to trial this time. It was a question that was unanswerable. It seemed they, like me, did not know what was taking place. Before they left, my sister handed me a bag containing cooked food and gave me money. She also told me that they only came down for a week, so therefore the next time they visited me they would bring the things they brought from England, along with some more food and other stuff. Lele, my children's mother also gave me money, both pounds and Jamaican dollars. The feeling of her body in my arms was as if I was holding onto a dream that I wished never to awake from, it felt so good. I remember kissing her again after I hugged and kissed my little sister goodbye.

Lele's lips, the softness of them. Believe me when I say, when a man hasn't had a woman's touch for a long time, especially when it's against his will, deep down the man can become more emotional than the woman herself.

I watched them as they walked off with the officer who had escorted them in. They both looked back at me before they turned the corner and disappeared out of sight.

"Come," said an officer to me.

I didn't speak, instead I held on to the photographic image my mind had captured of their faces as they stared at me before disappearing out of sight. Holding on to that picture, I took a deep breath, then turned and walked back on the block and into my cell.

"God kno mi never kno seh yuh have baby madda. Ah yuh sista dat, mi like her," said the police officer in a joking manner.

"Bad man sista no deh wid police, fool." National responded.

"Wha yuh mean by dat, yuh never kno seh mi ave baby madda." I asked in an unfriendly tone. Our eyes met as he locked the cell door. He then turned and walked off the block.

After I had eaten, I lay down on my bunk and thought about my little sister and my children's mother. I couldn't believe what had just occurred. The happiness I felt was indescribable. Minnie my adorable little sister and Lele had visited me. I couldn't help but silently rejoicing within. My mind recaptured all that had taken place, I saw myself holding my sister and my children's mother again in my arms. The taste of Lele's lips was a feeling that I'd longed for. Like a dam, it opened and allowed crystal-clear thoughts to gently travel and flow through. I began thinking about the love we shared and that too filled my body with joy. Relaxed and excited while dwelling in the realm of thought, I fell asleep. I don't recall when I fell asleep, but I do know I had never felt so good whilst behind bars, in fact emotionally, that was one of the greatest experiences.

It wasn't until the following morning when the police officer on duty opened our cell for us to shower that I looked at how much money I had. Damn, I thought to myself smiling, I looked up and out through the ceiling vent, eyes gazing through the bars at the sky and thanked God.

"Yuh cashie my yout, wha dat pound, mek mi see how English money tan," I handed the inmate a twenty-pound note. "Jah kno England money ugly, look how it big." He was referring to the old English notes.

For a brief second I looked up at the inmate and smiled as he showed another inmate the note I had handed him. I then resumed counting the rest of the money that I had in my hand. Only God knows how good it felt to be holding money after being broke for so long. I had received a little something from the British Embassy when I finally saw them, and it had helped me during my times of suffering and I was thankful for it; but in all honesty, I'd become accustomed to being broke, and therefore had kind of mentally adapted to my circumstances. In a funny way it made it easier for me to survive because I had nothing, therefore I looked to receive nothing, which enabled me to get on with life to the best of my ability. Now, knowing I would be receiving more frequently as reassured by my loved ones, I wondered would the anticipation and desire become another issue, the challenge was, how I would deal with it.

After I'd received back the twenty-pound note from the inmate, I folded it up with the money I had and shoved everything in my pocket, put my pants on my bunk, and then I headed to the shower. Although I would do it at times, in prison leaving money lying around wasn't exactly a smart move, it wasn't advisable. Then that depended on if you knew the individuals with whom you located, or if between you there was mutual respect. Then again, I learned in prison that even the best of friends can turn envious, this I witnessed on various occasions during my incarceration. Friendships destroyed over material gain and benefits. Not everyone shows genuine respect. On a personal note, since I began to get visits, my experience regarding money and inmates wasn't too bad; in fact, it wasn't bad at all.

Back in my cell, I lay down on my bunk and thought about the visit from my little sister and my children's mother. I pictured them visiting me again; warm thoughts flowed calmly through my mind as I created my own little scene of what was to come. I had not thought so peacefully for a long time and hoped that this would be a permanent feeling, though I knew in the back of my mind that it was temporary, so it was essential to enjoy, and make the best of the little peace of mind I was experiencing.

The time had come and Circuit court was now ending. The weeks spent in jail made no change to my circumstances, the judge remanded me back into custody yet again, and I was still oblivious as to where I stood. The only thing I knew was that I was to return to St Catherine Adult Correctional Centre, Remand Block GB 3. I was no longer sharing a cell with Puppa and Scoffla. The moment I left, someone else had entered the cell to make up the third cellmate. I was now located with National as we had just returned from circuit so we jumped in a man's single cell to make up three. As mentioned before, no two men ever located in a cell. It was either one man in a cell or three or more but never two, two men in a cell was and is unacceptable in the Jamaican prison system, the thought alone is a one-way ticket to hell.

As I lay in my cell, I thought about the two visits from my loved ones. Staring at the big bags and other items I now had, it reassured me that it was real and not a dream. I now had clothes, a new pair of Reeboks and loads of toiletries, not to mention food and money, enough of it to last me a good while too, for they gave me more money on their second visit. My sister also gave me her Walkman that she brought to listen to music on the plane. I'll never forget, the Walkman was slim and chrome, it had a rechargeable battery component that could attach to the bottom of it, and it came with volume controllable headphones. If I were a fool in prison, inmates would have taken it off me. Trust me when I say, everybody on my block adored it.

Thinking about my children's mother's lips against my own, and the feeling of her hands against my body, a warm feeling came over me, yet a feeling of sadness encompassed me. It felt like I had lost her all over again. I remember closing my eyes and just lying there, hoping the music would take my mind off the pain, when I felt someone nudge me.

"Israel, wha yuh ah sleep." National asked as I took one of the earpieces out of my ear.

"Nah, I'm just relaxing." I responded.

"Wha yuh ah do?" he began to laugh. "Wifie yuh ah tink bout?" I smiled. Trying to hide the hurt I felt. "Gwan think."

"Yuh see it National." I said before closing my eyes again. The thought of being so far away from the people I loved so much tortured me. By the way I felt inside, I realised prison was going to test my faith in more ways than one. My circumstances and situations were either going to build or break me physiologically. Lying there, I challenged my thoughts as I travelled this desirable, yet hurtful path.

"Bloodclaat, man hungry." I jumped up; the thoughts were too much at that moment. "National, blud unno wha biscuit?" I asked.

"Wha yuh seh, can't sleep, baby mudda ah ride yuh?" National responded with a smile. "Yeh, mi would ah eat sum biscuit yes."

I reached into my food bag and brought out a pack of biscuits. "Gwan share this."

"Bless Israel." National replied.

"Respect, Israel." Trelawny said, as National handed him the pack.

"Remand again my yout, the system wicked." National said.

"Wicked is an understatement, Jamaican system fuck up, man haffi wait months again til circuit."

"Wha happen down there?" Trelawny asked.

"Fuck all." I responded.

"Jamaican system a joke system my yout." Trelawny said.

I took a deep breath.

"Mi like dat still, mumi cum check yuh." National said. "She ah go wait pon yuh?" he asked.

"Nah mus." I replied.

"Dat good." National responded.

We got talking in the cell about various things when I heard a familiar voice shout "Israel, National!"

"Pappa." National responded towards the block.

"Ah wha unno ah seh?" he asked.

"Wi deh yah, ah wha yuh ah seh?" National shouted

"Man cool. Yo, Israel wha yuh seh wifie forward check yuh, ah yuh mean my yout."

On approaching the grille, I returned the shout. "Suffering days done my yout." I responded. "Man, bless."

"Man bless yes. Israel yuh wha sum driers?" Pappa asked.

"Man criss down ya, man ave food blud."

"How yuh mean Israel. Man ah lock off den, inna de morrows."

"Inna de strong." I replied.

The following morning after emptying my piss-bottle, I left the block and walked over to the Ship.

"Wha ah gwaan Speci"

"Israel, mi tink yuh gone." he replied. "Dem remand yuh again."

"A fuckery, yuh see it."

"Jus cool."

"Mi can gi yuh a likkle ting still my yout." I put my hand in my pocket. "Mi can gi yuh a hundred still, mi get some money down ah jail."

"Jus cool. Keep that." Speci replied.

"Yo, mi a check Screw. Likkle more." I said and walked off.

"Israel." Screw said as I approached his cell.

"Judge nah gi man no freedom blud, so wha ah gwan Ras."

"Nuttin nah gwan." Screw replied.

"Mi have a likkle ting, mi can gi yuh some ting still."

"That criss Israel, wha happen to yuh?" He kissed his teeth. "Man rate yuh, yuh kno dat, if man brok mi check yuh."

Screw was a hustler and knew how to make ends meet in prison, he was also respected by a lot of inmates on his block. We talked for a bit. "Mi soon forward, mi ah go check my yout and forward." I walked off. "Buju, wha a gwan Kirkist"

"Mi deh yah. So wha happen?" he asked.

"Judge no remand man again."

"So it go my yout. Man haffi just hold de fate, yuh done kno ah so it go inna dem place yah."

While in the Slaughterhouse, not only did I link those three inmates of whom I had made mention, but many others before returning to my block for morning lockdown. On New Hall, I had made many connections, both through my friends and through the way in which I carried myself as an individual. It was crazy, I had respect from guys who disliked one another, but were genuinely cool with me. What made the respect feel that much more real was that I had won it during the days of my suffering, when I had nothing. That solidified my feeling about the people I was connecting with.

Chapter 10:
Association & Growth

As weeks went by after returning from circuit court, I read and studied the Old Testament more frequently. The knowledge attained increased my curiosity about the Hebrew language and culture. I recalled that my mother's father always said he was a Jew, and that my mother always wore her gold chain with a Star of David on it. Those memories, along with the things I was reading in the laws, reminded me of certain utterances she made, and things she did, which heightened my curiosity. I had been reading the Bible before heading to St Ann kangaroo court, at that time I would read anywhere, any book, or chapter of the scriptures. Something led me to start reading the law only when I returned, and then I felt the need to re-evaluate my method of reading the Old Testament. I began reading from Genesis chapter one page one, and I intended to read the whole thirty-nine books, page by page.

I'll never forget, a month or so after I returned from court, there was talk on the block that one of the notorious hit men from Spanish Town's Klansman Gang was at the reception on South Block with other new inmates. As I sat there reading my Bible, inmates were talking about how dangerous this individual was, and the power him and his people had on the outside. The reality at that time was geographically, St Catherine Adult Correctional Centre was situated right next to one of Klansman's stronghold territories. Within the hour, the new inmates arrived on the block and were put in selected locations. I sat there and watched them as other inmates greeted, laughed and talked with this specific inmate who was a member of the Klansman Gang. As I stared, an inmate formally known as Al Capone (R.I.P) walked past me and spoke. "Di right ting yuh ah do, read yuh Bible."

I looked up at him. He looked back and smiled as he continued to walk. My eyes followed him for a second before I resumed reading.

Al Capone was a deportee from Canada; over time, we became very good friends. With a nickname like Al Capone, I think I need not say much more. He was known to live up to the reputation he had made for himself in both yard and abroad, not to mention he was a lethal kick boxer. He was big, muscular and tall to go with it. I had learnt about Al Capone's skill and knowledge of the art of kickboxing about a week after my return from circuit court. National, myself, Al Capone, C'roy and Moses had begun to train together. Each of us had martial arts backgrounds prior to us coming together, between us there were a few different styles being displayed which made it more exciting and creative.

It had all begun with National and I doing martial arts training in our cell and on the block in the passageway. National, like everyone else on the block knew I loved martial arts from the days I kept myself to myself and hardly spoke. I used to train alone in the hut next to the kitchen near the ball field, outside a place more commonly known as grass. One morning Moses came along and asked to join in. National said yes. That same day, Al Capone and C'roy participated too, and from then it became a regular thing.

Weeks went by from the moment this much talked about inmate from the Klansman Gang had come on the block. He and my friends had begun to click and so we began talking too. It was during a conversation that we both realised we knew one another from road.

"Yuh kno seh yuh face look familiar, and now yuh mention dem call yu Tata ah road mi member yuh," Waynie-Bones said. "Ah jus true ah Israel, mi hear dem call yuh, yeh man mi member yuh."

"Prison name, yuh dun kno. Yeh man, mi use to deh ah Spanish Town regular all bout, outta Jones Ave, over Daddy Meekie yard. Man use to love da Canal Banks, regular mi daya Train-line and over Rivoli. Dem still have the studio behind Canal Banks?" I asked.

"Yeah man." Waynie-Bones responded in a calm tone that matched his slim frame. Looks can be very deceiving, and he wasn't an inmate to be taken lightly.

Back in the days when I lived in Jamaica, I used to have a lot of DJ friends, and hung out at various studios in both Kingston and Spanish Town. In Spanish Town, Gilbert Studio on the plaza was the place to be. Miami Vice over Train-line behind Canal Banks was where my artist friends, Likkle Meekie and Daddy Meekie lived. Those were glorious days filled with great memories shared with many Spanish Town artists, both known and unknown.

It was Puppa, Sherlock, Scoffla, Waynie-Bones (R.I.P), National, and a few others that used to click on Remand Block. I was part of that clique, but still linked with my friends at New Hall; with them, I'd made an unbreakable connection and kept it real. Realistically I was a loner, and loved it like that, but I was now chilling with people on my block. Even though I was around people more and letting people into my personal space, learning to love my own company, I would take time out to do me, and that was to enjoy reflection time. Everyone knew that was how I got down, and they respected it. I had also begun taking and making calls on Remand Block now. Everything around me had changed, especially me. My guard wasn't as high, but as I mentioned, I still made time for myself. Personal time was important for self-identity and I needed to maintain my own space to allow and understand my own growth. I was now talking to my family in England regularly. It was more than a joy hearing their voices, though it brought about a feeling of sadness when the calls ended. But because I was now making these calls under lock, I was able to stay on the phone for hours, not like when I would go over to New Hall, where I'd have to cut the call to return to my block and prepare for lockdown. What I realised about this change in communications, was that the more I communicated with family and loved ones, the more the emotions; yet, I wouldn't have wanted it any other way. Hearing their voices was more than sweet music to my ears. Over a phone call, Minnie had given me the full hundred about my firstborn child's mother, the lady from Portmore, who resided in Runaway Bay. She said they had asked her to come and look for me, all expenses paid and she refused. I explained to her that none of the family in the UK should feel a way about the suffering I had faced during the earlier part of my imprisonment, how were they to know what I was going through. I totally understood that they thought all this time our family in JA were linking me, and they assumed as the High Commission had said I didn't want visits, that I was good. My barrister had also lied saying he was visiting me, yet I had only seen him at court appearances. So naturally, they assumed that I was fine. Neither my family nor the British Embassy knew at that time that I was suffering, as the warders lied saying that I had refused to see the embassy. So, everyone was getting played. The prison system as small as it is in Jamaica, can be spiteful and lose you if they wish. As for my barrister he was just out for money, he was a straight up thief.

Chapter 11:
Solider Induction

Apart from Kara, the biggest change to prison institutions was the introduction of soldiers in January 2000 to the major adult correctional centres on the island. If ever a warder uniform was considered intimidating, the sight of a group of soldiers dressed in camouflage clothing and long guns was far worse. Soldiers were sent into the prisons to replace the warders that had been suspended due to politics, and those who walked out on strike. Soldiers now controlled the century boxes and the prison grounds. There were still a small minority of warders working but it was clear that soldiers were in full control. Because of their military training and background, it was clear that they had a different mind-set that meant one would have to conduct oneself with them slightly differently, the intimidation and disrespect some warders may take, a soldier clearly wasn't about to, and I had to learn the hard way. I faced the wrath of soldiers and wished it had never occurred. We were placed under lock a little early one afternoon. Not all prisoners were in their cells yet, but I was in mine, and verbally expressed my disappointment about being rushed into my cell. My cellmates at that time also expressed their views, but were at the back of the cell. Two of us had not filled up our water bottles as of yet, and wanted to fill them. To be honest, we could have asked an inmate to fill them, but then the soldiers were rushing everyone. A soldier walked past and overheard us complaining. He pulled on the padlock, smirked and continued to the next cell. Angered by the smirk on his face, I called him a pussyhole; his colleagues heard me and called him back. They stood there laughing and displayed the odd pointing of the finger at me while entertaining themselves at my suffering. One of the soldiers asked me if I wanted to come out, I replied, "Yes." The one who smirked said, "Let him out". This time, a warder stood there observing. They had said something to another colleague who had walked past, he then walked towards me telling his colleagues to leave me. He stood at the cell and called me closer. Not knowing his intentions as I was going off his words to his comrades, I came right up to the cell door. Who told me to do that? He grabbed my locks banging my head against the grille as he pulled on them. All I could see was his big boot as I held my head down. He had one foot on the ground, the other braced against the grille. Trust me when I say he was really leaning back and pulling on my locks. The others started hitting me though the grille and laughing, I was angry as hell. I pulled the soldiers arm that had my hair into me and he let me go. On the ground were a few of my locks. I remember the soldier asking the warder to fly the gate. Reluctant to do it, I could see in his face he didn't want to but nevertheless he did it. The soldier told me to come out, I refused, so they came in and began to hit me as they drew me out. It wasn't until inmates repeatedly shouted, he's a foreigner that they stopped hitting me, and to be honest, it wasn't even straight away. When they eventually did, the look in their eyes was as if they wanted to kill me. That night and for days following, I was in pain. I had been hit with fists, slapped, kicked, and beaten with a baton and the strap from the SLR rifle and trust me, that strap reminded me of mamma's old-time beatings. I was bruised and my head was pounding. To be honest I don't know if it was due to my locks being pulled and ripped out, or the hits to my head and face, but the pain was real. I knew soldiers weren't to be played with. I had friends on the outside who were soldiers and they were as serious as judges, and as eagles, swift in carrying out judgement. I had seen soldiers beat police on the island before in St Ann and Kingston, so I knew the temperament that they could have. There are some things you can't take back. In fact, nothing said or done can really be taken back. The reality is, there are just lessons to be learnt from all things, and I learnt a valuable one that day.

Chapter 12:
Pleasant Surprises

Months passed and it was time for myself, National and other inmates that were on remand to appear at St Ann circuit court. While in St Ann, I had received two shocking visits. The first one was a member of my family from Kingston 8. Jaro's little sister and I were very close; in fact, Keisha and I were closer than anyone could imagine. We connected really well the first time I met her in 1997. At the time of my return in 1998, the year I was locked up in St Ann, she was away in the United States. It was more than a pleasure seeing her again. She said that a lady told my aunty that my little sister and my children's mother had visited me. I quickly concluded that the lady was Mitzie. Mitzie was the only person I told that my family from the UK had visited me, plus she was the only person who knew both my family in Kingston and I. Mitzie originally was from Kingston, but now residing in St Ann. She was kind and had a lovely personality. During the time I'd received a visit from my little sister Minnie and Lele, Mitzie also came to check me. She had brought me food, she also promised to visit me every circuit until I was either freed or sentenced, which I thought was extremely kind. Mitzie was my Aunt's boyfriend's cousin. The reason I thought it was extremely kind of her was because she was doing this off her own back, without any financial help from my family in England or Jamaica. I now had a source in St Ann, someone to visit me, and if I needed anything, I could give money to her to purchase it. I usually got her to buy me cooked food from the road. Keisha was happy I was now getting visits; furthermore, she was happy to see me. It wasn't just what she said; it was her smile and the look in her eyes that told me this. Before she left, she gave me food and a few things. She told me she wouldn't be able to visit me again as she would be returning to the States, but I must take care. I hugged and thanked her, and then she left.

I remember being woken from my sleep to receive the shock of my life. That night, I must have reflected so hard on life that during the day, I was gone. When you're in a station lock up like Ocho Rios, sleeping is all there is to do in that sweatbox. My cellmates woke me saying a policeman is calling me.

"Yes officer." I responded.

"Stephen, foreign visit." He said as he approached my cell door. Instantly I began thinking, last circuit my little sister and my children's mother had surprised me, but I had spoken to them both and neither of them mentioned to me that they were coming to Jamaica again. I was excited and curious at the same time.

"Yuh sista deya fi see yuh." The officer said as he locked the cell behind me after I stepped out. "Come."

Confused, I followed him to the gate. Not only did I stand at the exact same place as I had stood before which is where every inmate stands when they're waiting for a visit, but I experienced the same feeling. I had begun to wonder if it really was my visit, when suddenly my big sister came around the corner.

We smiled at one another. A sign of relief came over me, while excitement filled my body, "Wha ah gwaan sis?" I said as we hugged.

"Wha yuh sayin bro." Marie kissed me on my cheek. "Yuh alright?" she asked.

"Cool. Cyaan wait fi get outta dis hell hole." I smiled.

We began talking for a while. I had asked her about my case, and like everyone else, she had nothing concrete to tell me. Believe me, it never bothered me. It had reached the point where I had stopped believing in those insincere barristers getting me off, and had placed my destiny in God's hands, which I thought was the most logical thing to do. The Bible had become a trusted friend and if God was capable of doing what he had done for his people, the Israelites, making them a sign to the nations and a people unto himself even though they were a stubborn people, I thought to myself, if I was obedient to his word there was nothing he couldn't do for me. And if I were to be freed or sentenced, he'd make a symbol or a sign out of me to all that were wise enough to acknowledge. We laughed and joked about my barrister, which to be honest was good because it really lifted my spirit. She had told me she was coming to court and not to worry, by my response, she knew I wasn't. As I said, I had left my future in God's hands, and what was to be would be. Before leaving, she told me she had left some items for me and gave me two bags of food and money.

Again, I was remanded to appear at Kangaroo court next circuit. To be honest, I was getting used to it. I would tell myself, no result is neither positive nor negative, though deep down I wanted my freedom to see my loved ones back in the UK. My sister had come to court as promised; she had words with my so-called barrister. I refer to him in this manner, as he wasn't the barrister who my family had paid to represent me. It was kind of crazy; my family had paid for a QC to represent me and instead of a Queen's Council appearing on my behalf, he had given the case to a jester. The joke was definitely on us. My belief is he skimmed off some money and gave that clown the rest saying they were both representing me, and not once did I see this QC at court. The only times I ever saw him were when he came to the prison for me to sign over money to him saying it was for outstanding court fees. The family home had been sold at that time and he had quite a bit of money in holding for me. Unfortunately, I didn't see or spend much of it. Since being released from prison mid 2006, I've seen proof that my family paid my court fees from their own pocket. Jay has shown me evidence of this. So basically, I was robbed, but on the grand scale, I'm thankful I'm alive and free, that's all that counts.

Chapter 13:
Remand Block GB3

I had returned to St Catherine Adult Correctional Centre with more than enough clothes, toiletries and a next new pair of sneakers to add to the footwear I already had, not to mention money. National had gone into a cell with Waynie-Bones, Scoffla and Puppa. I decided to locate by myself and hopped into the cell right opposite where my friends located that was left empty for specific reasons. My friends had told me not to locate there but I had my excuse if it all came on top with the authorities. The truth was, I hated locating on the ground with other inmates. I preferred to go sky high, sky high was the term used to indicate that an inmate was ready to go up into his hammock or located in one. For me sky high had a slightly different meaning, it meant high above ground and out of sight. Despite being a people person, I was also the kind of guy that needed time for self. That's always been my personality, Stevie time was important, even though I may not have always used this alone time for good, being mischievous and quite confused as a youth, I was more than capable of doing all the wrong things without the need for companionship. From childhood, I enjoyed my own company and was never afraid to face a challenge by myself. I was now learning to look at life through different eyes, using this alone time more constructively, more focused in my thoughts. I needed time to gather, channel and reflect, all of which is quite hard to do when others are constantly in one's immediate space. I needed to feel less trapped in other inmate's energy, to me, when I located on the ground there was way too much exchange of energy, and never really time for self, there were always people in my face. Personally, I'm a deep thinker. At times, I just liked to lay back and look up at the ceiling, and if an inmate called me and I felt not to talk, I'd just not answer and they'd think I was asleep and talk between themselves. Unless it was something really important, then I'd answer, or they'd get up and nudge me. For this reason, I hated locating on ground, plus as I stated, what I disliked more than words, was the feeling of inappropriate energy. There was just way too much energy flying around, especially when one is aware of it, it can get quite uncomfortable, and I wasn't strong enough mentally at that time to not let it affect me. To be honest, I tried to distance myself, avoiding as much as I could in my early stages of reconditioning my mind, my thoughts and what I let affect me or not, so I opted for the hammock as the only physical way to escape, knowing it psychologically made me feel a little better about the situation. However, in a single cell, ground was an amazing place to be. In fact, it was physically and mentally spacious. One could do as one pleased and definitely experience a more relaxing feeling, leading to greater peace of mind, and nothing can compare to peace of mind. Greater power is obtained in stillness than in movement and I needed to be still.

In prison, to me it is impossible to live comfortably. There is a difference between living comfortably, searching for peace of mind and adjusting to one's environment. In my eyes, there is no living comfortably in prison, after all, I wasn't born a caged animal, or to be controlled, so I couldn't and wouldn't allow myself to see comfort in my situation. There is a big difference between comfort and adjusting. Having no control at all over one's own movement is quite an uncomfortable feeling. I mean, being confined to an encaged environment isn't natural. Even a bird once freed from an unnatural habitat will fly away to the heavens gladly, but prisoners, when let out of our cells, there is limited movement, restrictions apply, so on that note, I wasn't comfortable at any time, but learnt to adjust. Through adjusting to my environment, a completely different form of strength developed in the process. Accepting my reality, living in the present, the here and now at that time, I allowed myself to make the best of it, manoeuvring in ways necessary to help find inner peace, which I sought every day. This concludes why I took the single cell, even though risks came with locating in that specific cell, I had formulated a plan of action if needed. But at that time worrying or fear wasn't my companion nor my first thought, I needed me time, I needed space to download internal information, study, read and channel. Wanting the single cell wasn't to be comfortable; comfort had nothing to do with anything I ever did whilst behind bars. For me, this situation was more about necessity, to aid my mission for inner peace.

Selling and trading is a big business in prison, I mean really big. Some inmates sold anything and everything, even their souls. One of the main reasons for this was to satisfy their nose. Smoke was really important to a lot of prisoners; from high-grade weed down to raga, inmates were smoking, I guess for some it helped to ease the tension or escape the stresses of daily life, which can be quite traumatising, not to mention additional memories from situations that occurred before being incarcerated. Whether good or bad, some of these memories can be a lot to carry, so I could relate to why inmates loved to smoke. Personally, I kicked the habit of smoking all together when I hit prison. During my time in the jailhouse, I smoked cigarettes at times but after facing problems with the police in St Ann, I knew I was going to have it hard when I was sent to run my remand in Spanish Town prison. There was no way I would be able to financially maintain the habit of smoking and so I stopped just like that, in one day. Imagine on the road back in England, not to mention just before I was locked up, I was a ganja-baby, I used to smoke weed all the time; thank God I had the will to just stop.

In prison, trading for goods between inmates occurred, but selling was big business and a daily thing. It was on specific days the new shipment would arrive. In those days, inmates were allowed two visits a week for footwear, clothing items and toiletries. Depending on our surname, it was Monday and Thursday or Tuesday and Friday. Sunday was the only day there were no visits, unless you were sick and had the doctor's permission. Saturday was dry food day though some inmates got cooked food on the weekend too. Wednesday was the real food day; it was the day that many inmates who usually ate off the tray chose not to. Most people would try to get something from someone's bag if they themselves weren't getting visits, and believe me when I say, a lot of inmates weren't getting regular visits, but then hustling was big business, so receiving a visit wasn't always necessary, providing an inmate had money.

Due to my profile and where I had come from, in the sense of what I went through in the beginning, my respect grew even more, likewise my pocket. My visiting days back then fell on Mondays and Thursdays. My sister Marie had checked me, bringing more toiletries and more underwear on top of what was in the bags she had left at the front desk in Ocho Rios police station. I smiled to myself, in the space of two circuit court appearances I had received two foreign visits, it felt good not just to receive the things that were brought for me although God knows I needed the support, but it was the feeling of knowing I was missed and loved. That put a smile on my heart and of course on my face. Before going back to the UK my sister had organised with some friends of hers from Spanish Town to visit me frequently. On top of that, I was buying prisoners out, keeping what I wanted, while giving to the less fortunate. On a serious note, I was helping those who had nothing. Without asking, I could relate to what they were feeling, I had experienced what they were going through. God had opened a way for me to do so, and I thanked the Most High for the blessing and did it willingly.

One blessed morning, warders and soldiers decided to search the entire Remand Block, which is upstairs and downstairs. It wasn't the first search I would have gone through, but usually I personally had nothing illegal. In prison, every inmate has to take responsibility for his own shit, unless he's paying another inmate to do that. It was wise to make it known to someone else, at least then if the inmate who was getting paid didn't claim the prohibited item or items if found, he'd get a beating after the search was over, and maybe have to reimburse the original owner. However, if he claimed it, then he would get in trouble with the authorities and all would be well with his fellow inmates. Depending on what was found, the punishment varied. I had experienced physical punishment from authorities first hand, when my locks were ripped out by a soldier who held me against the grille while his comrades thumped me; not because they found anything illegal but because I was rude. But to give you a little insight, that is the kind of punishment an inmate can receive and worse, plus some kind of rights taken away on top of it.

Why I say that morning was blessed, my friends and I decided not to use our hotplate and boil tea. Another cell had offered us hot water so we took it, good thing. The cell I was in had a chappie, which is where illegal things are hidden in the wall or ground, making it hard for the authorities to find, especially if the cover is made firm and made to match the texture or colour of the surrounding areas. In the cell I chose to go in, the chappie was on the floor and the cover hadn't been made well. In fact, the cover didn't even fit. The guys had covered the ground with newspaper and left the cell empty, therefore, no one could be blamed. That was if the authorities ever chose to search the empty cell. Just before the authorities came on the block, my friends shouted for me to send on the bags that consisted of sticks of weed and the three-star rachets, which I did. Because money is illegal, although most prisoners have it, if the authorities wish, they can take yours from you and put it on your rit. Rit is the name for the book kept at the main office where money is signed in, and food vouchers known as booklets are issued out. The money I returned with from circuit court, I had hidden in a secret compartment that I made in my bag, and some I'd rolled up length ways and slid into the razor tear I had made in my jeans waist, and zip line. Because jeans are thick, I knew it would be hard for them to feel the money when the authorities got me out of my cell as part of their routine check. Our hotplate was too big and would have made lots of noise, as there was no time for either of us to send traffic. Traffic for those wondering, is a lengthy piece of rope with a bottle filled with water tied just under the mouthpiece. It gives weight to the rope allowing it to travel distance, which enables you to collect and send things to other cells, by throwing the bottle while holding the end of the string. I stood there smiling to myself as the warders unlocked the padlock for the main gate. The hotplate had not been used and was stone cold. My friends looked at me from their cell, I looked at them and nodded, I already knew what I was going to say. When the time came for my cell to be searched, I came out with my piss-bottle when they had told me to. This was the procedure. I stood and watched them as they began going through my bags and lifting up the sheets of newspaper on the floor. The authorities knew my suffering prior to me getting visits, due to the rotation shifts from block to block many had seen me, and knew me from the days I was in continuous fights and arguments.

"Yuh ah hide chappie?" A warder said.

"No officer." I responded, in a dumb tone of voice.

"Wha yuh ah play fool?" A green suit asked whom I had spoken with before for various reasons, on more than one occasion. "Yuh betta pray sey nuttin no in deh."

The warder came up with the hotplate. The green suit looked at me.

"Wha yuh ah do wid so much tings inmate?" A bad-minded warder asked.

Looking at the soldiers and warders around, I took no notice of the grey suit warder and made my peace with the green suit overseer, whose uniform signified higher authority.

"I had no idea that was there officer, believe me. Officer, you know I just came back from court in St Ann, you saw when I returned a couple of days ago. And you saw when the police handed money in at reception and I signed it into the book. In a space of a few days, why would I do something so stupid? I didn't even know anything was under there, it's only been a few days I've been back."

Those days I had a strong Jamaican accent, I don't know how I did it, but I spoke better English than the queen herself, which was funny now thinking back on it.

"Cum, cum, tek yuh piss-gal and go back inna yuh cell."

Picking my piss-bottle up, I walked back into my cell. The warder locked me in, and then moved on to the next cell. My friends smiled at me. I returned the smile, and then began putting my belongings back and fixing up my cell. In my mind, I told myself never again. I had taken physical risk to attain psychological peace of mind, and could have made situations worse. Being a deep thinker, I analysed what I had done, foolishly, I moved towards gaining what I wanted without looking at the bigger picture. Although I had a plan, and the intention was for good, it could have backfired on me if the warders wanted to be difficult. A wise man learns from his mistakes. Believe me I had learned from mine, not to say I would never make one again, but I was wiser not to make the same one that's for sure.

I'll never forget it was the same day as the search a soldier came on the block and asked for me. As I looked at my friends I stood there and said nothing, neither did they. The first thing that came to my mind was, is he here to terrorise me? Was he a part of the search party this morning? Thoughts of the beat down I had previously received from soldiers ran through my mind. Then I thought, why would he ask for me if he were one of the soldiers that were standing at my cell during the morning search? So, I answered him. The soldier then pulled me to one side and asked me what my sister's name was. For a second, I looked at him. He asked me again and told me he was a friend of the family in Spanish Town. So I told him her name. He then walked me to my cell and handed me some money. Yes, I thought to myself, a new link. At that time in prison, a soldier was the best and strongest link; they had control of the facility and were more respected by inmates.

Daily the soldier would check me, even though he could clearly see I didn't need that kind of looking after. I guess he just wanted to make everybody know we were connected. One day, he checked me with a few of his squadron, one of whom had punched me in my face, and kicked and stamped on me the day they beat me and pulled out a few of my dreadlocks. To be honest, I don't know how many times he hit me; I just know he helped kick my arse. His colleague apologised to me and told my soldier friend there and then, in front of me, what he and a few others had done. I spoke with the soldier who pulled out my locks on a different occasion, turning a foe into an ally. When my link wasn't around, the same soldier or one or two others were there that I could count on when necessary. To me that was prison, like life itself nothing stays the same. I was just glad for the link Marie had made for me before she returned to England.

Time had gone by and I was enjoying being able to survive financially which enabled me to buy whatever I needed. Money was coming from my family in England, I would ask for money only when needed, and I mean *only* when needed. One evening whilst under lock, Minnie told me on the phone, that two close friends of mine, Sophie and Bounty (R.I.P), God bless his soul, were coming to Jamaica and would visit me. Minnie also told me, one of my other sisters nicknamed Pudding (R.I.P beautiful) gave Bounty some money to buy me whatever I needed. I had mentioned to Minnie that I wanted a whole box of cup noodles, toiletries, and money snuck in to me so I could buy things in prison. I explained to her that things were cheaper to buy in prison, as inmates sell their belongings for less than nothing to support their nose. I remember her laughing and then telling me to be careful. Not that I had anything to worry about, I guess she was just worried I'd get into trouble or problems.

I was excited. How I saw it, God was blessing me, all the suffering I had faced in the beginning felt like it was a test of my faith. Turning to the Bible, well, that really opened my eyes.

Seeing the Holy Scriptures through different eyes, I was determined to learn to read biblical Hebrew, and speak the Hebrew language. I knew the language spoken today was modern Hebrew and not the exact language that the Old Testament people and prophets spoke; but it still fascinated me to understand this revised ancient language.

What I came to understand after reading the whole of Genesis, Exodus, Leviticus, Numbers, Deuteronomy, and Joshua from page to page, sometimes going over a verse or chapter more than once to make sure it stuck in my head changed me. I now had a totally different view on life. Religion in its modern context had blinded my sight, or should I say the concept, which I had grown to know affected my perception. The Rastafarian perspective of Tafari Makonnen being Christ, the fulfilment of Revelation 5:5 was no longer visible to my eyes; it was as unrealistic as the concept of a white Jesus. I still upheld the Emperor of Ethiopia as a great king, even the greatest of our time. Only before the Emperor, did the Queen of England bow, surely that would always be a sign of true royalty and strength, but he wasn't the biblical messiah who is prophesied to return and establish the kingdom, wherein it is written his people will dwell amongst him in peace.

The thing is, from all the books I had previously read about the Emperor of Ethiopia and delighting myself in his wonderful speeches, never once had he said or indicated he was the biblical messiah, but preconceived ideas and the philosophy in which I had grown, had led me not to see this. What I found interesting with the veil now removed from my eyes was that memories of the past came forth. I had forgotten a vital lesson I was taught, one that would make anyone of Jamaican ancestry very proud, especially when it comes to history. In my late teens whilst I lived in Jamaica, a few wise men explained to me why they themselves wore dreadlocks, the concept and Israelite connection according to them predated the Rastafarian movement. These Individuals considered themselves biblical Israelites, and explained that black people in Jamaica considered themselves Israelites centuries before any movement was established in Jamaica based on the Emperor of Ethiopia, and that the original Israelites were black. And that the concept of growing dreadlocks also existed before Tafari Makonnen was crowned Emperor, they had explained that various kingdoms and people in Africa grew locks before 1930. According to them, many Jamaican's had labelled themselves Rastafarians because of Tafari's crowning and the identity of being an Israelite faded into the background. How could I have forgotten such powerful information; Jamaica truly is a special little Island under the Sun. Since release from prison, I learnt about the Spanish and Portuguese inquisition, and the arrival of melanated Jews taken as slaves from Europe in the 15th century, and even before. Some of these black Jews arrived in Jamaica predating the transatlantic slave trade. Other Israelites referred to as Black Jews during the inquisition were sent to Angola, Congo and lands on the west coast of Africa, only later to end up on the western shores by force. Truly learning such valuable historical truth validated what these wise men once told me about the acknowledgment of Israelites in Jamaica before the Rastafarian movement. I have great respect for the Rastafarian way of life, any true Rasta will say they are Israelites, and connect with the Bible. No doubt the Rastafarian movement is truly a branch of the Israelite truth, however, returning to the root is key. Truly, history has not been taught, well, not been taught honestly to us that is. Mass misinformation, preconceived ideology and cultural relationship even if incorrect can be powerfully misleading, and so I had buried the true knowledge of the Jamaican spiritual ancestry shared with me, only to return to the truth of my Israelite identity. In prison, I was now reading and studying by myself, without preconceived ideas or thoughts. I had put ego, pride and the desire to follow any man's concept aside. I wanted a personal relationship with my Bible and that I had begun to do.

When I was around nineteen and returned to the UK because things were that bad in Jamaica, I got deep into studying Egyptology. In so doing, I'd seen the true pictures of the Pharaohs and hieroglyphics, their dark tone and hue was undeniable, the ancient Egyptians were undoubtedly melanated people. Using the knowledge I had studied, I put two and two together and came up with the solid conclusion. Namely, if Moses was taken by Pharaoh's daughter unto herself as writing in the book of Exodus, and Pharaoh believed this child was of his own flesh and blood, Moses not only had to be a melanated man, but very dark in complexion. Not to mention Zipporah the daughter of the Midian priest, who would later go on to be Moses wife told her father that an Egyptian had drawn the water for her. The realism of life had opened my eyes, like within the scriptures it was through situations and circumstances the weak were made strong, the blind made to see, and individuals rose to glory and understanding.

I recall on many occasions Al Capone would walk past and smile as I sat at my cell doorway reading my Bible. Very rarely would he disturb me when I was reading. When I think about it, most people wouldn't. He would always wait until I was walking on or off the block, or just chilling at my cell listening to my Walkman, or at my cell front doing nothing, then we would talk or should I say, he would start a conversation about the Bible and just allow me to talk. One day those interactions between us ended. I can't remember if he had served his time or if he got out on bail. All I know was, Al Capone had been released. I was happy for him, as I would be for any man. Prison is no place to feel good about being in. Al Capone had been through a lot, like myself he had many fights in prison, but his always ended with more serious and life-threatening outcomes. The most classic of them all was with a mutual friend of ours, known as Rema. They had fisted it out, and of course, Al Capone kicked the shit out of him. After that, they stabbed it out. It was crazy seeing the two of them sitting side by side at the hospital section together. I visited them a few times that day, and couldn't do anything more than shake my head; it is insane when you think how miscommunication between colleagues can result to such violent actions towards one another. Having experienced similar situations myself in the past, I can honestly say ego, pride and lack of self-reflection are just some of the pitfalls to name a few that we as a people have, as a people we need to find better ways of dealing with our issues. Al Capone himself had escaped death whilst located on Remand Block. He had slapped a prisoner in his face and the inmate's friend had stabbed Al Capone in his throat whilst he was asleep on his cell floor with his head turned to the grille. I asked him afterwards why he slept like that knowing he had enemies, his reply was laughter. I couldn't help but laugh too. Prison had many crazy moments like that.

Prison itself was unpredictable; you just never knew when friend could turn foe, or who really was for you from who was against you. Some inmates knew how to play the game. In Al Capone's situation, he and a friend allowed their disagreement about whatever to go too far, in prison you just never knew. To add to the madness, warders when ready would run on your block and dig down the whole place, or just stop an individual and ask for a random search. Inmates planning and plotting for other inmates, and I mean your friends, not just your enemies occurred from time to time, trust was a complicated thing. You just never could tell. Despite the respect I had and was continuously creating, I was always on my toes, ready for anything and everything.

On a more vibrant and happier note, music on the block was a twenty-four-hour thing. There was never a dull or quiet day. Inmates would play their prison made sound systems loud as if everybody wanted to hear what they were playing. To be honest many did, myself included at times, especially when competitions were taking place and I was in the mood to participate. Then there were those who didn't have their own music, whether radio, Walkman or system so escaping from one's thoughts and listening to someone else's music was therapeutic. I guess it was heaven for them. It was amazing what people were capable of doing with broken down car radios, old and new CD Walkmans, tape decks and a few wires and a prison made amp. Competitions were a regular thing, with inmates judged by the forward they received.

At times, the energy on the block was peaceful, though it was momentary. Because our cell doors weren't electronically opened by the push of a button but manually operated, we would knock the padlocks on our cell doors repeatedly. When metal clashed against metal, the amount of noise it created, could be heard on other blocks, not to mention on the streets of the surrounding areas. It was the loudest forward that won the competition, and believe me, the general public weren't escaping the celebration.

Banging our padlocks was the same method we used to get warders attention if an inmate was seriously sick under lock, but warders knew the difference from a cry for help and a cheer of joy.

There are undeniable, naturally talented electricians in Jamaica. I use the term naturally talented, because the inmates making or fixing systems for prisoners for a small price, mostly learnt their trade in prison. These inmates were like the actors from the old classic TV series the A-Team; they would make something out of nothing. Pieces of equipment that people in England and countries like America would take for granted, these inmates would test every component on and keep what worked. As for the shell or body of whatever the equipment was, it wasn't thrown away, and believe me, it came in handy one day. An electrician would rebuild it, adding new components he removed from whatever other equipment he received or bought from another inmate. What made me laugh, most times the pieces were from totally different objects, both in size and ability, but their mental genius would make it work. The more I think about it, Jamaica has some of the most naturally talented people on earth. It's just a shame so many I encountered in prison didn't remain on the road once freed or should I say, stick to the trade they found in prison when no longer incarcerated, rather than return to a life of crime. This is where I believe the Jamaican government needs to set up programmes like the countries that they so much want to be like, which will allow the youths, or at least give them the opportunity, to continue whatever trade they picked up in prison.

Personally, I believe this would help lower crime and the number of killings on the streets of the capital and other parishes. While on the topic of prison and trade, it's prisoners that teach other inmates the odd new trade or two, and not the poor rehabilitation system run by the prison. On that note, maximum respect has to be given to the inspirational and positive role models serving time behind bars.

Fitness and health were never a part of the rehabilitation programme when I first arrived at Spanish Town prison in 1999. It was never really encouraged, and it still isn't in Spanish Town, as far as I know that is. In General Penitentiary there is a gym built opposite the notorious block known as Building. Even in having the gym facility there, inmates aren't encouraged enough to train and focus on health. Especially not to the level of other countries Jamaica so much likes to mimic. In those days, St Catherine Adult Correctional Centre had no gym. They had no real weights, and the weights inmates did make filling empty paint tins with cement to harden were destroyed by warders for all manner of reasons, whether just being bad-mind or the most common excuse of all, which was inmates want to get big so they can overthrow warders. I used to find that hilarious, but that was prison for you, always something crazy going on. Inmates had no real way to physically release stress or anger on Remand Block other than on one another, or find another outlet like music, which would play on the block daily. I must say, as years went by, warders grew to understand us more and allowed us to keep small weights around and that's because they would watch my friends and I on the block train in both martial arts and weights and got a bit used to it and us. I guess they came to understand we were better behaved and less angry, this separated us from other inmates, who seemed always frustrated.

There was one inmate whom no warders or inmates played with; he wasn't located on my block, this inmate resided on B Block. We later became close friends, more like brothers, he was known as Mastro-Bull. He had made his own weights using cement and iron. I met him during the days I first began making walks to New Hall aka Slaughterhouse. Because inmates who located out on the grass and those who played football out there would see us working out sometimes in the hut, especially me, someone or people had told him about me. I guess more inmates than I realised during the time I wanted to be alone, were observing me, and respected my wishes. When we got talking, he told me my presence was brought to his attention and he had seen me training various times but just left me to it. Reasoning with this fitness fanatic on his block brought us closer, and we started to do our own little workout with his equipment. Mastro-Bull was one of those inmates that had spent a long time in prison and had a lot of respect. Without a doubt, that was how in those days early in 2000, he was able to accomplish building his own gym without warders smashing his weights up. When I wasn't training on the block with National and the others, I was with Mastro-Bull. Sometimes I was enjoying the best of both worlds and training on my block and with Mastro-Bull. Daily I would train, and if I didn't for some reason train my body, I was sure to train my mind.

There were nights when the only sound on Remand Block that could be heard was the sound of music and I would choose this opportunity to clear my mind and meditate, freeing myself from both prison and the world. When warders would condemn prisoners to their blocks for whatever reason, I would send and call for Mastro-Bull, or sometimes he would come off his own block and ask them to let me out, he was never told no. Honestly, it felt great; I was free to move around, while others were confined to the perimeter of the area fenced around GB 3 and 4. In my heart, I believed God always opened a way for me, providing my intentions were good.

Pleasurable pictures are still visual in my mind of Sophie and Bounty's visits to St Catherine Correctional Centre. The love I have for them is beyond words, it's not easy standing there in a long queue, waiting in the hot sun, then to be frisked by the authorities. Not to mention the intimidation one is liable to face, along with the sight of big guns right there before your eyes, especially if you're not used to seeing it. I've heard inmates repeatedly curse on the block, family members, friends, refusing to come back again. Some due to intimidation, others just can't stomach the procedure. Knowing these two individuals, who weren't blood related, visited me, with Bounty visiting more than once, both of them I consider special. On the visit, they brought me all the necessities an inmate would need, plus T-shirts, sneakers, fruits and food items, including my twenty-four cup noodles. Within the fruit bag, Bounty had hidden money for me. In the visiting box, he told me where he hid it.

That evening under lock, I spoke to my sisters and my children's mother; I thanked Pudding who I knew would *always* be there for me like the rest of my family. I knew deep down they felt bad for the way I suffered in the beginning, but I knew if they knew what was really going on from the get go, I would have had their full support from the start.

Reflecting back, I was as stubborn as a mule when I first arrived in prison. Keeping it real to my emotions, I contributed in a way to the suffering I went through. I acknowledged that, yet also saw it as a way in which I strengthened myself too. My actions may have caused me more pain, but it also changed me, and the way people looked at me. You see, there is never a right or wrong way to do things once one's intentions are good and true, life is just a learning course, I fully understand now.

All that week my friends and I cooked cup noodles and greens, cup noodles and mackerel, saltfish cooked down with cup noodle, we put cup noodle in everything. We were feasting daily down at GB3. Bounty brought the same amount of cup noodles when he revisited me, along with other stuff, and topped up my friend's mobile phone, one of the phones I used to use. I had everything I needed, money in my pocket and money on my rit. Most prisoners take in all money they get, whether they sneak it in, or get one of the authorities to bring it in for them and then give him or her a little something out of it. But me, I figured having money on my rit at all times always paid off, it was smart to work with the system while doing your own thing. Once in a while, I'd get a warder to escort me upstairs where I would sign for some money, green suit officials and other warders would see me collect a few five-hundred-dollar book stamps for the tuck shop. Though money was illegal, inmates could use money at the tuck shop which I thought was crazy, but that's the system for you. But my idea was, I'll support their business while doing my own, plus I loved eating Jamaican patties in coco bread, washed down with a cold eggnog, and that you can't buy from prisoners.

Things were looking up for me, but when things are good, forces will try to pull you down, the key is not to always rise to the occasion. The Ras who had drawn an allegation against me in the past, decided to start his shit again, and believing at that time on my journey of growth I had to respond, which I did, my reaction only added fuel to fire. From his cell, he would chant things like, "Fire bon, a false Rastaman. Bon ah Israel God. Jah Rastafari, Jah Rastafari, go down Satan. Trample de devil under man feet." Sometimes, while he was chanting his shit, I would stand at the front of my cell and look at my friends and laugh, and the more we laughed the more it pissed him off.

One day he approached me respectfully and we began to talk, he asked me about my belief and my views on God. So, I began breaking the Bible down to him, and addressing the concept and the philosophy of Tafari Makonnen being Christ in his kingly character, as well as God, which I myself once believed him to be. Wisdom had opened my eyes, and I tried to share some of it with him. Unfortunately, the conversation didn't go as I desired; I understand better now that there is a cut-off point that should be made when things get too intense. When barriers go up, conversation should come down. At that time, I didn't have the insight I now possess.

"I'm not really a New Testament person, but Revelation 5, verse 5, is one of the main scriptures Rastafarians use to make this connection that Tafari Makonnen is Christ, correct?" I asked.

"Continue." Nia replied.

"But don't de scriptures seh dis lamb so to speak, takes de book outta God's hand? Therefore the lamb, Christ, cannot be God if he takes de book outta God's hand. This signifies two individuals, and it clearly says Christ has the seven spirits of God, not his own spirits, so it doesn't mek him God nor partners wid God but has God's spirit. Don't Christ himself seh inna di Book of John there is none good but God, so Christ isn't God number one and according to de scriptures, Christ is a divine representation in earth, born seed of Abraham and David, and the Israelite throne of David was established in Jerusalem and shall be re-established in Jerusalem." He looked at me, as we stood there other inmates began to gather around.

"Wha ah gwan Israel?" an inmate known as Youtie asked.

"Mi and Nia ah reason." I responded then turned my attention back to Nia, "Yeh so Nia, yuh read inna Genesis seh Abraham is born in Ur, which is in modern day Iraq, not an Ethiopian. The scriptures teach seh de Hebrews are Shemites, not saying they're not mixed with Hamites. Plus, Queen Makeba, who is Queen of Sheba, is Abrahamic, although she has ties to Arabia as much as she is known as an Ethiopian. As we know, Ethiopia ruled Arabia, just stating her country and tribal affiliation, yuh kno dat right? Not to mention they were one country Ethiopia and Arabia especially places like Yemen, have a long-standing history with Ethiopia, and the land if you look at a map, Arabia fits right alongside east Africa; historically the people mixed. When you read Genesis 10, it makes clear Sheba's origin, that's also something to consider.

Nia looked at the other inmates that stood there listening to our conversation. Not wanting to look like the idiot, because everyone allows him to get away with verbal abuse and all type of foolishness for two various reasons, one is that he was feared and the other because he acted as if he was the most righteous man walking the earth, Nia began to speak on Psalms 87.

"Yeh yu right de Bible does seh the Lord loves de gates of Zion more than all de dwellings of Jacob" I responded "and yes Ethiopia was mentioned, and it does seh dis man was born there, but it's not referring to Tafari. Where is Zion?"

"Ethiopia!" he responded angrily.

"There is a Zion in Ethiopia, but it's not the Zion the Bible is talking about. How can it be if Zion is the city of David, and according to scriptures, David ruled in Jerusalem, the city of God? And geographically, de twelve tribes of Jacob or Israel whichever one yuh waan call dem, settled in their Promised Land, modern day Israel and Palestine region. Hence, Tafari sits on the Solomonic line and is 225th king from Menelik the first, who returned from da land of his father Solomon, according to history, and set up a kingdom in Ethiopia. Then he can't be sitting on David's throne in Jerusalem because one, he set up his own throne in another country according history, and plus the Bible speaks of other kings sitting on David's throne after Solomon's death in Jerusalem."

The conversation got intensively deep, and the vibes became extremely nasty, as Nia became verbally abusive towards me before walking off.

That evening he must have gone to sleep with me on his mind, the following day he begun cursing the Bible and me. Under lock,

Nia did something that shocked everyone including myself. From out of his cell, one of the small blue New Testament Bible went flying, and landed on the passageway on the block. All of a sudden pages and pieces from out of his full-size Bible landed on the floor. In his anger, he had ripped it up.

When the warders came to let us out of our cells, he said nothing to no one and walked off the block, my friends and I began to laugh. That I shouldn't have done, but at the time, I found it funny, in all reality it could be seen as provocation.

A few days later while on the block, Nia and I exchanged words. Not the kind of language friend's use towards one another when reasoning about scriptures and things really got heated. Looking back on it now, at that point I should have walked and left the conversation right there, but I guess my pride and ego wanted to prove him wrong. Knowing what I know now, did I really need to prove him wrong, we had spoken on the same thing previously; if I had not gotten through to him then, what made me think I would do now, that again was my ego desiring to prove him incorrect. Especially knowing he had his barriers up and so did I. One thing led to another, he went into his cell and came out with a bottle. I had not too long finished cooking and still had the bricks that I used to rest the hotplate on at the front of my cell, so I drew for one.

The two of us stood there in front of one another, exchanging words but no blows.

"Suck out yuh madda, English bwoy." Nia said.

"Suck yuh madda," I replied.

"Yuh wah mi lick yuh inna yuh head."

"If yuh lick mi, mi kill yuh inna dis pussy."

"English bwoy yuh wah mi kill yuh?"

"Done di argument." An inmate said, while others stood between us.

Looking back on it, he never really wanted to war with me, it was more of an intimidation act. If he really wanted to, he had more than enough time. But then again while all this was going on, some of my friends just stood there without saying a word, and I suppose he took that into consideration. The next day, my family who I had met through Puerto Rican, who located on the Slaughterhouse, came cross and spoke with Nia. Like many prisoners, Nia respected him and took heed to what he said. After G-Go had spoken to Nia, my cousin and I left the block and headed over to New Hall. From that day, Nia and I never clashed again. Well not like that anyway.

God is good, I always hear people say, especially my mother, that was her slogan no doubt. I had been reading the Bible so much and enjoying it too, I was finding comfort within its words. Every night and day, I would repeatedly wonder what it would be like to have a Hebrew Bible. As so one thinketh, so shall it be, and indeed it was about to occur. One evening my little sister Minnie told me she was planning to come back to Jamaica and visit me with one of my brothers. Overwhelmed I was going to get a visit from England again, it was the perfect opportunity to work towards my heart's desire. Speaking to my brother on the phone, I asked JT to buy me a Hebrew Text, one that has the English translation in small print, with Hebrew writing as the main print. I'd told him I was reading the Bible a lot and wanted to learn biblical Hebrew. While talking with him he asked me for the phone number of the family in Kingston 8 that I'd visited before being incarcerated. Unwilling to give him, I told him of some of our other family in Jamaica but he was adamant on their number. After explaining to me that he wanted to pick up my suitcase and bring it back to England and plus family is family, he wanted to meet them, I gave him the number. I myself wasn't too happy with one or two of my cousins for how they dealt with me, but he was right, family is family no matter what. That night I thought as usual under lock. Whether they were good or bad memories, mind travelling under lock was unpreventable. But that night, I wouldn't have dreamt of preventing thoughts of myself soon holding a Hebrew text in my hand. As usual, I thought about holding my children, their mother, my family, and just wondered what was happening back in the UK, but that night wasn't about anything more than my Hebrew book that would one day be in my hand.

Chapter 14:
Accepting Heartache

Around the same period everything began to happen for me, I lost the most important person in my life. My children's mother and I decided to separate. To be honest, Lele didn't want to, neither was it her that brought up the conversation about us going our separate ways. Roughly, the same time Lele moved out of the flat on the South Kilburn Estate, and her and our two children went to live in another area, we departed. It wasn't that she couldn't afford to stay in our home; she was fed up of too many people in our community asking about me, and what took place. I guess it became a bit too overwhelming.

Her devotion to our relationship was unquestionable, but I felt at that time I had to be realistic, I was looking life, maybe the possibility of no parole. Knowing the kangaroo system in Jamaica, if they wanted to make an example out of me, I would never see the light of day. In spite of us separating, she stayed around my family and spent a lot of time with them. I remember a long while after Lele told me that she had met someone, it was only the talking stages and they had not yet slept together. To me, them sleeping together was only a matter of time. It hurt, but I had to think about me, I had to be strong for myself. After all, *I* told her to move on. I couldn't be selfish and ask her to wait for me I felt at that time. I still never knew where I stood, and surely wasn't going to make thoughts of our relationship weaken me. In fact, our separating did quite the opposite. Strangely, I became more focused on myself, and thought less about her. My children were my rock and were now everything to me. I never stopped loving her, and never will. We didn't separate because of bad energy, but protecting my emotions and the fear of her leaving one-day, or having an affair was too much to think about. I honestly felt she was a good woman who deserved to be happy, and not caught up in a long-distance relationship not knowing when we would see one another. It just didn't seem fair, especially on her. I was the reason we were in this predicament, and she didn't sign up for this. If I remember correctly, I promised I would always be there for her. I wished I had thought of her and our children *before* I reacted, instead of acting on impulse, but this was my reality. I wasn't always a thinking guy, and now I was paying for it in more ways than one. I wanted her to be happy, truly happy and not feel, do or act out of character then cheat and feel guilty about it afterwards. After all, she has needs. I needed to, and did let her go, to prevent any sorrowful actions from blurring the beautiful memories we held and shared.

Adding to the psychological pain I was experiencing; someone I was deeply associated with around the same time I broke up with my children's mother had been killed on his block. His throat had been slashed, and he was stabbed a couple of times. He was pretty strong for a skinny guy. From where he was attacked, he had run downstairs and collapsed outside the building. It was a pretty good distance. There was nothing anyone could do, he had lost way too much blood from his stab wounds, and blood oozed from his throat, which had been badly severed. These are the types of murders, which took place in prison, especially on the Ship. Other popular styles of execution used were to leave the inmate seated in an upright position in their cell, as if they were reading a book, or just chilling. The Ship aka Slaughterhouse was renowned for its style of killings, and he had become a victim of the Slaughterhouse. He disrespected the order, and paid the same price that someone else would have paid, if they'd violated other inmates in the way that he did. So, I guess he knew something was coming, we all did, but being a top guy and respected as a striker, which is a prison term for killer, just maybe he never thought death was the final result. Emotionally, it hit me hard. I felt it for him, but the order is the order and it was wise not to go against it. Clarke aka Rema (R.I.P), gone but not forgotten.

As months went by, I came face to face with much emotional hurt. I was hearing less and less from my children's mother. It wasn't even the fact that I wasn't in communication with her; it was paining me that I was hardly hearing from my children. That used to eat me up at times, nevertheless, I told myself I had to remain strong. I had gone so long during my suffering days without hearing from anyone, especially them, and then to be speaking regularly and now have that slow down rapidly, was affecting me. It took some serious mental reprogramming to re-adjust. We would talk occasionally, and when we did, I made no fuss about it. I understood it was hard for her too. I knew deep down she felt I was pushing her away and the reality is I was to a certain extent, hence why I finished it, yet I needed her to keep contact regularly with me too, but that didn't go the way I hoped. Maybe it was too hurtful for her or she was too busy with her new life and trying to get over me. Whichever way, I never asked, and kept things cool for the sake of our children and friendship. My real contact to my children over the years to come was through my family and especially my friend Dee, who was also Lele's cousin.

Not that Lele never contacted me, of course, we spoke, but it wasn't as much as I would have loved or needed it to be, or as much as I believed our children needed to know and hear their father's voice. The importance of them hearing me telling them how much I love them, even more importantly, listening to them and allowing them to express what's going on in their lives, growth and development, to me was essential, we needed it, them and I. Thanks to my family and Dee they made it happen.

Dee was the most amazing friend I could ever have asked for whilst I was incarcerated. At that time, Dee lived at her parent's house and one day I decided to reverse call her and they accepted the charge. We talked and talked. She really comforted me and showed me a lot of compassion. I had known Dee before I knew my children's mother; in fact, it was because of Dee that I met Lele. Dee and I grew up in South Kilburn, we knew one another from childhood, we all went to junior school together, and she and Minnie were close like sisters. I would call her mum and dad uncle and aunt, that's how close our families were. Dee and I, we had a natural bond to begin with. But calling her for the first time showed me how close we really were. She had told me she would keep the link tight and believe me she did. My children's mother would give Dee my children from time to time as they were family, and God bless her, she began taking them regularly and every time she would take them whether they stayed the night or not she'd phone me. Dee was amazing like that. This she had done for years. When I think about it, the amount of money she must have spent on calls must of mounted, but was money of importance to her is the real question, honestly I don't think so, our friendship, her love and compassion showed me so much, and from it I learnt so much about her too.

Chapter 15:
Spiders Web

The thing about being behind bars and having more time on one's hands to think about life, is that it could either affect you in a positive or negative way. I mean thinking too much without channelling those emotions correctly can lead to madness. Not necessarily sending an individual crazy, but if the foundation behind the thought or reasoning wasn't positive it could make the situation worse, heighten the emotion and lead to a more devastating outcome. Conversations and association within confinement are contributory factors causing some inmates to go in as petty criminals, and come out as hardened robbers and killers. On the flipside, others turn their lives around. In my case, inmates, some who would never see road again, expressed a lot of positive words, encouragement and respectful insight to me over many years, at various times. A prime example was my return from circuit court where friends and I conversed on our troubled pasts, I don't remember who started it or how the conversation started, but it led to us reflecting on our occurrences of childhood growing up, to our lives on the streets and individual experiences, all of which interlocked like a spiders web.

I explained that unlike myself, my brothers and sisters in England weren't at all familiar with Jamaica or the Jamaican system; they weren't even familiar with their own flesh and blood in Jamaica. It just was not a place they visited regularly, and those who did, stayed in St Ann initially up until the point of my incarceration. It was only then that they began to venture into Spanish Town and Kingston. My blood relatives are not from St Ann, but our connection to that parish will become clear as to why we spent a lot of time down there, especially me. I don't know much about the Graham side of my family, what I have been told is that I have relatives in Clark's Town, Falmouth and Mo-Bay, and my father's dad was Cuban. On my father's side of the family, we were Cuban-Jamaican, and I believe Maroon too, or so I've been told. My father spent his adulthood in Kingston before coming to the UK. As for my mother, her family and parents were from Kingston, some of them branched out to Spanish Town. My mother was born in Kingston; she grew up in East Kingston. My big sister Marie, during her childhood had lived in the family home on Somerset Avenue, Franklin Town Kingston 16, where my mother grew up with her mum and my uncle Jappy, before coming to England. But my sister Marie left Jamaica when she was a young girl, and therefore had not kept in contact with anyone.

Reflecting on my childhood, I thought about the root of my problematic behaviour, which I believe stemmed from home. A father's contribution to the upbringing of a child, especially a boy is so important, words can't even express. Simple things like the natural tone of voice when directing a command towards an offspring to do something will cause them to carry out the act. Whereas with mothers, it just may not have the same affect. Masculine energy has its role. Unfortunately, my experiences of positive masculine energy fell short when I was around seven or eight years of age, and contributed massively to me spiralling out of control. Some men just don't understand how much their children need them, how important that paternal energy and presence is, and the impact it has on a child. Relationships don't always work and aren't supposed to or destined to. As mortals, we can't always make what's *not* to occur, manifest. Although the root causes of the breakdown of some relationships aren't really bad, it's more stubbornness, or lack of communication, which makes individuals then incompatible. Nevertheless, it takes two to work at it, and if both parties aren't willing, then separation may just be better than a toxic environment wherein two parents become the mirror of destruction through which their child sees itself. Whatever the outcome of a relationship wherein a child or children were conceived, responsibility of fatherhood is a duty and promise made with the universe that this soul that has entered earth, born into one's loins, is your obligation to nurture. A covenant so many forget they have made.

I give respect to any man who takes on another man's seed, playing the role of father. Whether he knows it or not, conscious or unconscious of his actions, he has reached out to the universe asking permission to be a special guide unto this soul, aiding him or her in their journey. For such individuals, great is their reward. The problem is when the individual doesn't realise the severity of his request. Anything less than total devotion brings about energetic confusion, creating further disharmony not just in the home but also in the universe. Every issue or problem that has a negative effect on an individual's life, is never confined to the four walls, but will seep out into every environment one finds themselves in, and as every human is connected in the universal web of life, it's easy to see the reaction from bad decisions can affect others.

A child isn't born ill mannered, rude or violent; that just doesn't exist in the natural order of life. These are learnt traits due to conditioning, circumstances, and environmental attributes; unfortunately, I had over exposure to all of these and more.

My stepfather, blinded to the covenant he had made with the universe, took on responsibility for a few souls and got with my mother. I don't know if between us our soul disconnection was from the very first time he saw me, or due to him and my biological father coming to blows, which would then be a contributing factor to the way he would go on to mistreat me. However, I do know the disharmony he brought into the home, definitely flowed out into the world and my actions, creating chaos, hurt and pain for many who were on the receiving end of my deeds.

Reminiscing on my youth, I tried hard in my own silence to think of good times between my stepfather and myself. To be honest, I couldn't remember a time when I genuinely felt like I loved him nor had any strong feelings of care towards him; there were none. Whether my mind had blocked out any good memories, or there were never any to begin with, the only thing I can remember was the way he dealt with me when my mother wasn't around. He had a sly look of dislike in his eyes when she was there; he was good at hiding his feelings, but I could always read him. I read him like a book. Too young to understand energies as I do now, but not too young to know I had a bad feeling about him. I wondered many times if my mother felt what I felt, but expressing myself was something I rarely ever did. I had a bad habit of suffering in silence and reacting in the wrong way, I guess that contributed to him continuing to behave the way he did towards me. There are many youths and even adults in relationships that don't make anyone aware of the situation at hand, or personally don't confront their abuser when being abused. Whether physically or verbally, abuse is abuse and it is wrong. Being on the receiving end, expressing my emotions through my newfound strength, I plead with you not to suffer in silence; I encourage you to speak up. My stepfather was the kind of man that would blame me for everything even when it wasn't me. He had beaten me with his cricket boot, I was ten years old at that time and unable to understand the psychological affect it and other circumstances were having on me, all I knew was I hurting. There is a common theory in psychology that the abused will go on to abuse. A theory is a theory until proven; in my case, it's a fact. I was abused and became an abuser, causing pain to many people directly and indirectly, over a span of many years. What's crazy about it is, I found more satisfaction in participating in specific violent acts on the streets than even making money from it. I believe if money was my drive and not just to do harm, I'd be a very rich guy because I had the ability and will to do things that many wouldn't do, but the desire to get away and unnoticed was a more rewarding thrill. My violent tendencies and love for causing pain and hurt to others who I thought did me wrong, or in other circumstances just felt to be troublesome, led me to carry out various actions I believe stemmed from being beaten and abused. Not just because of the physical beating I encountered, but also the mental torment I faced. My stepfather was good at doing things and acting all nice afterwards, looking back on myself I believe such actions rubbed off on me. I could be messed up, violent and very aggressive out on the streets, and at the same time, be this little angelic youth adored by everyone. Neither of my personalities were an act. I was extremely loving as a child. All who encountered me could and would generally fall in love with me, but then there was a side to me that was very dark and troubled. Even within my own head, there were conflicting thoughts as I pictured and visualized very disturbing images in my mind. Some specialists believe everyone has wild imaginations and conflicting thoughts, but what makes people different, depends on if these thoughts remain thoughts and then disperse, or if they are nurtured into manifestation. Society labels this as problematic behaviour; unfortunately, I became a problem child from young.

Prisoners had a way of driving one another into this crazy realm of thought. As one spoke of his experience, another could connect, triggering emotions even though we were just reasoning, but the intensity and the way in which the pitch in our voices changed depending on the topic, it wouldn't take a psychologist to know there were a lot of unresolved issues. The level of connection was insane. Not in the sense of going through the exact same thing, but similarities that can make one relate to where they're coming from, or what they've been though. Sadly, for me, I could relate to so much of it, which made it more intense emotionally. As I stated before, no child is born ill mannered, rude or violent, it just isn't natural, these characteristics are patterns learnt over time. On a normal day-to-day basis, I wasn't a bad child in the sense of being ill mannered or disrespectful to people, in fact I was always loved and adored. I was the kind of person who can make friends anywhere and fit in everywhere, black or white, rich or poor, people checked for me, people of all races felt comfortable around me. As people would say to me, I had this likeable character that was easy to click with. I guess somewhere inside I felt hollow about things. A good child doesn't just decide to be bad over night for no reason. I definitely was angry due to not having my biological dad around, within there was a void that needed to be filled. My stepfather didn't help the situation; in fact, not understanding the contract he was entering into with the universe, he made it worse. In a big way, he contributed to my change, this I totally understood before my incarceration. What I have come to question due to maturity and in experiencing my own journey, is what unresolved issues did my stepfather have when he came into my mother's life. Were they also contributing factors to how he dealt with me? Could it be more than the physical altercation and verbal issues between him and my biological father? Did he have his own issues to deal with and either not knowing how to deal with them, or not accepting them as his own issues, carried them willingly or unwillingly into a union with my mother, and spiritual contract with the universe where he swore to protect these souls, and of course was unable? Although they are his problems to solve and deal with, it is something that crossed my mind many times. But as these thoughts came, I constantly reminded myself, only individuals can free themselves.

Children will be children, and depending what one sees and is exposed to or even curious about can cause one to get up to mischief. Sometimes with my siblings and close friends, we would get up to mischief. Reflecting back on those funny days, I can say I felt sorry for those who would babysit us. Between my brothers and sisters who lived in my mother's home, we could be quite a handful to manage, unless you were my aunty Colonel B! Now she's another story, but some of my uncles had a very hard time looking after us. I was known form Kilburn Park Junior School as a fighter, as someone who could handle himself. At that time, I was getting a lot of unnecessary disciplining and blame at home for things I hadn't done, so reacting to anyone at school, or boys from any other school who opposed me or my friends, was a good opportunity to release some pent-up frustration. I was also considered quite humorous and a joker at school, someone who was funny to be around. I was also pretty mischievous and a bit reckless, at the same time, I could get my work done. I was far from dumb; getting good grades was an easy task. As I said, I was never really an ill-mannered child, a little mischievous, hurt and confused yes, but ill-mannered no.

I was eleven when I really got into street life, bunking off from high school, getting up to no good and engaging in violent crime. Acts of violence and serious acts of anti-social behaviour passed for amusement. The money wasn't really my drive. It was the joy I got from inflicting pain; it brought about a serious rush of adrenaline. The excitement and pleasure were so desirable. I would go home at times and think about whatever had happened and smile to myself, sometimes I smiled at my stepfather, who I'd think about hurting. If he wasn't there, I remember days I'd just think about doing whatever I did on the streets to him and gain a sense of satisfaction from it. Looking back on my life, I really see how he weighed heavily on my soul, in the sense of energy. I thought more about the things he'd done and how he treated me, than looking to the brighter side of things and proving him wrong about me, and what I could achieve. Still, I was young, not mentally matured, and wasn't supposed to be, I needed love, not to feel neglected, yet I felt neglected in so many ways. I remember those childhood mornings like yesterday; man, I loved bonbons, sweet peanuts and rhubarb and custard sweets. I would ask for money for school and most times it was my mother who gave me, he always seemed to express that he had no change whilst he showed me notes, but funnily enough, when my elder brothers, little and big sister would ask, he'd seem to magically find a few quid to give them. Whenever he did give me small change, I could feel how reluctant he was in doing so. What he didn't understand or enjoyed, was the psychological pain I felt in seeing the paper money, yet being told always there was no small change, which most of the times he ended up finding, just not for me. Such sights sent an electrical impulse to my spinal cord via my brain telling me I'm nothing, worth nothing, the suggestion to go to the corner shop and get what I wanted and bring back the rest of the money before I headed off to school was never an option unless it came from my mother. I disliked him so much for his actions, but in disliking him, I ended up hating myself in my continuous silence and violent outbursts and actions, all stemming from lack of self-love and not feeling loved by him. All I ever wanted was what all children want and that was to be loved by those supposed to protect them. Instead, I received hate and secretly grew with hatred in my heart.

As a youth, I was known as Stephen Brown, all throughout my junior school and high school years I was using my stepfather's surname, up until I went to my fourth and final high school. It sounds terrible right, being expelled from four high schools, the dramas that led to continuous terminations from school to school, I will explain in a bit. According to my sister Pudding, I was three years of age when my mother married my stepfather, and I guess somewhere around then, my name changed from Graham, and I was given the surname Brown. None the wiser, I walked proud with it until I came to the realisation during junior school that Brown wasn't my surname, nor was it my true identity. Honestly, I don't remember why or how I came to the realisation at or around the tender age of ten, but I knew I wasn't a Brown. The change of surname was never done officially at the registration office, just on my school application. Deep down, I hated the fact that I was using his name, which I carried for a few years after finding out. I used to wonder why this man even wanted me to carry his name when he hated me that much, was it a power thing, psychological, and to some degree physical control over me? You would have to be in my head then to know how confused I was. My mother's intention I know was not to do harm, but as many women do expect and hope, it makes the man feel a true sense of belonging. The greatest downfall with expectations of others is that when they let you down it can be more damaging than the eye can see. The anger in me at times, leaving the home with such energy knowing I'm not a Brown, wasn't a great start to the day, especially when he upset me, or when a teacher called me Brown in class it troubled me deeply, yet I kept it to myself. For years, I tormented myself, unwilling to share my emotions with friends or family. I can't say all my negative actions as a youth were based on him, but he was definitely a big contributory factor to my behaviour at junior school and also to why I became heavily involved in the streets during my first venture into high school at eleven years of age.

It was in 1988 at the age of thirteen the veil was lifted and my true identity was revealed. I remember that year clearly, because it was the year my mother took out my passport, and my brother JT, mother and I flew to New York to see relatives from East Kingston who had migrated to the States. Here I was, no school to attend after being booted out of my third school, Aylestone High, but still smiling. All that anger and confusion bottled within, questioning myself carrying this evil man's surname in secret for years was out in the open. I had in my possession a document with my true identity on it. I'm a Graham, there was no way in heaven or hell was I going to use Brown anymore. At some point before starting my final high school, I built up the courage to speak with my mother about my feelings in relation to carrying my stepfather's surname at school. Not that my mother was a hard person to talk to, quite the opposite, she was the most loving, kind and sweetest lady to grace the earth, but I wasn't the kind of person to express my emotions. I could be very talkative dependent on the topic of conversation, but about things that really bothered me, I found it hard to speak, and that was a major downfall in my personality back then. I used to bottle a lot in and channel my feelings in all the wrong ways. I don't remember when we discussed it, but I do know I entered Queens Park Community School in 1989, the year of its grand opening, as Stephen Graham. The transformation of surname brought about a feeling of joy, unfortunately the dislike between my stepfather and I stayed the same, in fact it got worse I would say. The psychological games weren't always played as before, verbal expressions of his dislike became more apparent and we had our fair share of arguments, mostly when my mother wasn't around. I began standing up to him at times. Mostly we just never spoke anyway, there was nothing to talk about, so it would seem like nothing was going on or there was no problem, but the unseen was and is more active than the seen, and so was the tension between us.

So many things in the family home bothered me. The more I came to acknowledge certain situations through either age, seeing or hearing, the more questions I asked myself. One of the main things I questioned myself with was why a beautiful educated woman like my mother, someone who had two degrees one in nursing and the other in accountancy married a man who could hardly spell his own name, I mean literally couldn't spell his own name and to add to that she bought him a car. What would make a woman who had worked in some really great places leave her job and let someone who couldn't bring in as much as her provide for her. A man who you would find in the local betting shop on a regular day became her main provider. I couldn't get my head around that then; I still don't know or have all the answers today. What I do know after having my own experiences and coming to my own realisation about life now as a man, that the desire for love, old fashion morals, culture and a false representation of religion can cause some people to go through experiences that are questionable and quite unnatural, all leading them to act way out of character. I guess my beautiful mother in her youthful days or at some point in her life had her own experiences or principles that she either took on or had prior to her encounter with my stepfather that would later reflect on why she allowed certain things to manifest in her life. Then again, it may run even deeper than her

117

childhood experience, connected to some distant ancestral memory, where love or the need to be loved had a key role in that time. Whatever it was, undoubtedly my mother wasn't the first. History and current life choices show many people go through things and allow things to occur; some of us can't understand why or how they even allowed them to happen. The underlying issues are deeper than meets the eye. May God bless her soul, my rock, gone but not forgotten; I love you mummy always.

My mother was one person I could always count on to love me. Such thoughts brought smiles to the deepest part of my heart. I remember just sitting there sucking my thumb and cuddling next to my mother. It's weird to look back and think of all the crazy things I'd do, especially when I started high school and my passion for senseless violence began to spiral out of control. The comfort of my mother's shoulder, as I sucked my thumb after a violent act on the streets where friends and I would've kicked the shit out of someone, for whatever reason, whether it was for money or just because they said something or looked at us wrong. Whatever it may be, that shoulder and her warmth made me feel great and took away all the pain.

Watching my mother cry at times when bills came also angered me as a little boy and was a contributing factor to me hitting the streets. I hated seeing tears flowing from my mother's eyes, only God knows how it made my blood boil. My real father, not only being absent but never in contact, didn't help the situation. My big brother Jay, who lived at home at that time, took on the responsibility of playing dad. He began beating me when I did wrong, not understanding he was only making things worse, which added to the problem. I just knew some innocent person walking God's green earth was going to pay for it. Even though my actions were wrong, the underlying issues at that time were never understood, so in truth, the disciplinary actions were in vain. One of the factors in my life was the lack of a real positive male role model. My big brother Jay was acting the part out of the goodness of his heart, yet at the same time didn't know how to handle the situation. I mean, you can't be hitting someone and expect them to tell you why they're doing what they're doing at the same time. Maybe it's the old-fashioned way, but it definitely defeats the objective. No real answer or result will come out of it; there is no level of empathic communication. Now I'm not just talking about speaking to someone using words, I mean the importance of using empathy to communicate to get a positive result. The reality is, this can only be achieved when both are calm and in the correct frame of mind to talk. This is a more rewarding approach, and my brother Jay at that time didn't understand me, the situation, or what was really going on. The truth is, his old-fashioned approach, was doomed from the start, plus the fact that in my eyes he didn't contribute to the home as much as he could have, these were also factors relating to and contributing to why I hit the road. You see, I didn't choose the road because it was cool, or just wanted to be a bit of a naughty boy for respect or any other reason other than having serious issues within the home, personal issues, and at times feeling misunderstood at school. Additionally, other external contributory factors led me to turn to the streets. The streets were a way to channel some of my anger. What road did for me psychologically was greater than the physical gain from the little money made here and there as a youth. As I stated before, money wasn't my drive, it was the excitement of pain, hurt, sorrow inflicted on others that lifted my mood, bringing my stress levels down. It's quite disturbing when looking back at what it took to ease the pain I felt. The reality is, I'm not the only child to ever feel and know that a buzz exists stemming from doing something wrong or illegal. On the flipside, when one is awoken, and truly begins to see the world we live in for what it really is, the feel-good factor generated is only a temporary illusion leading to more pain. As a mature man on a destiny, and understanding energies now and how one channels energy, I see my actions and methods as a youth through to my adulthood regarding my emotions, was actually an energetic cycle of destruction. Anyone I inflicted pain on carried their pain into someone else's life, whether directly or indirectly, a husband to wife, children or friends. I mean, who really wants to know someone they love or care about has been attacked or killed. It's a no brainer. The low-level vibration I was pushing from one person to another, sending pain and hurt through the veins of many, stemmed from me transferring onto the victim and seeping to their loved ones. This same destructive cycle of pain I helped promote over the years, wasn't only via personal pain I inflicted on others but also through other street related dealings, wherein I aided and supported various friends in their missions to do all manner of wrongs. What people don't realise is, even if one hasn't personally inflicted pain, but encouraged or aided by any means, it's also a burden on your shoulders. In fact, it comes with a double burden, spiritually one is connected to both the victim and the perpetrator whom one encouraged or aided; reality gets deep. I was truly contributing to the destructive cycle of mankind's problematic whirlpool. Walking around absentmindedly, totally oblivious that the unseen is more powerful than the seen; I was drawing spiritual entities to myself and creating havoc, whilst adding to the energetic misalignment, which causes the earth and the universe to work harder to bring us back into alignment. The effect of our actions is so much deeper than the eye can see.

The depth of this problem is immeasurable, but not all is lost, we just need to acknowledge things from a different and deeper perspective. Similar to my problematic childhood experiences the seen and unseen cycle of destruction is at work. Who's truly acknowledging the destructive behaviour of the youths today for what it really is? Beyond the psychological and emotional cry for help, it's the experiencing of some sort of stress disorder; more importantly, who understands the spiritual shift and fight that's taking place, the unseen entities trying to latch onto the young and confused. Is mankind only seeing through lost eyes to judge the youth, labelling them through systematic spectacles? Even those who know the youths best, judging their own children, because they themselves are disconnected from the spiritual warfare taking place in the seen and unseen; they're unarmed and absentminded, so therefore unable to fight in their children's aid to help realign us as a people. The world truly is a crazy place. That's correct, adults too are caught in this spiritual warfare, facing their own trials and tribulations, some faced with situations so great, the attention required to support the young is not available. The reggae legend could never have said any greater, indeed, there is so much trouble in the world. It's not the young or old who are sick, but society itself. The so-called leaders who have created the very web in which many are caught; spinning destruction at the root, and reaping havoc knowingly or unconsciously, who is really to blame?

I had just reached my teens when I first ran away from home; unfortunately, I did it a few times, and in the process, hurt a few good souls. The reason for my actions the first time I did it, was a direct reflection based on my stepfather's words. I'll never forget what he said to me that caused me to get out of the car and disappear. We were parked outside Kilburn Park Underground Station, my mother had popped out of the car, he began talking with me about my court case, and then suddenly his tone changed. In a very cold, heartless manner he looked me in the eye and told me that he hoped that I get found guilty and go to prison, he went on to say the home would be better without me. At that time, I had a robbery change hanging over my head. I mean, how can a so-called parent wish for their child or stepchild to be incarcerated. I didn't even respond. I still remember the numbness I felt within, the tears in my eyes were unable to flow as anger mixed with sadness filled me up. I was in no fit state to express myself, removing myself from his midst was the only thing that came to mind. I just got out the car and left.

Looking back on it now, I can only imagine how distressed my mother must have felt coming back to the car and seeing that her son was no longer where she'd left him. The tears, the sadness; the uncertainty of the unknown is more distressful than understanding the reason and cause, because it gives no closure to a situation. My disappearance for hours on end, worrying and wondering what the hell had happened. Knowing my stepfather, he would never have told her the truth; my mother would have been an emotional mess. On my return, my mother and I never really discussed what happened in the car, the night I came home with my big brother on my father's side, whose house I found myself at way in East London. My mother was just too happy to have me home. As I said, these occurrences kept happening, and I'd find myself at my sister Marie's partner's house in Kensal Green and wherever else I just felt I needed to go and get away for a moment. As the pattern continued, my mother would ask me what the problem was, but I wasn't the kind of person to open up. I didn't or just wouldn't, so it seemed like the problem was me, and I was just unruly, but my stepfather and I had our secrets, secrets that were ripping my family apart, scarring me, while sending me into a deep chaotic abyss in the process. As I mentioned previously, Jay, one of my older brothers born to my mother, decided after a while to get involved. He thought it was his responsibility to take matters into his own hands and would literally beat me to talk when I ran away from home or did something wrong. Physically it would hurt me, but inside I'd just shut down and take it. To me, talking with him made no sense, I just knew someone on the road was going to feel the pain he was inflicting on me, or later I'd inflict pain on myself. I had crazy ways of relaxing and channelling my anger if I wasn't hurting somebody else. Most of my brothers never really understood me, I knew they loved me deeply but just couldn't really relate to what was going on in my head, but then how were they to, if I didn't open up. My eldest brother on my father's side living in East London at that time could relate to me, when I think about it, he was psychologically smart too; he played the reverse counselling role. It's not that I would talk to him, but he would tell me about his own life experiences as a method to get me to know I'm not the only one faced with trauma and pain. I guess it's because we shared so much in common including experiences why I felt so close to him.

Speaking with inmates highlighted just how much our own experiences were so relatable; emotionally it was crazy how we could bounce off one another even though some of the things expressed were so traumatic it could make a grown man cry. At the same time, such emotions expressed could bond us through the pain felt, and make us see and understand where each could have done something differently. Psychologically, we were addressing our issues. Counselling ourselves, not that we would call it that, but making one another see where we could have done better and acknowledging why we did what we did. The conversations would get dcep as we looked at those who contributed to our poor life choices. We questioned whether it was something they themselves had been through and thought was OK or normal behaviour to inflict hurt, whether physical or mental. Maybe they weren't aware of the damaging effects it had on others; or even family members who were also going through the same experiences, yet who may have handled it differently. Such in-depth reasoning had me expressing my home life and youthful experiences with my peers, and for a hot minute, I couldn't stop thinking about everything I had shared. On the topic of smoking, I expressed that I had my first experience of taking a drag from a cigarette when I was eight years old. This happened under the podium, just by the garages on the old South Kilburn estate, way before the local council thought to knock it down. It seemed like so many had smoked from young, but being in Jamaica, weed was our main topic on that note. I shared with my peers that I was smoking weed from before I hit my teens. We joked about eating and drinking fluids to hide the smell from our parents and carers, and waiting until the buzz died down and our red eyes returned to normal. There was a time in my life as a youth I thought it was cool to smoke, sometimes showing off in front of others. I would roll up a spliff at the back of the bus where we would smoke it; such actions got me and school friends into trouble sometimes. House dances and parties, depending on whose event it was, was another place I used to smoke, and smoke heavily. Of course, being so young, I hid it from certain people, including my mother and stepfather, just not my brothers and sisters. I was about thirteen when I found myself in dances acting like I was a man, when really, I was just a schoolboy, growing up too fast. It was my early teens when I smoked, or should I say sampled my first cocktail joint. Man, I felt a buzz like nothing else, but I was young and in the wrong frame of mind, trying out things seemed cool, especially if a person or people you looked up to or admired did it, it was much easier to be influenced. My first experience was based around a close family friend who didn't even know I'd smoked the remainder of his season spliff. It was only up unto recently when I told him during a conversation that he didn't misplace it, I had taken it and smoked it. I was young, mischievous and a bit of a wild child; most definitely due to my experiences I was drawn to all the wrong things. He had left it in the ashtray, and me being the youth I was, just went and fasted with it. Today I feel great knowing I haven't smoked anything for almost twenty years and have no intention to do so. As mentioned before, when I left St Ann police lock up, ordered to run my remand at Spanish Town prison, I stopped smoking weed. A place where most people felt the desire to smoke more, or even start smoking for the first time, I quitted under the circumstances. Due to the early financial struggle faced behind bars, and also wanting to clean my system, there was no better time than then, it was a test of my will.

When we spoke about school, that got emotional because one or two peers didn't even attend an educational establishment past All Age School, which is like primary school in the UK, others like myself got kicked out of school. When my colleagues heard I was booted out of four schools and the reasons behind it, they all called me bad-brock (unruly).

I became seriously active in anti-social behaviour and violent crime at the tender age of eleven. It's hilarious when you think about what is classified as a tender age, and then you have individuals like me who are robbed of our youth, or some may judge and say we robbed ourselves of a childhood. Nevertheless, this tender age range seems far from a beautiful moment in life, based on my experience it was a nightmare, and I was the star of my own horror.

I found the streets attractive for all too many reasons, looking back at myself, it wasn't just about my family home, that definitely had its role, but I was also misunderstood at school. The energy I displayed was never recognised in the educational establishment as positive, I couldn't sit still, nor did I really enjoy learning specific subjects, the constant sitting and less creative lessons really frustrated me. Not bashing school nor the schooling system, but as I've grown to understand, there are various ways to communicate with a person, such as verbal, facial expressions, body language, gestures, the list goes on. There are also various learning styles, not every child learns in the same way, so one methodology expressed is none appealing, and it was just not cutting it for me. Not to mention the lack of empathy I experienced throughout my schooling. Not all teachers acted the same, but there were those that may see me slouching in my chair or not in a talking mood. Despite this being the wrong attitude and energy to bring into a classroom setting, for indeed it is a place of learning, how many teachers throughout my years of learning considered if I had issues, problems or troubles, instead of seeing me as disruptive? If they did ask, did I feel they generally gave a damn about me for me to open up? This was another problematic situation, which led me to bunk off on some days, walk out of school at certain periods, or just skip that specific class. This was because their approach to my behaviour wasn't in my best interest, but rather, what the teacher thought was best for all. What they failed to realise however, is the chain is as only as strong as its weakest link. If I was down and emotionally weak, then not only was *I* let down, but so were the other *students*, whether they needed that moral support and care that I did or not. The point is, the underlying empathetic foundation wasn't there to begin with, and it is problematic that so many teachers didn't comprehend that my troubles stemmed from beyond the classroom. My absence, disruptive behaviour when present, or body language were signs, yet they were unable to see, or dismissed the idea that I had issues outside of the school grounds, or that I may need another learning style to comprehend what was taught, or just another outlet to channel my energy. It was problematic then and I still see it as problematic today in some cases.

The first high school I attended was John Kelly Boys' in Neasden, Crest Rd, today known as Crest Academy. Back then, it was an all-boys school, and next door was John Kelly Girls' and man I hated watching the girls just disappear out of sight, and we had some really nice girls in school too. Me being me, I had a few fights early out and established my name as one of the strongest in my year. In fact, only one guy was considered stronger than me, but we were the best of friends, and we were not going to fight to see who was really stronger. To be honest, I believe he would have wrapped me up. Sometimes I played the class clown and other times my anger got the better of me, so teachers found me hard to discipline, I just wasn't listening, I had my own issues going on. When I did do work, I was considered exceptionally bright, and expressive, though I would make many grammatical errors, but the context of my work was great. I had brains, the problem was that I just got bored easily, and hence used to bunk off school to chill with some of the local boys, many of whom were a few years older than me. We looked out for one another. My favourite topic in school no doubt had to be Physical Education (PE). I was on the school football team and we smashed every school we played back then, my best friend and I were star ballers at school. Football was one thing I had a passion for; another not so positive passion was fighting. Unfortunately, this passion got me suspended from school a good few times, it was also the same reason I was permanently excluded from my first high school at the age of eleven. One of the main South Kilburn guys also went to John Kelly; Sky (R.I.P) was two years older than me, and usually a few of the squad would come up after school. I don't remember how it started, but two carloads of local Asian men had something with a friend of ours, either he stepped out into the road in front of one of their cars, or they pulled out in front of him. Whichever way, they had picked the wrong youth with whom to argue. We were young and hot-headed, and that I believe was one of our biggest downfalls. That evening their cars were smashed, one worse than the other. Fearless like lions, like hyenas we attacked in a pack reacting without remorse. Whatever we could pick up we throw at them, they wanted none of it. A few of them ran leaving one car, while the other car drove off. The police were not called funnily enough, but teachers on site saw me in my uniform going crazy; that was it, I was out.

From John Kelly, I want to Hampstead High. During my initial interview, I received the benefit of the doubt and was accepted into the school. A pupil had seen me entering the building with my mother the day of my interview, and complained to the teachers that I supposedly had robbed him outside the school prior to being accepted. I admitted to the head teacher in the interview that I had been there on numerous occasions to meet friends, but had no knowledge of what I was being accused of. They gave me the benefit of the doubt, and I'm sure they regretted it in the long run. As usual, I got myself into trouble, fighting and just being me. Looking back on it, I put my mother through hell. She had been asked to come to the school a few times, for fighting, truancy and for me being accused of stealing from the teacher's bag. There was no proof to support the allegation of theft so the police were never called. However, some teachers' patience was running out, and I could feel that I wasn't really wanted there anymore, could I blame them? To be honest, I did, I accused even the innocent of not liking me. There were teachers who generally hated me, but then when I think about it, there was the odd teacher who really tried, but in truth, I didn't like myself, and was just looking to pass the buck. But then, if they knew what was going on in my head would those who disliked me still have felt the same, or would they have had empathy? The unknown root of my problems ran deep. This was to be my mother's last trip to Hampstead High. I was on the verge of facing exclusion for fighting; my mother told me to be on my best behaviour, and I aimed to. The time for our meeting was set just before lunchtime, as we were on our way upstairs, the alarm went off and of course children being children they came rushing out of their classes and towards us. Looking back on it now, I know it was accidental, even back then I'm sure I knew it too. A few of them brushed hard against my mother, and my mind just flipped. I chased them downstairs and gave a flying kick to one of them in his back; the others ran off leaving their friend who I beat up, *badly*. They expelled me instantly. There were no excuses accepted, whether my mother was pushed or not, and they were right too. I was a problem child, but to be honest, I didn't need more rejections. I had way too many rejections as a youth already, I guess that was why I didn't care, my father, stepfather, certain so-called friends; I felt rejected. The impact was burdensome especially coming from both my father and stepfather, whose actions affected me in two different ways. More rejections I suppose only sent me deeper into my own understanding of life, which coming from a child's mind, isn't going to be that great. Although I held on to the thought, wanting to believe that my father loved me, lack of communication had me in mixed emotions, not hearing from him at all definitely brought about a feeling of rejection and anger.

From there I went to Aylestone High in Kensal Rise. I was booted out yet again for fighting. To be honest, I was hardly at school. I spent more time in Kensal Green chilling, smoking weed and gambling with friends, but these weren't my guys from South Kilburn, but more Church End Estate, Stonebridge, Kensal Rise and Kensal Green youths. I used to get around a lot, I loved the streets and rolled with people from all over, I was a wild child. After my expulsion from Aylestone High, my mother took JT and me to New York to visit family. She was considering us staying in the States back then. My uncle in Connecticut had offered her one of his houses, at times I wish she had made the transition, maybe I would have had a much better life, but then maybe I wouldn't have. What I do know, is that my experiences have laid the foundation for who I am today. I'm not saying road life is a good experience, not at all, because I have a lot of sad memories, some I'd prefer to forget, and wish hadn't happened. But surviving, and having now turned my life around, I can and do understand why I took this journey.

Not all hope was lost regarding school, my mother had meetings with the educational board concerning me, and I believe they were getting fed up with me too. My bad experiences were not over, not by a long shot, destiny knew better. I still had much to learn about myself, my anger, and misplaced loyalty, and I was going to mess the opportunity up as I did before. Damn, I did this in record time, at least in Hampstead and Aylestone I lasted around two school terms, if I'm correct, at John Kelly Boys' I lasted the longest.

After being kicked out of Aylestone, later that year it merged with the old South Kilburn High and Brondesbury High to re-open after the summer as Queens Park Community High school. Yes, I was in, but as I said destiny knew better. Within a month, I was kicked out for fighting again. Even today, I look back on it and think, over a pound, my last opportunity for a good education went out of the window, over a single pound coin. One of my friends from Church Road lost all his money as we played pound up the wall one early school morning. Mocking and laughing at him because he was now broke; he then left to borrow some money from a friend to continue playing. On his return, little did we know he roughed up a classmate and took his money. After school, we would usually wait for each other and walk down together, sometimes they might come to South Kilburn or I may go to Church Road and Stonebridge with them, we rolled tight and were close like family. The victim's elder brother had come over and accused my friend of taking his little brother's money. One thing led to another, and we attacked both brothers. To be honest, if my frame of mind was how it is today, I would have run back the money and put extra on top, apologised and kept it moving. It wasn't worth us getting kicked out of school for. Throwing this educational opportunity away or getting into conflict over a pound just seemed petty; but that wasn't my mind-set back then. All I saw was disrespect, his tone of voice registered violation, when in truth he was right to be angry, but then in our way of thinking back then which wasn't correct, we saw red, and violence solved everything. One pound, one bloody pound, and now I would be out of school permanently with nowhere to go. No establishment wanted me. What is seriously scary though, is that I see the same pattern today when I mentor youths that have been permanently excluded. The establishment can keep you out of education for months. I was out of school for almost a year and all was well, but if a parent keeps you out of school for a few days, they're in big problems. That rule hasn't only recently applied, maybe officially it has, but my mother was threatened numerous times because I played truant and didn't attend school. The interesting thing is that systematically it's law that a child attends school, at least receives some form of education. Weekdays are allocated to schools, no matter what a parent says, so if the *authorities* couldn't keep me there with all their meetings, warnings and every other trick they played, then *why* should my mother be told by the educational welfare that they would come down *hard* on her. In all honesty, I was moving quite selfishly, unwillingly I had my issues, nevertheless I wasn't really thinking about the hurt I was causing, but even then, it didn't make any sense. They knew my mother had no real control over me, she would send me to school, and it was *not* her fault I wasn't attending. I would leave out in my uniform not saying I remained in it, but I left in it nevertheless. According to the government policies and compulsory educational laws during certain hours of the day it's mandatory that every child receives an education, whether state, public or home schooling, this is the requirement. It was my personal views and experiences within the system that led me not to attend. Numerous emotions kept me away from the classroom, such as lack of support and encouragement from teachers, feeling neglected within the class, not to mention some subjects I just found boring. Additionally, I had my own troubles, internal conflicts that affected my desire to be there. Instead of trying to penalise my mother for her attempts at getting me to school, why not aid her. All parties must and should take responsibility to find the best solution without anyone feeling singled out or persecuted, this is and will always be the best way. It's more than important not to point the finger, and note that the method of choice must be acceptable to all parties involved in the child's welfare.

The reality was, I had been kicked out of four high schools, and was on the verge of going to prison or dying on the streets because of my choices. The question is; did knowing those consequences frighten me? Unfortunately, it didn't. Although that sounds ignorant and childish, one can say that I was both, or just confused about my morals and what was good or bad for me. Yet when one can't see danger as a bad thing because the vision allows you to deny what's before you, we have to question, what powers these triggers to establish such psychological destabilisation causing one not to care, or at least act as if one doesn't?

Back in the days, the police had their fair share of fun stopping me. I humoured them without knowing it, exciting their day because I was too ignorant and *lacked* the insight that this is what they wanted. They loved and still love mind games. Same tricks different era, sadly our youth are still playing into their hands. Me getting upset and angry was a joy for them; the police dealt the hand and I took the card. Nothing wound me up worse than the police calling me by my first name as if we were friends. I hated that with a passion.

Before my first trip to Jamaica in 1989, I had a horrible encounter with my stepfather in the kitchen, one of many back then. I don't remember how it started, all I do know is he bent Marie's arm asking about a book, which belonged to my mother, and I saw red. Grabbing a knife I went for him, my mother jumped in between us and stopped me from taking his life, which I would have done in a heartbeat, and felt no way about it at that time. I remember another occasion where I picked up a vase and threw it at him, because of how he dealt with my mother. It was crazy. He would be put out of the house when certain incidents occurred, but then after a while, my mother would let him back into the home. Whether it was days, weeks or months, like a snake he would slither his way back into our lives. I guess she loved him or had issues with love, but then who doesn't have issues? My mother was taken by her father from her mother at a young age and came to live in the United Kingdom. My mother was highly educated, sweet and articulate, not to mention extremely beautiful to look at, but she didn't have the best luck with men. Could any of this have played a role in her choices? My grandmother was half-Indian, very attractive and wealthy. I guess my mother was blessed with looks, because my grandfather was also a very handsome black Jew, and to some degree, he had a strong emotional connection with women. My grandmother was undoubtedly loving and had nurtured my grandfather's children. My mother, being the only biological child of her mother, grew up without her, while her siblings who her father had with other women, remained in Jamaica with my grandmother. For whatever reason, my grandfather wanted my mother with him in the UK. Could this early departure from her mother have had an effect on her? The lack of sibling bonding, my mother not returning for her mother's funeral, knowing that she was the true and only biological child, but unable to attend for specific reasons, could these be contributing factors and more? There is so much to consider as to why we do things. I'm grown, I'm mature now, and I see life differently today. Back then, I was just angry and hated having him around. For the life of me, I couldn't see why she allowed him to return to the family home when my elder brothers would remove him and sometimes my mother herself would tell him to go, but as I said, he would slither his way back into our house. This silently drove me mad. The reality is, I was not the only child to have ever felt like that, there are many out there in the world, nor was my mother the only woman to act out of character, neither was my stepfather the only man to be messed up and mess up other women's lives or homes. Society is full of broken homes and dysfunctional families to some degree. It's becoming a norm and that's the scary part; even though back then, especially in Caribbean families, we tried to hide it, sweeping it under the carpet, not that it helped, in fact it only made it worse.

As a youth I suffered from blackouts, dizziness and nosebleeds. Sometimes very bad nose bleeds too, they just would come, but I believe they were triggered by my anger. It was never diagnosed, concrete scientific evidence was never given as to why I would get nosebleeds or blackouts, but I always believed it was something to do with my pent-up frustration. I remember dropping one day in front of my stepfather, sometimes I wouldn't just drop, I could actually feel it coming, I'm sure others could see it too, as my body would give way. His grin spoke volumes, as my mother rushed to my aid, while he pretentiously assisted. Occurrences like that and others built up so much hatred for my stepfather back then, but in the same breath, it destroyed the loving little boy that existed within me. Well, destroyed is a bit of a harsh term to use on

131

myself, but the use of such terminology only relates to and emphasises the psychological damage, emotional trauma and hidden pain I encountered. It manifested negatively, creating unproductive thoughts, patterns and reactions.

In June 1989 at the age of fourteen, I shocked everyone, especially the police when I walked out of court for robbery and theft with 12 months conditional discharge, in no time I was on the plane. That should have been an eye opener for me, everyone knew the police wanted me badly, and my mother wasn't going to allow them to get me. Back then, I wished I had her optimism. Due to circumstances, which led me to leave England in the first place, she didn't want me to reside in Kingston city and get into more trouble, so she asked my stepfather's family in the country to put me up. Not having a great relationship or connection of any sort with my stepfather, I was reluctant and sceptical of his people. My preconceived ideas of them were based on how I saw him; I knew he had a dislike for me, and mine was equally as strong towards him. The way I saw it, I couldn't trust him, so how was I to trust his family. That little month and a bit holiday to the Island in the Sun was epic and filled with drama, hence why I found myself back at square one, back in the UK, getting up to mischief, which led to me having to leave London again to return to Jamaica. It only gets worse.

Early 1990, unable to stay out of trouble, not to mention conflict and arguments with my stepfather's family members, I returned to the UK and couldn't settle as I had promised, and again I was off. I had to leave the UK or should I say run away, only to return to face a robbery charge and carry out the most senseless and crazy act in the process.

Those who really knew me back then would say I had a messed-up childhood. Then not many knew me, well, the real me was not shared with anyone. I was great at keeping things bottled in with regards to personal issues and family life; at least I thought I was, and that was my biggest mistake. It's only now I'm older, or better should I say, having matured mentally and spiritually due to self-reflection, that I've realised keeping my thoughts and feelings bottled up was somewhat damaging psychologically. Really, I should have shared them, but anyone who has been through real hurtful situations, knows it's not always the easiest option, talking about certain kinds of problems with people, although it may be the correct method. Many things can cause an individual to act out of character; there are just too many triggers. It's not always easy to pinpoint the underlying cause, even for parents and siblings who many would expect to detect the pattern of behaviour, and this is where it gets tricky. I was fifteen years old in the year 1990. Unlike average children, focusing on exams, preparing for their futures, me being me, I was a product of my environment, circumstances and situations, which affected the way I thought about life, manifesting in my actions. This caused me to be thousands of miles away from London, facing the possibility of a prison sentence for the intent to export marijuana from Jamaica. The situation I found myself in was a prime example of a deep, dark issue affecting my thinking. Looking on my past actions through clear vision today, who'd have predicted back then me attempting to export weed and risking my freedom when the purpose of my return to the UK, was to face a court hearing for robbery. My mother had been given the heads up that I should return to face trial, in spite of the excessive harassment I was getting from police back then in London, and believe me it was ridiculous. The family solicitor assured my mother there was no way I'd go to prison for what I was being accused of, the evidence wasn't substantial and me returning would be best. I had been sent to Jamaica more than once prior to this robbery case in 1990, which I was to then stand trial for. As I mentioned, this is the same time I attempted to export Cannabis.

According to the solicitor, it was better I faced the system again, and then return to Jamaica once the case was over. To stay abroad, skip bail conditions and avoid the court system, would do more harm than good in the long haul. As any loving mother would do out of love, she sent me abroad, with no thought of the consequences for her actions, all she could think about was saving me. Seeing her child going through things she herself could neither totally understand nor control, it created a feeling of helplessness, which caused her to risk being penalised. In my mother's eyes, I was still her Tibo, which is my family name. I was her son, kind, loving and sensitive and believe me I was, but I was also a very troubled young man with many issues buried deep within. After being kicked out of four high schools, sometimes experiencing dizziness and blackouts when I got too angry, occasionally even when I stood up from a seated position, this tells you a lot was going on in my head. Not to mention the times I would inflict pain on myself, punching walls, doors and all manner of things. Some would call it self-harming, but for me it was a way to ease my anger or frustration. That should tell you a lot was occurring psychologically with me behind closed doors, doors that were even closed to those nearest to me. The thought of me going to prison I guess was just something my mother couldn't and wouldn't allow herself to see, not that it bothered *me* or did it? I really didn't care I told myself, in a crazy way, I felt that going to prison was kind of cool. To be honest, that was the ego expressing the lack of self-love and self-worth. To answer if I cared or not, reflecting back on my youthful acts tells me everything; if I really didn't care, why did I run from the police, why not just stand and fight all the time? What's really disturbing looking back on it, is that I convinced myself I didn't care, believing I actually didn't care if I went to prison. To accept the realisation that I really didn't mind doing time, bugs me out, but that's where I was mentally. However, my mother did care and there was no way she was accepting it.

Being a father now myself, I definitely understand the measures a loving parent will take to help their child. Some may say if a child does the crime, they should do the time. I say tell that to a parent who experiences a child ripped from their arms by the system in the past *not* due to crime, and then is faced again with the possibility of their youngest son being taken and locked away. Although the circumstances were and are different, people react to triggers. If the issue that presents itself connects to a trigger, or past memory, whether they're the same or not, similar situations alert the brain, awakening a buried and painful memory, the only thing one comprehends is to protect. In my mother's case, protecting the child of her womb was all she could think of.

Looking back, man I created a lot of pain for my mother as a youth. The reality is, unintentionally I was very selfish, yet didn't see it as being selfish at that time. I really had issues. Understanding myself better now, I would say I had serious issues, many of which stemmed from experiences I'd faced both at home and on the streets.

It's funny how the most disturbed of us can be the nicest among us too. To my mother and all grownups on South Kilburn estate where I lived back then, there are nothing but loving things said about me even until today. When I pass through, I still receive a lot of love. As a youth, I showed respect in front of my people, and the block loved me back. I indeed had two personalities, the grownups, ladies and girls and some close friends saw the nicer side; others? Well, they saw me how they saw me.

You can never get time back, that's real talk; but I wish my mother were alive to see me now. Nevertheless, I know she looks down on me with a smile; the truth is I wasn't in a good state mentally back then even though at that time I thought I was.

If trying to take marijuana to England in 1990, knowing why I ran, and the purpose of returning being to face court for robbery, *isn't* a prime example of an individual making irrational and silly decisions, then what is? I mean fifteen isn't too young to understand right from wrong. When weighing the odds and considering the risk I was taking, knowing my circumstances, it says it all about my state of mind. I got arrested at Kingston Airport as I checked-in, taken to the holding cell and then the following day I was shipped to Kingston Central police station, more commonly referred to as Central police station, or Central Lock-Up. Those days in Central police station, weed on the block was referred to as tranquilliser, and the weak were forced to use a piece of garment and fan their cellmates. That individual was made to 'spin propeller' as it was called back then. At the age of fifteen, I wasn't new to police custody, I'd been arrested in Britain on numerous occasions as I mentioned before for a range of things. Being totally honest, it really didn't worry me one bit, as I stated earlier, in a weird way it was cool, I felt good. I guess a lack of self-love attracted me to the hype of street rep or maybe my desire for acceptance and a place of belonging. But it was my initiation into 'Heaven', as upstairs in Central police station was called back then, that became the revelation for me.

Fifteen and charged for attempting to smuggle weed to the United Kingdom. My mind was definitely not functioning to the best of my ability, I had tunnel vision and it was extremely short, I couldn't see the bigger picture. I had no real consideration for the reason I was returning to the UK. Even though I knew it was to stand before the judge and prove myself innocent whether guilty or not, risking my freedom before I had even won it back wasn't smart. The real truth behind the exportation of weed from the beginning in itself was a massive risk. I'd found out my stepfather was carrying weed back and so I decided to do likewise. It had not been wrapped nor compressed for some time to kill the scent, neither was the weed packed in my Clarks shoes properly. My stepfather's cousin had told me to leave it until next time, but I was determined, which led to me being caught at customs during a search. The end result was, both my stepfather and I were held at Central police station.

My mother was a highly respected woman and very well connected. She knew a lot of people in Jamaica and the right people too. She made her way to Jamaica instantaneously on hearing what had happened to me. Whatever Mommy did, it worked and I was a free man to return to England. In a short space of time, Central police Station had reformed my mental image of a rude boy. All that I saw and heard, I downloaded and processed like a computer. My release from Central police station was followed by my encounter at the airport with some of Jamaica's most talented entertainers back in 1990 such as, Mad Cobra, Capleton, Panhead (R.I.P), Likkle Meekie, and Ghost and Culture. Conversation led to us linking up in the UK, where myself and other family members accompanied them on their tour and some of the artists spent time with my family and I at our home. They came to England to do some shows for someone my mother and I knew personally, R.I.P General Vigo. The thought of hanging around with some of Jamaica's hottest names at that time, mixed with the mental adaptations I'd taken from my experience in Central Lock-Up, being young and crazy, this silently boosted my ego. To be honest in fact, it majorly boosted my ego, I felt like the big man on the block.

My interaction with police came to a halt in 1991, after they came to my house determined to get me after my acquittal from that robbery case in 1990. The same case I was returning to England to face when I decided to export weed and was caught at the airport, placed in Central Lock-Up, and on my release met with some of Jamaica's most talented artists. Winning that case in 1990 truly angered the police, after that I was stopped and harassed, even arrested numerous times but never charged. It was now 1991, and the police were determined more than ever to lock me down, but higher forces were protecting me even in my wrongdoings; but in this situation I was innocent and the Most High was on my side.

In the early hours of the morning, the police arrived with dogs and everything. On numerous occasions, things they said I'd done I hadn't, and for what I *knew* I'd done they wouldn't come for me. Honestly, I'm glad they didn't, or I wouldn't be writing this book. I would most probably still be an angry individual delighting in my pent-up frustration from all that I had been through as a youth. No exaggeration, half of Queen's Park police station came to my house, dogs, the works, saying I did an armed robbery. As they were about to take me, my mother asked them, on what day did I do this robbery I was supposed to have committed, and the answer they gave her I remember my mother thanking God before she even told them why. That evening when I was supposed to have committed the armed robbery, I was at Brixton police station on an ID parade for a case that had been dropped prior to them coming to my house, due to the witness being unable to identify me. What greater alibi could a man ask for? I smiled to myself as I thought about the way in which God was always showing me signs, many of which I refused to see until I ended up incarcerated with more time on my hands than I wished for. However, I see it now, that sentence was a moment for me to reflect.

Because of what I was going through, and that last incident with the police coming to my home as if I was number one on their crime list, it led to my final departure. My mother sent me to my brother's home in East London to chill out for a while, to lay low and then sent me packing. I was shipped off to Jamaica again, but this time she explained that there was no way she was bringing me back, so I'd better make it work out there.

As I mentioned earlier, between late 1989 up until early 1991 when I left from East London to finally settle in Jamaica, I had travelled to the Island in the Sun more times than necessary, all because of my state of mind. Thinking about all the back and forth and the financial pressure I placed on my mother, looking back on it, it was a lot, not to mention a lot of stress too. Money didn't grow on trees, and I knew my mother had to reorganise and sort things out before she would send me, but like any loving parent she found a way, and from East London I headed straight for the airport.

Emotionally disconnected from my stepfather, and not feeling to be amongst his family, I was sent to where I didn't want to be. Honouring my mother, I did as she had asked and went to stay in St Ann. Little did I know, to a certain extent, my prejudgement regarding my stepfather's family wasn't wrong, or did I *will* problems into my life? At times, I found myself in disagreements and arguments with specific family members. I would be lying if I said every situation stemmed from one of them, partly my mindset back then played it role no doubt.

Not too long after my arrival on the Island in the Sun in 1991, my little sister Minnie joined me in Jamaica where she would now attend high school. Minnie and I being very close and only a few years apart in age, I guess my mother thought it was a good idea to ship her off so that I wasn't alone I assume. Minnie wasn't troubled like me, so I believe she was sent for no specific reason other than to keep me company, or when I think about it, maybe to make me feel responsible with the intent that it would keep me focused. Looking back on it, I'm sure she was cool coming to Jamaica, but her whole life was uprooted, and my life definitely had an impact on why she was there. After all, she had no issues with school or home life in England, so there undoubtedly was a connection between me being there, and her for no reason, having to relocate too. It's crazy how one's actions and life can affect another in a massive way, whether good or bad. How it affected her, being uprooted due to me going there, is something we've never talked about, so only she knows the effect it had, or even still has, due to her own experiences while there. One thing I can say, when she was there, I did protect and look after her to the best of my ability back then, no one messed with her, we were tight back in those days. The only time Minnie visited Spanish Town or Kingston was when I brought her there; and most of the time I wouldn't. I was a street youth, doing road things and getting up to a lot of no good activities. Totally aware of the danger, I refused to put my little sister in harm's way. I am now man enough to recognise and say, I was living irresponsibly and dangerously at that time in my life, yet protectively. As I mentioned, I would never put my sister in danger; I loved her way too much. Looking back on it, I wasn't as protective as I thought I was. Although I'd leave her in Runaway Bay where we resided with my son's mother, who was only my girlfriend then, assuming she was in good hands, I didn't think far enough ahead to consider if she heard something happened to me, how she'd take it, knowing I was her only true family around her. It was quite careless and irresponsible of me, but then that's why I said I was protective to the best of my ability back then. That's the downfall of a lot of us out on the streets. Even when we think we're protecting our loved ones, we're not thinking of what we put them through, or the potential sorrow we could cause them. The fact remains, I had left my birth country due to my negative behaviour and picked up the same habits instead of understanding I was given a fresh start. I have come to the realisation that change of mind-set is much more powerful and important that change of environment. As you read for yourself, no real change or difference with me came from a new environment, and I'm sure there are many when they really think about it, would say the same. It may contribute, but true change comes through one's way of thinking, that is the key. As a youth, I just loved the streets. I was always in search of something, and on that note, I just loved Spanish Town, Portmore and Kingston. I could be found anywhere from Rivoli, Train-line to Jones Ave. When it came to Portmore, I would visit Cumberland where my son's mother once resided, also Gregory Park too, but I loved Waterford, Boston, and Third World were the places where I just loved to chill. As for Kingston itself, I was just all over the place. I was like a dog without a home, but had genuine love in so many areas it was unreal. Well, it depends on who's defining love and what one perceives as and attributes to their concept of love. Looking back on certain occurrences, situations and what one considers enjoyment, one's vision of love wasn't as clear; in fact, it was blurry. Addicted to streets everywhere I went, whether England or Jamaica, I always found myself with the wrong crowd, wrong company and getting up to no good. So many things have occurred in my life, many of which I wouldn't write about, nor even *think* to put on paper; not just because my own life and freedom would be jeopardised, but the lives of others too. Not to mention damaging the names of those who've turned their lives around, as well as friends and associates both living and deceased who would just prefer not to be made public for whatever reason.

Over my years in Jamaica, I struggled to see the good, the troubles of my past were deeper rooted than I understood, and with time I would make a mess of the opportunity. In 1994, my mother had no choice but to come to Jamaica and bring me back to the UK. I had caused enough problems for myself in Jamaica, my little sister Minnie had returned to the UK before our mother came for me. Not that Minnie had done anything wrong, it was her wish. Problems were mounting for me and my mother knew she had to sort something out, as me residing in Jamaica just wasn't working. Some of my stepfather's family were getting frustrated with me. My mother heard about the violent act I did outside the local bar to someone who had literally saved my life one evening on the beach, when I encountered an enemy and his friends. With all that she heard, my mother wasn't too keen on me going to Kingston to live with her family, which in truth, is what I really wanted. I didn't really want to leave Jamaica, I just wanted out of St Ann. I really wanted to live in Kingston or St Catherine permanently. During her short trip, my mother considered it. She was going to take me, but then decided it was better I come home with her, she explained her worries and reasons and so I ended up back in the UK.

Sitting in my cell, I thought about everything, unlimited memories ran through my mind. I was now under lock. Being in a single cell on GB3, meant I was left to converse with my own experiences that came rushing to the forefront of my mind, awoken by numerous triggers. Like so many other smart and intelligent youths, situations and circumstances that appose some of us, lead one to slowly stray from the path that parents and guardians so badly want for us. I had been caught up in emotions stemming from trauma, and entangled in the web of illusion, believing that the streets had something to offer me. Man was I wrong. But when I think about all the things that happened and were occurring within my life and surroundings, they affected me deeply, clouding my judgement of right and wrong, darkening my vision, blinding my sight. Looking back, I can say I was like a tornado or a tempest, but then even they know their purpose. I didn't know what mine was, well I *thought* I did, but obviously, I didn't.

One thing I learnt in prison was that facing the troubles of my past enabled me to begin to see my future. I began to learn to fight the true fight that everyone needs to face someday in their life causing one to raise beyond the limitations of others expectations. Also, I learnt, only by stepping up to fight the *single real battle* one faces, against self, does the world seem like such a small place, and easily conquerable. However, the battle of self is not an easy task to conquer. Untangling oneself from the spider's web wasn't easy. The ways in which the dynamics of society are set, and the contributing factors weaving around many, trapping them in darkness, aren't to be overlooked. What I came to understand was, the more I accepted and challenged my habits, acts, and most of all, thought patterns, the more I grew mentally stronger, and it showed. Even when returning to old habits or thoughts, the awareness pertaining to the situation was clearer. I was seeing and accepting that I had much more work to do on myself. The joy for me, on this transformational journey disentangling from the spider's web, was the acknowledgement and fact that I was recognising self-awareness regarding whatever the issue. This most definitely was a step forward, not backwards. The saying that *old habits don't die easily*, was very much true, I was living it. But I knew I was in a better place than before. That was my strength; that was my drive. Believing in myself, acceptance of errors and keeping it moving, I was learning to love me. I knew the process wasn't going to be an easy one, but a life long journey. Both old and young had found the grave and still never knew or loved themselves wholeheartedly. The desire to achieve true self-love was going to be my greatest challenge. Some bad habits are extremely hard to kick, and masking or putting emotions in their boxes is very different from addressing and dealing with them, this I knew from experience. I have told myself before, time after time, I've changed, I'm no longer an angry soul, and have walked away from situations, only to one day just blow up; a ticking time bomb, exploding just like that from zero to a thousand, with no control. I was afraid of this, along with other self-issues stemming from childhood. Change was my purpose; this I understood was my greatest task. I wanted different not just for myself but for others too. I was slowly moving from being that traumatised troubled young man who was unconsciously or should I say subconsciously selfish, to becoming a deep thinker, set to align self through reflection, and acceptance of errors, enabling me to relate sincerely to those whom I encountered on my journey.

Hand on heart, I know that all my experiences and lessons are what made me into the powerful, self-believing man I am, therefore I'm grateful. The journey has been very painful in many ways, and that also isn't to be underestimated or forgotten. From pain comes strength. Even today, setbacks still arise, but it's how I perceive them differently that makes me know I've come a long way, and there is still a journey to travel to truly cut through the web of confusion and illusions. But I am truly thankful. Not all of my loved ones and friends are still here in flesh, in this realm to say, feel and testify to such conclusions regarding the purpose of life. There are just so many experiences I went through as a youth that played a role in fashioning the person I'm becoming, all were either connected to, or stemmed from the family home. I truly believe that with the breakdown of family structure, lack of communication in the home, things we're exposed to, whether within the family or external influences, there are just too many factors contributing to the behavioural characteristics our youths are displaying today. You just can't pinpoint the root. It can be truly difficult to find or understand. Breaking the surface is hard enough; everything takes time, effort and devotion.

Surviving all that I've experienced, seen and been through, and doing the work I'm currently doing, not just in my local community, but throughout the global community, I'm truly thankful for the accomplishments. Nevertheless, would I be as affective and driven if I had not been through so many tribulations, and experienced so much in life? Honestly, I don't believe so. Me saying this, doesn't mean and should not encourage others to believe that they can also walk that dark road and live to share their story. Every man has his journey, the key is to live your own, not follow another man's path. Personally, I feel I had to experience what I went through. It brings me to the conclusion that nothing I've experienced, all the madness, the pain; nothing was in vain. I had to understand how to become the master of spinning my own web. I saw the system for what it really was. For some of us it can feel like there's no going around their web. The many issues spun throughout our lives aligned one after another, whether straight or indirectly, causes the mass of the web to seem so enormous. When trying to break free, one can feel like a fly trapped for eternity. The many factors attached to the spider's web weigh heavily on us creating so much confusion, pain, internal and external suffering; psychological and spiritual freedom seems impossible to achieve. Caught in their web, I looked at its core, at my core, they both reflected darkness. No longer did I want to nor could I live with myself mirroring the image of destruction that was set for me and passed down through generations and through nations, tribes and people. I needed a change. It was there and then that I realised I must walk in a way that not only begins to untangle me from their web, but I must also learn to create my own web. Attaching everything positive to my web that I needed for growth both spiritual and physical, holding close to me that which would not only enable me, and show deep down who I am and my worth, but in the process help others through my creative works, sharing personal struggles, showing the ancestors' fighting spirit, displaying strength and never laying down. My heart is now aligned to the greater purpose. In the mirror, I see life, I am living and my core reflects light.

Chapter 16:
Oval Rock

I had just returned from Kangaroo court; same result different day. I was back at Prison Oval Rock, which was another name for Spanish Town prison. I was becoming pretty fed up of this back and forth, back and forth procedure that seemed to be getting me nowhere. I had no choice but to accept it and wait it out. What I dreaded was being sentenced, and not having the remand time spent taken into account. I was developing faith and prayed that wouldn't occur. However, knowing how corrupt the system was, and after speaking to inmates who said their remand time meant nothing once sentenced, I'd be lying if I said I didn't consider what would happen. My own preconceived ideas ran away with me, and not always the most positive of thoughts might I add. It would be another few months again, before facing the judge. In the meantime, I had to face my reality, which was going through the process of being locked down, fly ups, at least one guaranteed search on the block, and the odd random individual search here and there. That was the regime, and it came with the territory, not to mention the odd little action or violent outburst caused by the least of things, but creating the greatest confusion. Prison life sucked, unfortunately and sadly I got used to it, but never saw myself as a part of it. Psychologically, emotionally, I always tried my best to zone out, or better I should say zone *within*.

Circuit court and its kangaroo actions were one thing, thinking about prison is another thing, the prison system overall is all messed up. The things they would find during a search, knives, phones, cigarettes, weed and other illegal substances, and act as if prisoners were the only people breaking the law, yeah right! Once in a while, money was found. Was it always confiscated? Well, the truth is, it depended on which warder found it, and who the inmate was. Most inmates hid their money really well, so it wasn't always a big issue. News travelled far when bizarre illegal substances were found. Nothing crazy was ever found on my block or on regular bases, but at times warders would find the odd stick of dynamite during their search on New Hall. And when you know something like that can make its way onto a block, it leaves you to think what *can't* an inmate get brought into the facility, providing he has the money and the right connection?

Prison had me constantly thinking even when I wasn't under lock. I mean in prison what more is there to do. Yeah, you can exercise in your cell, you can study, you can listen to music, play the radio, watch TV, watch a DVD, these are some of the comforts we had in prison on the Island in the Sun, providing you had someone who would buy these items for you. But there is only so much of it one can do. Although having access to a TV in one's cell, and later it becoming legal to have a portable DVD player, the fact remains, how much of it can one watch before the mind starts running away? As for having a cellmate if you have one, there is only so much you and your cellmates can talk about, that's if you're not at each other's throats' half the times. The number of fights that break out under lock in prison is ridiculous. Petty disagreements can cause blood to run. I've heard the screams of many, and witnessed numerous attacks; as mentioned earlier, I saw my own blood run whilst behind bars. The prison system is a den of frustration.

One of the most common reasons fights breakout between inmates under lock is food and smoke. A prisoner in a Jamaican institution will kill over his nose, and depending on the individual, he will envy you over your food bag. The amount of fights I witnessed locating with frass-heads, it's a joke. Frass was a terminology used in prison when an inmate doesn't have anything to smoke and needs to relax, which is when problems between inmates are likely to occur. You would think these people were on hard drugs the way they carried on. To me it was funny because I never ever had anybody try to take my belongings once I began to get visits, worse try bad me up to buy them weed, cigarettes or raga. Now that was a classic in prison, good old raga. Raga was the trash of the cigarette that would be thrown away by the corporations and companies that make and pack the cigarettes, yet lots of these inmates were smoking this poison that they would buy for two dollars a ball. It was a sad sight, but also a learning curve for me and those wise enough to acknowledge the destruction occurring before their eyes, the demoralisation of character and manhood, resulting from actions and reactions that were just uncalled for. I observed everything and stayed away from most things unless necessary. Strong headed or stubborn, call it what they wished, always I did things my way, either way, I was self-willed, determined to do me.

Sometimes I'd think about some of my friends back in England, and where most of us were really going. Many of the friends I had in Northwest London like myself were caught up on the wrong side of the system, or should I say the side the system painted. It was a masterpiece of illusion, upon which they spent years of programming and designing for us to fall into the trap, and like blind mice we were captured, products of their illusions, volatile criminals. We were chasing after something that wasn't really there, something that we could never really control or hold onto. It doesn't take a genius to work it out, street youths anywhere in the world that remain on this road, always end up in one of a few places, dead house, prison, or if not mentally strong the odd individual will end up in the madhouse, this is the harsh cold reality. The power of this illusion is so captivating that even though many of us totally understand where this road leads to, we are still drawn to it. The addiction to the streets is similar to a smoker but worse, a cigarette packet says clearly smoking kills, yet people still smoke. We knew what we were getting into, if not at first, surely after the first encounter with the police or other street youths. The realisation was there, but the desire to remain on the path was more alluring, and the addiction to the illusion was incredible. So incredible that I can honestly say, I knew I could never win, but still loved to participate in the illusion, and that thought pattern truly leads to problematic behaviour. The key is to understand how to tackle it and reverse it, putting a plaster over a deep wound is not going to make it heal correctly, nor is throwing youths into prison the answer, it may be financially rewarding for some, but it surely won't change the way individuals see life. I mean, the amount of things I've personally been through, I'm talking serious encounters with other street guys as well as the police, yet I remained on road. I have undergone surgery where doctors entered through the side of my head to enable them to apply titanium to my shattered cheekbone, had my nose broken on a separate occasion, been stabbed in the leg, escaped death and prison numerous times, and taken my fair share of beatings from police. In fact, my front teeth were severely damaged and chipped due to an encounter with police, after being arrested and accused of pulling a firearm out on two officers on Church Road in Northwest London. According to them, I had jumped out of a cab that they intended to pull over, and with my hand under my T-shirt that bulged before their eyes, I waved something at them, which caused them to stop in their tracks and radio for back-up, allowing me time to run. That was their account of what happened. When they did arrest me a moment later in the estate, no weapon was found, nevertheless I was beaten, taken to Harlesden police station and later released without charge, as they couldn't produce an illegal weapon although they searched the area. What they did find was a stick of weed on me, but a bloody face and damaged teeth, wouldn't really look good in court over a stick of weed, so of course I was released without charge. Before they let me go, they told me I got away this time, but won't be so lucky again. The officers made it very clear they believed I threw it or gave someone the firearm. Looking back on it I say, whether I did or didn't have a firearm on me was not the root problem, but the unstable thought pattern of my state of mind was. And those few things I've mentioned that happened in my life are only the tip of the iceberg with regards to my experiences being on the receiving end of situations. Not that there isn't just as much danger and problems that can occur when one desires to dish out pain, who knows, things may not always go as planned, the outcome can be horrifically unpredictable, even the innocent can get hurt. One would think I would have learnt my lesson and jumped ship based on my experiences. Instead, mentally I learnt to steer the boat, not saying I sailed in a direction that was beneficial or promising, in fact, back then I seemed to be attracted to rough seas and storms, calm rivers and canals did nothing for me. I thought about all the craziness that I encountered as a youth before I was shipped off to Jamaica in my early teens, and all that I had got up to whilst in JA and on my returns to the UK in my late teens to early twenties, before being sentenced for manslaughter. It was utter madness, where was I mentally, really, I had to question myself.

One thing I do know is, when you're in the circle you can never really understand the holistic effect of one's actions and the deeply rooted detrimental impact, until you step outside it. There were so many things I reflected on, reanalysed and thought about whilst behind bars. Some things I wished didn't happen, while other things I could see where they stemmed from, and to a degree, rationalise the process of the event. At the end of the day, every action has consequences and that ran through my mind. Why things happened, what I escaped, and what I could have avoided all together, prison really had me reflecting hard. The truth is, prison was my saviour. I needed it. I needed something disastrous or drastic to really shake my world up, and cause me to step back. It's only then that I realised the danger that not only I was in, but also what those that loved me were going through. The sad thing is, not everyone lives long enough to see or come to the realisation of this, while others may repeat the cycle over and over again, dragging loved ones and friends through mucky waters, and never see the truth of the matter. Could anyone say they didn't care? Addressing this from personal experience, I know I cared and loved my family, but I had issues, fighting my own personal demons. In my struggles to understand what I was facing; I just couldn't make decisions that many would have hoped I made. It didn't mean I didn't care, it just meant I was unable to care about them or myself. Prison made me realise there's so much judgement handed out, and not enough understanding and acknowledgement of the underlying issues at the root of one's actions. It's pretty sad when thinking about it. Prison had me looking at life through different lenses, analysing society, my surroundings and most of all myself. I was hating and loving things about myself. All this, while learning new things and challenging some bad habits that weren't going to be easy to shake, as well as specific thought processes, while others just melted away like snow exposed to the truth of the scorching heat of the sun. Every moment and everything were a challenge, some sort of test. The more I thought, the more I believed the world was just one big testing ground and if this was so true, with the old mindset I was definitely failing, but the tables were turning. What lay beyond these thoughts for me? Where would tomorrow lead me? My mind travelled there also. Prison had me really thinking.

Women in my past were an unforgettable and comforting journey back in time, yet regrettable and pleasurable depending upon whom and where my mind travelled. I had made numerous mistakes in my past, played and acted up, while at the same time created so much joy and wonderful memories, all of which were shared with me during phone conversations. Numerous partners from my past and women with whom I had intimate encounters would take me down memory lane, some conversations leading to what we would be doing to one another if we had that moment right now. Such conversations behind bars are more than pleasurable, yet tormenting to the imagination, one would have to have forcibly been taken away from an opportunity so sweet, to know how it feels. In prison nothing beats speaking to a woman on so many levels, the degree of comfort is crazy, yet it plays on the mind when the call ends and one is all alone. This is factual and there's no getting around it. But for me, I loved the self-afflicting torture it brought; I loved the verbal companionship and also the vibe that came with it. It was nice hearing from them, it was hearing their voices and conversations that would cause me to think about what we had and where we went wrong. It would trigger me to start thinking about other situations and similar circumstances that applied in other relationships or so called one-night stands. On this topic, I'd think long and hard. On numerous occasions, I remember asking myself what I really wanted out of a relationship back then, and whenever I get out of this hell hole what would I do differently. To be honest, it took me a while to conclude, and even then, my answer wasn't solid. I didn't know who I was, and what I really wanted out of life, or how I was going to go about getting it. I just knew I wanted better than what I was doing before, and knew as long as I carried certain psychological issues, I could slip up and fall into previous habits. I was coming to accept that loving self is key. With all this going on in my mind, could I ever really know what I wanted from a woman and a relationship until I knew what I wanted for myself and where I was going? Nevertheless, the thought of being with a woman again was comforting, and I visualised freedom and sexual encounters on numerous occasions.

Chapter 17:
Circuit Court

It was time for circuit again, time to hop on down and come straight back up. I knew I wasn't going home or getting sentenced any time soon in this kangaroo court. The system had me hopping back and forth like a joker. The cards were shuffled and dealt out unfairly. Many times, I wondered if those representing me had something to do with it, prolonging my case for more money, just too lazy to do their job, or was it just total systemic corruption. Whatever the case be, I was on my way to St Ann. When I think about the dysfunctional setup of the system and some things that went down whilst I was incarcerated, I feel I am truly blessed and protected. When I reminisce on certain occurrences, I believe I was removed from harm's way by a higher force for whatever the reason. Although I witnessed and participated in a lot of things in prison, there were also many crazy situations that went down that I escaped from untarnished, without a mark to my name or my body. Like for instance, my circuit court appearance before the previous one, wherein Marie had surprised me. During that circuit, all hell broke loose in prison, while I was down at St Ann. I had escaped the madness by nothing but share blessings. I had avoided an entire prison beating. Friends had filled me in on my return, telling me I escaped one of the wickedest beatings to take place in prison history. Warders and soldiers had battered inmates for days, just opening cells, swinging, and hitting them like crazy with all manner of objects. All my close friends had been beaten, apart from Waynie-Bones, and Puppa. Sherlock had been battered badly I was told. I believe it was because of the charge he was on, that they'd dealt with him so harshly. He was awaiting trial for the murder of a warder's daughter. Because I never asked, I never learned how it all started, and why the authorities had dealt with inmates like that. All I do know is, the Human Rights Resource was called in, and so many prisoners made complaints. Only God knows why no justice was ever given. Well, as far as I can recall, nobody said anything positive came out of it. All I realised was, I had escaped a lot of things in prison and continued to escape more trouble. One thing I know for sure, my own hand wasn't the power that was willing it, God was definitely watching over me.

The previous circuit court I had just returned from, removed me from a situation that had been bubbling for a while. Only God knows why I wasn't to be there. I was placed on the first truckload of circuit court inmates sent down to St Ann to appear before Judge Wolf. Whether that was his real name or was just a nickname prisoners gave him, I have no idea. National and a few other circuit inmates had not gone down with me. A few days later, National reached Ocho Rios police station and had told me that some of our friends stabbed up Nia, and he thought he was going to press charges. National told me, when I left, Nia tried to disrespect the link, so they put him in his place. Something told me that if I was there, I would have been involved or caught up somehow, and most probably, I would have.

Here I was again in St Ann on the circuit preparing to face kangaroo court, and the tension on the block down at Ocho Rios police station was high, the humidity of the place didn't help. Everyone was frustrated. The heat outside was scorching, the walls sweaty, and as for vibes on the block, no matter how inmates cracked a joke or two, the energy vibration was low. Visiting time always saw a lift in prisoners' spirits; there was nothing like a long bag filled with snacks and cooked food. These occasions always put a smile on prisoners' faces even if it was just temporary. I wasn't looking a visit, didn't expect one either, but to be honest, I was good. If I needed anything, I would give the duty officer or an inmate's visiting family member money to buy it for me. Little did I know a repeat of two circuits back would happen. I was going to get a foreign visit; it wasn't Marie this time, but her daughter Natz instead.

152

One day, an officer called me shouting, "Visit Graham, Stephen visit." Smiling to myself, I wondered who it was, no longer shocked as I was with Minnie and Lele or surprised by Marie. I was excited to see who it was; I just felt it was a foreign visit. Just when I thought I couldn't be shocked or surprised, again, it happened, it took me a split second to gather my words as my beautiful niece approached me. "Hello uncle Stevie", she said. Before my very eyes was Marie's daughter. I was both shocked and surprised, no heads up nor warning from my big sister, I was on a high. We spoke for a bit and then she gave me all that she'd brought from England for me, as well as some English pounds. With the currency so strong back then, it felt good to hold some more of the queen's head, which is what Jamaican's called British money, due to the queen's face being printed on it. During the conversation, my niece told me she was coming to court and I would be seeing her again, she's here to take care of me. To me, it was like damn, my little niece came all this way to see her uncle. I was happy yet felt honoured. As my niece disappeared, the midweek excitement vanished and the mood swings and tension started to build again. Even *I* found myself getting restless and aggravated. Honestly, I found it hard to hold onto that beautiful feeling my niece brought to the station, the day was just a bad one.

When it was time to be let out of our cells, it was more of a demand than a request. Inmates requested the opening of all cells on our side, so we could shower before eating. Officers agreed although it wasn't the norm, I guess they wanted to keep the peace. How Ocho Rios police station is situated is in two sections, normal jailhouse prisoners were never kept with us circuit prisoners for security reasons. Believe me when I say everyone's minds were working overtime, the humidity, clamminess and negative energy within the atmosphere filled our section. To add to the low-level vibration we were all projecting, there were a few already sentenced men with us serving some serious time. Yet they still had outstanding charges for robbery, firearms and shooting with intent to kill hanging over them. The block was mad. While most inmates aired their frustration, cussed police and pushed their weight around on one another, certain inmates had another agenda. Thoughts of freedom weren't just words expressed through anger.

Weeks went by, and the block ran the same way; madness and frustration. The police had no real control and literally gave us an easy run. As much as I was captured by my new love for the Bible, thinking of scriptures I read regularly and reanalysing aspects of my life, I was far from a perfect being. Surrounded by heavy energy and feeling strong negative emotions myself, I was in constant battles with my inner being. During that circuit appearance, I would say the better side of me lost the battle, but not the war. The person I am, have been, and continues to grow to be, testifies of my changes. But during that moment, it was no doubt energetically one of the worst circuit court appearances I had faced; I allowed negativity to rule, which brought out my darker side.

All circuit inmates had seen the judge, few had been sentenced, and others were remanded to next circuit court. That meant another set of months to run in prison; believe, many weren't feeling that, including me. I'd been called from the bullpen otherwise known as the holding cell, where my niece as promised had come to court and see me. Natz witnessed first-hand the sheer corruption of the kangaroo system I was entangled in. After speaking with my barrister, I knew I wasn't going to stand trial that day. I was angry and pissed; the life of limbo I lived would go on and on.

Early morning a few days before circuit ended, the whole police station came on the block. Someone had tipped them off saying inmates were going to escape, and the grille in the roof had been cut. Someone amongst the circuit prisoners was an informer and had alerted the police. We were all rushed back to prison a few days before schedule. Nobody was ever charged and nothing came out of it. As circuit inmates, we all knew we would never get leeway on the block at Ocho Rios police station again, that's *if* we were ever to return to that police station for another circuit court appearance.

Chapter 18:
Circuit Again

Because of the attempted escape that took place at our last visit to St Ann circuit court, circuit inmates were no longer held at Ocho Rios police station, as others and I had anticipated. We were transported to St Ann's Bay police station in the parish centre. Like before, National and some other inmates at Spanish Town and GP came down late. So there were only a few of us on the block including some jailhouse inmates who became circuit inmates by the authority of whichever judge they had seen. Happy for a bit of peace and quiet, I lay there on my bunk in a half empty cell thinking about Dee, she had been a true friend to me over the months. I'd spoken so many times with my children it just felt amazing. What was even more amazing is that she was in Jamaica with a friend and they were coming to look for me. While at prison, I talked with my children's mother on two occasions back to back, and both times she had sent me fifty pounds, which I thought was kind of Lele, being that she was with someone else and had my children to maintain. Knowing Dee was coming to Jamaica, I asked Lele to buy me a small chain with the Star of David pendant on it and a few vests, and to give them to Dee for me, which she did. As I lay thinking about Dee, I thought about the Star of David pendant. I was really looking forward to receiving it. I had asked my children's mother to let my daughter and son kiss the chain before she sent it. I guess emotionally, I wanted to feel close to them, a symbol of comfort, oneness, engulfed in a spiritual bond with my offspring. A passage in the Torah, in book of Numbers came to mind as I thought these thoughts, which led me to start thinking about the words of Balaam prophesising that a

Star shall come out of Jacob and a sceptre out of Israel. Then I thought about what Jacob prophesied saying the sceptre shall not part from Judea. My spirit really resonated with the scriptures, I felt comforted.

As days passed, tension arose between a long-time circuit inmate who was an ex-soldier charged with four murders, and a jailhouse inmate named Killa, whom we all knew from Ocho Rios station, via our circuit court appearances. He used to locate on the opposite side in the police station, but had now been put on the circuit and therefore shipped off to St Ann's Bay station where he was to join other circuit inmates and await trial. This new circuit inmate, myself, and a few others including an inmate named Boom, who almost lost his life because of misinformation, trained every morning and evening on the passage before we showered. Killa was a Jamaican who grew up in L.A and was a member of a Crips set based in Compton. He was awaiting trial for attempted murder. I had maintained the peace between both inmates for days, when my long-time circuit friend called to the police to lockdown the first three cells. He himself located in the first, Boom in the second, who at that time had no problem will Killa, well least I thought not. I was located in the third cell. The ex-soldier had told Boom to come in his cell, whilst we were all on the passage. Boom's original cell was locked down, and then mine. The thought of the ex-soldier plotting never crossed my mind, as inmates at times would run the day in a different cell for whatever the reason, so others and myself went under lock as normal. Then I heard the ex-soldier's cell lock, yet his voice and Boom's could be heard on the passage as they ordered the officer to open the other cells. Instantly, I knew something was about to go down. Killa had clocked the play. The plan backfired drastically, almost causing Boom to lose his life. Usually flip-flops or sliders are worn on the passage and sneakers when we were preparing to go to court. Honestly, I don't think any of them noticed Killa had his sneakers on as he stepped out of his cell. From within my cell it was impossible to see everything taking place, all I could hear was chaos on the passage. Apparently, a few inmates, Boom being one of them along with the ex-soldier had approached Killa. With his hands down his pants, Boom stepped to Killa who reacted and held Boom's hand so that he was unable to pull his knife out from his pants. Killa dipped in his own waist and pulled out his shank as he held Boom's weapon hand in his pants and the rest is history. The inmate had received two vital stabs. One to the lower part of his neck, and the other just missed his heart. Because he had raised his arm up a notch, it guided the knife away from piercing directly through his heart. His reaction led to him being stabbed in the arm during the attack on his vital organ; if he had not raised his arm Boom would have died that day no doubt.

The inmate was a strong guy; he was taken to hospital immediately and returned days later. While the inmate was at hospital, his cousin known as Gunmout and the other circuit inmates came from GP, and a few of them wanted to take out Killa. I told him to cool until his cousin came back, because all was not as it seemed. We argued for a while. Understanding his frustration and anger, I stood back and refrained from talking at that point, as I knew I wasn't getting anywhere. He was just too heated. Gunmout was a real hot head and a serious individual. He was the kind of guy who would smile and laugh with you, then do the unexpected out of the blue. He was given his name because he had been shot in his face and survived. The following day Gunmout and I spoke, and he said he would wait until Boom returned, only to go back on his word. They wanted to get to Killa, but were unsuccessful. Deep in my heart, I knew the ex-soldier had caused the conflict, so I had words with him, but he denied it. Days later when Boom returned from hospital, he came straight to his cousin, a few others and me and told us exactly what I'd assumed. It was pretty obvious from where I stood, he had been manipulated and controlled, as we'd say in Jamaica, he took press. After all, it was only the day before the stabbing occurred that both men were exercising on the block. Boom blamed himself for taking press from the ex-soldier, and told me personally that he wasn't going to retaliate. I told him to thank God he was still alive, and just live.

Some prisoners just don't learn. Because there were inmates from both General Penitentiary and Spanish Town prison at circuit court, even though Boom himself and Gunmout were planning to leave it alone, some decided to jump on the bandwagon. They hyped up themselves and escalated things, planning to murder Killa if he was sentenced, or told to run remand at prison if his case was adjourned, which would mean he'd go to one of the abovementioned adult correctional centres.

I knew he was going to be sentenced after hearing about his case from the horse's mouth and he was. His case was pretty straightforward; it was unlikely to be adjourned. Everyone on the block knew he would end up in prison, but what no one knew was, who his friends in the system were.

That circuit court was a disaster through and through. Inmates were turning on each other; I was remanded yet again, back to prison with no knowledge of when my trial would start. Unfortunately, I didn't get to see Dee, so I was well pissed and upset. The only good things that formulated were what I learnt from my daily study of Hebrew. Despite what was going on, I studied, as I had mad passion for knowledge. Enjoyable also was the regular Sunday home cooked food I got when Mitzie came, God bless her, she fulfilled and kept her promise. Those of us who had money sometimes would ask someone's visitor to buy us patties from the food shop across the road from the police station, depending on the vibe, man's pocket and appetite, we would order breakfast, lunch and evening meals. No doubt, circuit time was when I ate the best. I ate from ackee and salt fish for breakfast to jerk chicken, oxtail and butter beans with rice for lunch or dinner, sometimes both. The reality is, no matter how well I ate at times; I never truly felt good, or happy. I mean, how could I? Every time I looked out the grille, I saw people going about their daily lives, I felt like a dog in a cage. Feed me all you want; the truth is I wasn't going anywhere too fast.

Chapter 19:
More Remand

Back at prison, I spoke with Dee and she explained to me what had happened. I was cool with it, although deep down I was pretty saddened, as I wanted to see her. Her support, consideration and affection towards me, made her a champion in my heart. I could only imagine what it would be like to see her in person, to thank her and look at the smile on her face. It's amazing how a simple thing such as a beautiful imagery of a smiling face, can create such warmth; almost comforting, seeing her would have truly lifted my spirit, nevertheless, I was just as happy that my chain and things were left down in the countryside with her uncle who'd bring it to me next circuit court.

My brothers and sisters had sold the family home on the South Kilburn estate, which our mother left for us when she transitioned from this realm, and my share was in the hands of my QC barrister. It was transferred to him by our family lawyer in the UK in case I needed anything, but believe me, I didn't see much of the thousands of pounds he was holding for me, but that's another story. From time to time, I would send my cousin Jaro to collect a hundred here and a few hundred there. I figured it would take a little pressure off my family in England; after all, they had paid my court fees, not that the barrister told me that, as I already expressed. A few times the barrister had me sign over money, saying there was outstanding balance that needed clearing. None the wiser, I paid it off. I give them that, my barrister and anyone involved were hustlers, and I say it without humour. In addition, my family were flying out to visit me and sending things regularly. Taking a little pressure off them by using my own money from time to time was the least I could do. The odd few times I made Jaro pick up more than a hundred pounds, I made it stretch over a period of time. At that time, it was only sixty something dollars to the pound, so two hundred pounds worked out to be just over $12,000 Jamaican dollars. Whenever money was collected, I would tell her to bring cash and send it in. For example, out of two hundred pounds, half would be roughly $6,000 dollars, in prison that's good money and could go a long way if spent correctly. The other half of the money was spent on cooked food; nothing like road food, as we would call a home cooked meal. We would also buy snacks. Snacks under lock are comfort foods. Depending on the days, she would bring me food, or toiletries, as certain things are only allowed to come into the prison on various days depending on your surname, it was all in alphabetical order. When it came to money, that was sneaked in, we had our ways of getting it in, for some of us, we didn't need to hide it, everything was patterned easy.

I can never forget what one of my cousins did to me. Adding to the daily stress and pain faced due to incarceration, my cousin made it worse by stealing my money. Back then, I thought to myself, how low can one stoop, thieving from family, especially when I needed every penny I could get. She was on road, I was locked down, it upset me, but looking back on it, and although principle is principle, the money should of run; but who knows her struggles and why she did it. I mean, the level of suffering and stress some people face; not righting her wrongs, but only God knows what she was facing at the time, or if it was just greed.

When Jaro couldn't visit me, she would send Marilyn, my original sweet sistren from Hungry Town; we were close from road. Sometimes she'd visit me with Jaro if she wasn't busy. One day both of them were busy and had something to do, so one of my other cousins from a place called Angola in Jungle was staying at Manning's Hill and had checked me instead.

I remember the food bag coming in and no money handed over to me by the orderly. Instantly I got mad and asked him where's the money? He said he wasn't given any money, and before I walked off, I told him he knew the consequences of holding out and trying to scam me. He swore he had not taken any money from my cousin, but I just continued to walk. Straight into New Hall I

160

walked with my bag, I didn't even go to Remand Block to put it down. I told my friend to give me the phone. Listening to my conversation as he watched out for warders for me; he alerted an inmate and sent him to call a few of the orderlies. I was so angry, that day I was looking to kill someone, and it wasn't me alone feeling like that. I knew for the violation my friends would've made sure money ran back and the orderly get a few good box and kick for the violation at the least. Worst-case scenario, blood runs. Orderlies arrived one after the other, as they were working the whole prison. I pointed out the orderly that had given me my bag and straight away, my friend responded to that orderly's defence. He wouldn't violate us he told me, and told him to leave. I was so angry, I remember him telling me, either your cousin never gave him for whatever reason, for fear or something, or she thieved the money. I was called to go back in the cell as my cousin Roy (R.I.P) up at Hungry Town called back. Straight away, he told me he believed she had taken it; and to think, she denied taking the money when I spoke to her at first, putting an innocent life at risk. What confirmed that *she* took the money, was when Roy said my cousin brought some items on her return to the area, and was crying she was broke earlier that morning.

The desire of the inmates who were at St Ann's Bay jailhouse during circuit court disappeared into thin air once Killa reached prison. Because of the stabbing that took place at the police station, when the prison truck brought us circuit prisoners back to both Spanish Town District Prison and General Penitentiary, Killa was not on the truck with us. Anticipating his arrival, inmates in Spanish Town were saying, when he arrives what they were going to do if he comes to Prison Oval Rock. This caused vibes between others and me, because I saw it as if Boom was leaving it and he is the one who was stabbed, why are others pursuing it. The ex-soldier was located on South Block, which is the first block you pass through when entering the prison. All new inmates' check-ins took place in an office on the block's compound before allocation, so the ex-soldier and others would know when Killa arrived. I had visited South Block and spoken with them, and left it like that. My involvement was purely about creating peace, I could see where it would lead to, and the angel of death would collect someone's soul if it persisted. Days later Killa arrived at Spanish Town prison. News reached me that instantly; Killa had linked up with Sexi-Paul who was an associate of his, which made him cool with Buck-Wheel and the rest of South Block bigger heads. The ex-soldier's dreams crumbled like a cookie and him along with it. Taking Killa's life would never be a reality. Killa also had ties with two of the most dangerous prisoners in the system, both of whom located out on grass at that time, Lord-Evil and Damian. So, plotting to or attacking Killa was a suicide mission, one which neither the ex-soldier, nor anyone who he thought would aid him were willing to do.

In Spanish Town prison, I knew everyone at the top in the game, but what made me stand out from a lot of inmates was the way I lived and how real I kept it. Despite whom I knew, I would never show off or throw my weight around. I had friends on every block in the prison apart from Boys Town, and my link with New Hall was tight. One thing I never did was throw money at the big men. Everything and anything I had given away was always to the poor. My respect had a solid foundation it was built from the ground up, and that made it unshakeable. To myself I was always true, and was always willing to give good advice, which made a lot of prisoners talk with me. No matter how bad a person is or acts in front of others, in every human there is a part of us that cries to express itself and needs to communicate with someone else. I acknowledged that, and would lend an ear, always giving sound advice and strong reasoning, which made me someone that people felt comfortable speaking too. My foundation stemmed from my days of suffering. Many saw and knew I wasn't taken aback by what people would say, or how they mocked me during my suffering days, which was when, as stated before, people began realising my stance was more out of share strength and not weakness. Not to mention everyone knew I would fight for my rights and never bow to any man. Allow me to be me, that was always my belief and I walked in it with pride and respect for others and myself.

I had lost a close friend whilst I was at St Ann on circuit; Puppa had gone to court and was sentenced for illegal possession and shooting with intent. I felt it for him, he was the first inmate who I'd not known from road that I'd put a little trust in, not to mention ate from. Apart from Puppa, up until the time of my sentencing, I had only eaten cooked food from Max and Waynie-Bones. If an inmate was ever planning to kill me, believe me they weren't going to get to me through my belly. My will and the way in which I profiled, made sure of that. Food would be my last down fall behind these crummy walls.

Honestly, I found it hard to eat from inmates, unless we were cooking together in the cell and of course I'd watch it get prepared or I'd be doing the preparation myself. But food from road, you never knew what is running through the minds of prisoners, worse the minds of the family members on road. Who's to say if they don't really love that specific member of the family for whatever he has done on road towards them or others, and desire to poison him, and because of your belly you die like a bitch. Then again, they may be working obeah to help the inmate in some way or another, and you get *helped* too. As I've stated before, I'm a deep thinker, some may say paranoid, but I'd rather be paranoid and safe than chilled and thrilled. The reality is because I've seen it with my own eyes; an inmate shared his food and everyone who he gave it to, defecated like ducks through the night into the next morning. I don't trust easily.

The wickedest thing I know to take place is when an inmate crushes and grinds a light bulb into power, and then adds it to whatever was cooked; the most dangerous combination is when it is mixed into a hot bowl of cornmeal porridge. Such porridge is known to cut up an inmate's intestines and cause him to excrete blood. It's not hard to acknowledge why I never trusted any and every one, when knowing things like that have taken place. I prefer to watch my food being cooked and believe me; I'm not taking an eye off it. As I stated before, it was only Puppa, Waynie-Bones and National I trusted, they were the only people who could cook food and I would allow to send on to me. If there was a shortage of hotplate to go around and I wanted food under lock, believe me I was holding my own until fly-up and whilst I was there that food was being dealt with. In truth, I only used other people's hotplate to reheat something quick or I cooked myself, which was something I could do with my eyes closed. I used to cook a lot, not that I didn't trust my friends, but they liked my hand, as they would say. I had been cooking from young, fourteen to be precise, not just for the family at home, but for my mother's business too. Before my mother had her own shop, she used to run a catering business from within a busy cab station in Kensal Rise back in the days. Pots were empty when she'd come home and I'd smile. Looking back on it, cooking was something I really enjoyed, and still do. Back in the days when I moved out of the family home on the South Kilburn estate, across the road into Fielding house, whenever fish was fried and the local guys on the ends knew I cooked, it was sharing time. Everyone respected my cooking skills. Tata Ranking some of them would say, send some fish down, and of course I would more than happily oblige. The love amongst us back in those days on the block was amazing. South Kilburn was one big family; I think that's the easiest way to describe us. Numerous times, I'd sit in my cell just reminiscing on the good old days. Wishing I could turn back the hands of time, whilst facing the fact that the past is the past for a reason, realisation of my circumstances and where I was had to be accepted. I could do no less than adjust to the times and ride it out. The reality was, behind these walls is where I'd constantly eat, whether it was me cooking it, food provided by close friends, or I was getting road food in my long bag on visiting day, the unshakable truth was, I was a prisoner and everything else was just thoughts and memories.

I didn't always eat prison food. Once I begun to get regular visits, we cooked most of the time, but there were the days when something would come on the tray and I'd be like yeah, I want some of that.

One day Kara had cooked stew peas and rice, and I'd taken a little in my bowl. That night it was like I had taken a wash out. The funny thing about it was that it wasn't only me that was affected by the meal, but the general population that also ate it. The amount of cargo (bag of doo doo) that one inmate came out of his cell with was ludicrous. Cargo is a prison term for defecating in a bag.

As disgusting as this topic is, the idea is to give you an inside look at what we had to, and some still have to go through. There was nothing comfortable about squatting in a cell corner over a plastic bag lined with newspaper. Toilet tissue rolled up long ways or plaited which is how your wick is made, and then lit, in order to

164

cut the scent down as you take a dump. Whether located by yourself or not, your blanket is your screen, so other inmates are unable to see you. Then in the morning, you have to wash your cell out, worse if you're located with others. That morning, every block was washed and not just the cells, it was a complete disaster.

Whilst on this topic, on a normal day an inmate who located in a cell where there was no understanding between cellmates would have to hold his number two until the morning. I have witnessed inmates forced to hold their faeces so long, they produced cold sweat and started shaking. Others crapped themselves. That was the sad thing for some; certain inmates didn't tolerate the doing of number two under lock, whilst others understood its nature, that you've just got to go when you've got to go. In truth, this was easier said than done, especially for someone located with an asshole.

On to more pleasant memories, I remember being called for a visit and wondering who it was, because nearly all my visits were planned ones and I wasn't expecting anybody, nevertheless I was looking forward to it. I recall standing in the box and seeing one of my close friends from NW10, I'd more describe him as a brother. Raymond smiled at me. For those few minutes, we spoke and he made it clear that he got me, and I would be seeing him always until I was free. I laughed and nodded my head. Raymond had sent in the latest pair of Nike and designer jeans and tops, when I say he kitted me out, it was like I was on road and just come out of jail. You know how real connects deal with one another, so he dealt with me; not to mention he sent in money for me too. I can honestly say, he kept his word, yearly I saw him, sometimes twice for the year.

Happy moments never last long in prison. National began to lose weight suddenly; it was noticeable as he was a big strong brother, mad strong, if I were to express my observation of his power. However, National would say it's the training, even though he did train extensively hard, I was worried about him. Prior to losing the weight he developed a rash, which the prison hospital gave him cream and tablets for, but it began to spread further around his body. I used to encourage him to tell them to send him to a real hospital, but being the warrior he was, and pretty stubborn like me, National would just overlook it, scratch some part of his body and just get on with it. In my heart, I knew there was something more to it. One day they took National out of his cell by this time he was much smaller in structure than before, still muscular but just not himself, the warders were taking him to hospital we all believed. National never returned, and word came back to the block that he had died. That broke me up inside and out, tears were unable to hold back and I didn't want to hold them back either. I wholeheartedly believe if I did try to withhold them, I'd have gone crazy literally, if I tried fronting in the midst of the block. I had lost a close friend, someone I considered a brother, someone in whom I trusted, and believe me although I talked to many at this stage on the block as my respect was there amongst my peers, National was someone whom I dealt with on a whole different level. I had opened up to him when I trusted no one; the loss hit me real hard and deep.

Chapter 20:
Remanded Again

As usual, I would speak with various members of my family, a few ladies from my past and of course Dee, she was my rock. Like my family, Dee kept me informed about what was going on in England and in constant communication with my offspring. Hearing from my children's mother became a thing of the past. Our communication had gone down the drain, at times it felt like our love went with it. Though deep inside I knew I still loved her for all that we once shared. I also considered it might be hard on her, knowing she loved me too, which I didn't doubt, but now she had moved on. Keeping her distance might have been the way she dealt with her emotions, the least communication the better, or easier it may have been for her, or maybe her new man. To be honest, I didn't give it all too much thought; I respected her and left it like that. I was man enough to put all that to one side and focus on more positive things, like my children's wellbeing, and if and whenever I got the hell out of prison, what I'd do to make changes in my life. Mental and emotional growth was definitely occurring, I was learning and getting to know me, and was at that point in my life where I knew there was more to me than what I exposed. Steps were being taken, the transition period had begun, the process necessary to turn me into the man I felt I needed to be was in motion. I also knew it wouldn't be achieved over night and there was much work on self to do, after all, from within I was a broken man. I needed healing, mending, and comforting, all of which had to come from within first. I knew that not all of my answers would be found within those walls, as the true test of time would be whenever I was free.

So I understood the outside world had a lot to teach and show me. I just wondered when and what it would be; unwilling to kid myself, I knew my anger, and my love for sex were going to be big challenges when I was free from that hell hole. In prison it was easy to overcome it, the sex part that is, based on the fact there were no women to have sexual intercourse with. The only entertainment was what one saw in porno magazines and videos, but all that led to hand jobs, and to tell the truth, keeping strength in prison is a wise move. You never knew when you might have to fight, so with me thinking like that it wasn't a regular thing to say hello to Mrs palmer and her five daughters. The greatest challenge was more when the build-up of sexual frustration came during mad conversations with women, or when the conversation was over and the mind began working overtime and nature decides to rise and won't set like the sun. That was when true willpower needed to kick in, and believe, it didn't always win. Therefore, sunset isn't appearing without one's help. The mind is a powerful thing, and can will its own creation, worst-case scenario if you didn't help the sunset, your dreams would. The imagery that can formulate during dream state can seem very realistic. As for anger, that was another thing, at times inmates could act crazily. Not necessarily to me, but in front of me, and I hated a bully, so there were times I couldn't help but get involved in an argument or even get physical. I didn't always react to inmate's actions, nor did I get involved regularly, although I was fighting myself not to. I was trying to understand me, so going into myself and reinforcing thoughts of why I shouldn't get involved was key, but there were times I'd just flip. I guess while I was seeking myself, I'd suppress thoughts instead of dealing with them, pushing them to the back of my mind and thinking I'm good and then just blow up, which was bad for me and didn't do me any good. I knew I sincerely hated seeing inmates bully the weak or unfortunate, but my response wasn't always because I hated bullies. The more I analysed myself, I knew I wasn't the best at channelling my emotions. Thoughts of my past experiences would play on my mind and I carried a lot. I thought I had dealt with these emotions, when in truth, I just pushed them to the back of my mind. Additionally, I had bad anger problems, and the smallest and sometimes insignificant things could set me off; somehow, they were triggers. The root of the problem was my emotion and how I channelled it. I had lived with this for years. In fact, even today I realise there are still things I haven't fully gotten over, and really only pushed to the back of my mind or placed in a box, not knowing that it can open at any time, and this is dangerous. Emotions overall are something that people are not taught how to deal with, whether within the education system or in society. Our emotions and pain harness great energy, if not channelled rightly, the end result can be worse than a tsunami. In school, I remember teachers flipping on students, I've seen police officers lashing out on civilians who they're sworn to protect. Daily I saw warders take their frustration out on inmates; I guarantee that all of the abovementioned have issues in their lives and just need an outlet for their frustration. The sad thing is, incorrectly channelled emotions can be destructive, not to mention transferrable, and someone is going to carry that energy somewhere else and to someone else. Thinking in this manner, I looked and hoped to find freedom, so I could explore myself and my state of mind in a world wherein so many different temptations and trials waited. I wanted to know my strengths, weaknesses and myself. I wanted to understand who I was. Even with these thoughts going through my head, I was still prone to do crazy things behind these bars and act out of character, slipping back into bad habits. The only difference was, at the end of it, I'd know and acknowledge where I went wrong or right. It didn't mean I wouldn't do it again, it just meant I was a bit more conscious of what I was doing and why. I guess it was a part of me learning about myself, hence I desired to be physically free and face new challenges to enable me to keep growing mentally that is.

Circuit court was just around the corner and I was more than looking forward to it. Dee had left my things with her uncle and he told me whilst I was in prison that he'd bring the stuff to St Ann's Bay police station, so I had much to look forward to this time round. I didn't want to keep living in limbo, I just wanted to be sentenced or freed, to set my mind at rest and on whatever path and mindset I needed to further my growth.

Taken from Spanish Town Adult Correctional Centre, the prison truck made its way to St Ann's Bay police station and pulled up right at the front gate where it came to a halt. One by one, they led us out, usual procedure. After they'd booked us in, we located ourselves, which was also a usual procedure. The police never ever told us at any time which cell on the passage to go into; inmates chose to locate with whom they chose. I can't speak for circuit prisoners before my time or after, but during my circuit appearances at St Ann, the police had to work with us, and that is the God's honest truth. Allowing us to locate in which cell we desired made their lives and our stay much less stressful. One thing I must say is there was cooperation between police and us, apart from the odd pulling on clothing during a quick test of manhood, or tough talk between an inmate and a police officer that is. Such situations always stemmed from some young officer that wants to flex a little muscle on the block and create havoc for himself and his colleagues. There were quite a few of us that trained daily whilst we were at jail, and knowing they couldn't bring their guns on the block they understood battens weren't going to be much use against say ten to fifteen strong willed brothers. Situations always were squashed, but none of that led to any of us inmates trying to take liberties. We were respectful; after all, they allowed us to order road food from the restaurant morning, noon and night. Every man loved their belly, so we always cooperated, unless, like I stated, one of them acted out of character, and that rarely happened.

It was court morning and I was in the bullpen with the other inmates. What Jamaican's call the bullpen, is known as the holding cell in England. That morning I sat in the back where I always sat. I was never one to shove my face against the grille and beg, nor stand there and watch inmates' family members and friends go to and fro. It was only if I felt a bit peckish, I'd ask someone to buy food for me, providing they said yes which they always did, and even then, I chose wisely who I trusted to go to the shop and buy me food. For anything not sealed in a packet such as a box food, I trusted my spirit or knew exactly who it was, as I said before I didn't and don't trust easily. Money was handed to the police on watch, and he or she would hand it to her or him, as direct contact with civilians was not allowed. Although with certain situations, they'd turn a blind eye and allow us to touch our girls or a female who took a liking to an inmate. In which department I had no problems. Although some people from St Ann, especially in

Runaway Bay disliked me, back in the days I had strong links in Saint Ann's Bay in the ghetto and in and around the area due to my affiliation with certain youths, more specifically, my brother from another mother Percy (R.I.P). Percy was a local dancehall artist, real ghetto youth and a close friend, so I got to know the right people in the parish capital, and was familiar with a few ladies, so seeing the odd person I knew while at court would lead to a conversation. Plus, women just seemed to like me; I guess they saw something in me.

Remanded again, it wasn't what I wanted. I was tired of it; living with the unknown. It's literally impossible to direct feelings and emotions towards something when you don't know where to channel it. I felt lost at times, even though I held faith. I was tired of seeing the judge. I just wanted the nightmare to be over, to know where I stood and keep it moving. I wanted direction; I needed mental mapping and couldn't do it whilst in limbo. It never stopped me from thinking positively and hoping one day to do this and that, but the reality was, I had no idea of what I'd do nor when, and most importantly how I would go about it, as limbo gave no fixed answer to my problem. I just had to keep living and dreaming.

Dee's uncle checked me one Sunday at St Ann's Bay police station during visiting hours. He brought the things Dee left with him for me, and brought me a cooked meal and drink from the street, which I thought was extremely kind of him. I received the vests that my children's mother had sent and a pair of sneakers Nosh sent for me. When Dee's uncle first handed an officer my chain, by the officer's reaction I could see he was wondering if he should give it to me. Immediately, another policeman told him to hand it to the inmate, everything is all right. It felt good to get it in my hands. I know the young officer was looking at it from a point of view that if anything happened to me, for instance if I was robbed, or stabbed over it, it would go against him. He failed to understand that the chances of me being robbed in jail were as slim as the chance of me walking off my charge scot-free; somehow, I just knew it wasn't going to happen. Me walking off this case, deep down I just knew wouldn't happen for various reasons. Not that there would be any complaints if I did, but in my mind, I just wanted to know how much sentence I'd get, to set my mind towards it, and then start living. To live, was to ask questions, to feel alive was to have found the answers. I knew I could really hold on to the sensation of feeling alive in my new understanding of life even in prison, I just needed to know what I was living for. Believe me, the time spent alone soul searching, reading the scriptures and practising and learning biblical Hebrew, had me looking at myself in ways I had never done before. I just knew there was more to me.

Just over a month had passed since my return to Remand Block, when news came that Puppa had escaped from General Penitentiary. He had beaten the prison walls of Tower Street Adult Correctional Centre and found freedom. My heart was more than happy for him. To be honest, I prayed that they'd never catch him and that anywhere he was, God was with him. Puppa was and will always be seen by me as one of a kind, the respectful manner in which he dealt with me will always reflect positively.

During that same period of me returning from St Ann circuit court, Waynie-Bones had also landed on road. He had gone to court and successfully found freedom street. We all felt good for him, and hoped he remained out there. It was a powerful moment, Puppa and Waynie-Bones both on road. Freedom was what inmates desired, you'd have to be crazy not to desire it, though believe me at times you'd have to wonder about some inmates. The way some would carry on, you'd think they had a death wish and wanted to be killed while incarcerated. Others you'd think they had nothing to go back to, or were wanted on the outside and had people just waiting to kill them. However, my philosophy was I'd rather take my chances out there than die in here; prison was somewhere I just didn't want to be.

In the space of a few months, two of my close links in prison had found Freedom Street. Other inmates that I dealt with and knew on our block had also been either bailed or freed. It felt like a good luck streak was running on our block, at one time nearly everyone had a single cell due to the number of inmates that were rightfully released back into society. Such strong vibes led me to think about my case and the three musketeers that would ride on the devil's back into the courthouse every time without fail. I just knew they weren't going to leave it alone. Two out of three of the guys that were pursuing my case were family to my son in Jamaica; they were his direct cousins. The third was dating their cousin, which made them all practically family; without a thought of my son in mind, they were determined to see me go down. But there was more to it, a long, lengthy history of altercations between us added fuel to the fire, even my son's mother had written a statement against me but later withdrew it. I'm not totally innocent in all this, I had my role to play, and again it was where I was mentally back then, and how I saw life that caused me to act in certain ways which triggered or should I say added to the situation.

Chapter 21:
UK Linkup

Waynie-Bones had gone, Puppa had gone, as Jamaican inmates were leaving, it seemed like more English citizens were being sentenced and now faced the experience of prison life on the Island in the Sun. I was on South Block one day when I saw an inmate who looked really familiar, there was something about this inmate and I had to know what it was. On approaching him I asked him a question and his accent gave me the answer to my curiosity. As we begun to talk, we both realised we knew one another from Harlesden. He was a local recording artist from NW10. He had told me there were other English inmates from the ends on the block and a few on NCB, which was a block to the left of the Slaughterhouse aka Ship. I asked him where the other English were on South Block. Due to the answer he gave me, I followed him into the building. I laughed when I saw who the other English was as we approached his cell. Right away, Harrow-Jay and I began to talk. It isn't easy for foreigners to go through prison without paying tax, and getting bullied, but Harrow-Jay I can honestly say held his like a soldier.

The next day the artist had brought me to another English that I knew from Stonebridge back in the days, he was the foundation selector of the local popular sound system Vigilante. Days after, I bumped into Abba (R.I.P), another popular Stonebridge man whom I had also known for a long time. For the little time we were in the same prison, there was nothing but love between us. We walked as a unit even though we were on separate blocks, new friends or prison friends never came between the respect we showed one another and that is how I knew the genuine hearts that were in each of them. One day, Harrow-Jay told me that some guys on Abba's block were trying to disrespect him, so I visited Abba and told him we can make big problems over this, but he was leaving soon and didn't want that, plus he was going to transfer to South Block where Harrow-Jay located. So on that note, I made it slide. But that was the love between us. Being the longest prisoner there out of all the foreigners and having strong links, for Abba, I would have done whatever had to be done to protect him and assure he had a safe exit out of prison, the same goes for any of them.

It was pretty funny because in those days I was getting visits, not weekly, but I was still getting them, yet the way I'd dress in prison was always rough, you'd think I wasn't getting visits at all. I hardly put on my designers that Raymond brought, or the garments my family sent previously; the odd one garment and that was it. Most times, it was shorts and T-shirts. I just didn't see the point of dressing up. Who was I impressing? My money would run down at times due to spending daily on food and other stuff, but I didn't make it bother me. After all, in the beginning, I had suffered and went through that hardship like a soldier, there was no way I was going to cry when the well went dry, especially when I knew my family and a few close friends would always pour water in there to quench my thirst. I had a strong support network and I was grateful. Plus, my English friends also had me the little time we spent together, we moved as a unit as I mentioned before.

As for the Jamaican inmates, pity I couldn't say the same thing. A war was in the process of developing on Remand Block as tension was rising between certain long-time remand prisoners and three new inmates who had just come off Death Row after winning their appeal. Inmates came to me and explained what was going on. I had won a certain degree of respect for myself not only on my block but also within the prison itself. Certain inmates and I talked and everything was cool. But little did anyone know the level of influence certain individuals were under by a set of prisoners that desired war and not peace. Seeing where it was going, I told individuals I was on a different wave, and if it's not a plan to escape, I wasn't involved. Realistically, I was showing them the waste man life in prison is a joke because no one's a winner at the end of the day, if you're going to fight against anybody then fight against the system.

Problems escalated, and one day about two weeks later, all hell broke out on the block. One of the Death row appellants stabbed an inmate and ran out of the block. A few of us were working out at the time and continued to do so, while many inmates followed the excitement. There I was doing my pull-ups as I saw him exit the building and run around the corner out of my sight, I guess towards the fence, which was where I heard he was stabbed. The Death Row inmate was caught in a catch twenty-two situation, he could either attempt to climb the fence and make a run for it or stand and face an enemy that was approaching hot on his tail. The decision he chose caused him to lose his life that day. He attempted to climb the fence and was laid to rest. The war on the block that had escalated outside came to an end. His two friends who were also in war ran to pick him up, and began to walk briskly with him. I walked over with my friends and looked at him. He was barely conscious, he had lost a lot of blood, and the way they held him, you could see they were carrying dead weight. I turned to my friends and shook my head. There was no way in hell he was going to live and I was right. His comrades, the two ex-Death Row inmates were transported to General Penitentiary and the other inmates that were his friends were kept under lock for a few days, segregated for their own safety.

That evening under lock, I thought about life. It was so easy to get involved in prison politics and suffer the consequences. Not to say I wouldn't war in prison for a good reason or purpose, because I would. In fact, I would do whatever it was that needed to be done in order to survive or protect someone very close to me, but my children and the thought of a new life was my priority. Although I knew I had it in me to do everything anyone else would do, I saw a bigger vision, I always tried to remain in a mindset extending beyond the prison walls. In prison it's so easy to slip and if you slip, believe you will slide, the problem is, how far. I tried my best not to risk falling into the trap, unless it was totally necessary. The truth is, if necessary, I would take that deep breath and gear up, war is war, one either stands or drops. My belief was that if for one split second I allowed my mind to lose track or focus, there was the possibility I'd kill someone without hesitation. I knew my temper I was battling with, and how uncontrollable I could become at times when I really lost it. Yet I could be very controlled to the point of precision. Nevertheless, if I had to take a life and the authorities found out it was me, I'd end up spending the rest of my life behind bars or die by someone's hands within the walls due to retaliation, or someone may look to take my stripe. There's always a risk, hence I tried to remain in my own head all the time and stepped wise. I had a famous line I used to say when a prisoner would try to hype up himself with me, not that it happened regularly but I would say, "Man ah no zebra for yuh cum tek man stripes, if yuh ah look stripe, gwaan ah zoo." Everyone knew I wasn't into the hype thing and could handle myself if necessary, but I was seeing more to life and wanted more from life than this.

Speaking as an ex-prisoner, Jamaican inmates fight as much mentally with one another as they do physically, which means you have to be strong through and through to overcome the set up. I knew that no matter how many months, years or whatever it be, somewhere down the road, I'd face temptations as I did in the past. I also knew somewhere along the line I'd fall right into temptation's hand. I prayed to God always to deliver me, as I had my children, family and an unpredictable future ahead of me.

The next day, all the top men in prison came to our block, spoke with the inmates and called a truce. The same day a few others and I reasoned with the same set of individuals and got the full hundred on what was really going on.

Time had passed, and we all went back to living a relatively normal scheduled life. It was crazy seeing how some inmates just didn't give a damn, and were acting as if they were at home. I used to curse inmates at times, when they would come in my presence and act or talk their shit, until I learnt to just laugh, not in their faces that is, but within myself. My laughter had nothing to do with them at all, it was more about my mental freedom, and I could see the difference between us and could tell I saw life differently. They were lost to the reality of the real world and were definitely either going to come back to prison when they were released, or meet their maker. With the high gun crime rate on the streets of

Jamaica, especially in the parishes of St Catherine, Kingston and Mo Bay, meeting their maker was a statistical fact for these young black males that were throwing their lives away. I didn't want this life anymore, not only for myself but for them too. The reality is, I could only inspire others while saving my own soul, and thought, what better way to teach or show a changed mindset than to walk differently, so I did. I just wanted my freedom to start over again and build from the ground up, but this time on solid ground and not sand. Nobody was going to wash away all that I wanted to build. Regularly, I spoke with a lot of lifers and ex-Death Row prisoners, some whom would never see road again. The encouragement they gave and insight into why I should change, made me know they saw something in me I never saw in myself as a youth, and this constantly had me on my toes, thinking and analysing my life. Listening to their mistakes, upbringing and struggles, as well as sharing my own, brought about a different perspective on many things, which had me re-think about occurrences and opportunities I had not grasped for various reasons, and how past experiences had clouded my mind.

Circuit court was drawing near and I had gone over to South Block to check Harrow-Jay and the others. Whilst at my friend's cell, I felt the urge to make a call and left him to go upstairs and ask another brethren of mine if he had his phone on him. For certain inmates the risk of being caught was a daily thing, due to them hardly ever locking their phones away. He had it. In his cell, I dialled one of my close friends back in England.

"Wha ah gwaan Nosh." I asked.

"What you saying Tats." Nosh replied.

We began talking for a while about what was happening back home. I was always interested to know; keeping in the loop was important to me, it made me feel a sense of connection to the outside world. During our conversation, Nosh changed the topic and told me that he and my sister had visited my children's mother's house, and he saw Lele holding a newborn. When he told me that, I remember pausing for a second and then recalled to mind her sister was pregnant as I was told previously when I had asked about her wellbeing. So instantly, I told him and myself, Lele was holding her sister's baby. We left that conversation there and talked about other things. After speaking with him, I phoned England again but this time someone who would know. As they answered the phone, I asked the person if Lele had a baby with her new partner. I was now taken out of darkness and brought in the light. When I asked how comes no one told me, the explanation was, they knew how much I still loved her and just wanted me to focus on me and not think about anything that might trigger me off or upset me, which I understood. I respected where they were coming from. The truth is, the news of this reality really hurt, but it was something I knew deep down would happen one day. Nevertheless, emotions are powerful and Lele was for a moment in my life a very significant part. If I say I didn't feel anything I'd be lying, but I reassured and comforted myself with the reality of our situation, plus I reminded myself it was me who had told her to move on in the first place. I was happy for her, but saddened at the same time. One has to have been in my position, to truly understand my emotions at that moment. I still had mad love for her. After all, we didn't break up because we fell out of love; it was the distance and circumstances that made it pretty impossible for us to have any form of real relationship, so I perceived. With that in mind, it would be natural I'd feel hurt knowing if I was on road, that beautiful little girl she'd given birth to would've been mine, believe me that hurt deeply. There was no bitterness in my hurt, it was based on love and reflective thoughts of our past, and this is what made it hurt so badly. There were never any bad feelings towards her, the guy or child. In fact, because of the respect we had and have for one another then and today, her daughter's father and I are friends, and her daughter and I have an amazing relationship like that of a father and daughter, and for this I'm truly thankful.

Chapter 22:
Fatherhood & Relationships

Thinking as a father and not a sperm donor, I've always told myself I'm going to be there for my children. Knowing my father wasn't there for me, I didn't want to repeat the cycle. When I was young, I used to tell myself I wanted all my children with one woman, but things don't always go as planned. Even though in my youth and wild stages I attracted a lot of female attention and had a lot of fun, I didn't want to repeat my biological father's footsteps and have many children with different women. I had watched my mother struggle with us, and didn't want to put a woman through that, neither did I want to have children and never see them. After all, I knew what it felt like, my father hadn't seen me since I was very young, nor any of his other children he'd left in the UK, and to me that sucked. I would ask myself why he never kept communication; words of encouragement are more powerful than even money. As a youth, I believe I needed to hear his encouragement and words of discipline even if it was over the phone; at least try, but I heard and got neither. Shaken by the reality of my circumstances, life choices made sure it was pretty obvious things were drifting far away from my dream. I was incarcerated, with two different women having my offspring, one in Jamaica and another in the UK where my daughter and son resided. I knew whenever I touched road again, not only did I want to reconnect and build relationships with the children I had from previous partners, but I was bound to end up in a relationship and want a child with that woman too. I knew no matter how long it took after I touched road and sorted myself out, that I'd want a serious relationship, as no one really wants to be alone. The question was just when. I questioned myself many times regarding my steps in life, was I walking in my biological father's footsteps. I'd always tell myself there's no way I would become him, as I'd always be there and love my children. However, the thought of spreading myself thinly between three homes was a challenge in itself and I concluded that even if I would be there for my children, like my biological father, I had messed up. Even though I'd be there for the children, it would never be that perfect picture of my childhood dream. Nevertheless, I would always love and be there for my seeds, even if it was only via phone for some time, due to distance created by seas and oceans. I was determined to ensure that they knew I loved them, and this was key. I had no knowledge of whether my father continued to love me once he left England in the early eighties. It wasn't until I was twenty-one, that's like fifteen years later, that I saw and heard from my biological father again, and to me, that just wasn't good enough. So much had happened in my life, including me being locked up in Jamaica in my teens, and he knew nothing of it, or the drama and horrors I had faced and dealt with on the streets. The wrongs I had gotten up to, and secrets that haunted me; he knew nothing of the pressures I faced daily, and I didn't want to be that man that repeated his errors and not know my children. I had to do better, even though it would never be them waking up and seeing me every day. I knew they would see me as much as possible and even stay at mine once I had my own place when I was free. I was determined to spend time and as much time as possible. For my son in Jamaica, things would be different. I knew that once free; I was going straight back to the United Kingdom. I wasn't in connection with his family like that, but I believed and trusted something would work out, and we would be reunited. It was messed up, but I was determined not to repeat that cycle of disconnection. It was way too late to give them the perfect happy family home a child deserves. Still, I knew that as long as Lele, myself and whichever woman I'd be with in the future were good, and respected one another, we had a fighting chance. Namely, that our children would grow up knowing, although mum and dad aren't together, they do the best by us the children as always. It was for this that I prayed. As for my son's mother in Jamaica, well, that was a completely different story. A lot of work needed to be done, to begin to heal the wounds in both of us before that level of communication and relation could occur.

Coming from a broken home and longing for my biological dad as a youth, only to suffer an unfulfilled desire of wanting him in my life, made me quite angry, and I didn't want that for any of my children. Unfortunately, I myself was unable to accomplish the perfect home, but as stated previously, one's presence and contribution despite not living in the home, also plays a major role, and can have a massive impact. Regarding my own childhood, it was something I needed but didn't get. From the day my children were born, I was there for them. As for my son in Jamaica, unlike the two in England, I was unable to be at his birth due to me returning to the United Kingdom. Nevertheless, I would send down things and money to his mother. As for my two children in the UK, I was present at both of their births, and delighted in their lives and home as a family unit up until the time of my incarceration. Even then, I thought about reuniting with them one day, one day returning and having my children in my life. Sometimes that thought would come with their mother and I reuniting, then I would remind myself of her partner and tell myself it's all about starting fresh, but my thoughts were conflicted at times. To be honest, I'd want her back in one set of thoughts and in another, someone different. No matter what I thought, my children were at the centre, and everything revolved around them like the sun, they were my source of energy. It's crazy how the mind can make one think to the point of over analysing a situation, even creating hypothetical scenarios, and believe me, prison doesn't make it easier, it affords one too much time to think. But that's not necessarily bad, too much time to think that is, it all boils down to the individual. With such thoughts going through my head, it kept me strong, and it was because of happier times to come, and through the connection we shared, I was able to find the inner strength to begin looking into myself. So, I would say my past life of momentary happiness contributed in a big way to my change.

Reminiscing on relationships, I would definitely say as a man I could have been better to both of my daughters' mothers. I used to tell myself they both would agree that I was kind, funny, sweet and warm; but my ability to be faithful had let me down the odd time. From my opinion, it had even gone as far to contribute to my downfall. There was one situation that affected both my children's mothers. My children's mother and partner at that time in the UK forgave me, but my ex-partner from Jamaica wasn't so forgiving and it was the same situation, which indirectly contributed to my incarceration further down the road. It was in situations like these I saw my father in me, his love and weakness for women. I would prefer to have inherited his work skills, he was a great tradesman, but I didn't hear much about this aspect of him from young. As a little boy, I was always introduced to another brother or sister and a woman who I'd look at as another mother figure. I guess this had an impact on my psyche somehow and would manifest in my actions. The situation worsened, by being a popular boy in school from Kilburn Park Infants to Kilburn Park Juniors, wherein, the exploration of girlfriends and the desire to explore the female body came to be. High school was just full of crazy times. I was exposed to so much, and too much too fast. It kind of made me wild, although I could hold it down, I just had that extra desire at times, which could lead me into trouble, and it did on various occasions. My stepfather showed me nothing, nothing at all, but pain and misery, so I wasn't getting any lessons on manhood and fatherhood from him. In fact, he taught me how *not* to love and I was definitely not following his footsteps. The streets taught me a thing or two, not that they were great lessons either, nevertheless, they taught me and gave me the good, bad, nasty and funny. Thinking hard in prison, I concluded that, everywhere and anywhere, lessons come; it's just about which ones you took at the end of the day. Being a young man on my own, kind of left to my own devices, as my mother would try talk to me about relationships and sex, I'd steer the topic away, or sometimes just tell her what I thought she wanted to hear. This wasn't always beneficial. Not that I never spoke with my mother, in fact we did, but there is nothing like talking to a father, or a male figure. I needed that interaction, and would therefore share thoughts with friends. The only downfall with that, if they're mentally in the same place as you, or got your back full hundred, they can be more dangerous than good. In the sense that most times, they side with you, and that doesn't help when you're wrong or plan to do something wrong. For example, encouraging multiple partners when they know you have someone who really has got you, when in truth they should tell you to hold it down. Then there is the lack of respect for female time and companionship, being made to feel there is nothing wrong with changing plans last minute, with no consideration of the effort the other party may have made. It isn't quite the mature thing to do, but then who was there to guide me or any of us, we only had ourselves.

What I know I got right; was the way I would spend time with my children while their mother worked. Thoughts of the fun we would have together made me smile numerous times behind bars. I was my children's everything, my daughter loved me endlessly, no one could put her to sleep but her dad, she wouldn't sleep without me. Anyone can get her to puss nap, but sleep like out for the count, that wasn't happening until daddy was home. Night or day, especially night, if I'm out, my little princess would meet me at the door once she heard the lift opening on our floor. Always jumping out of her sleep, she would wake suddenly and fly to the door. My daughter always slept on my chest, then I'd put her down and hold Lele until we fell asleep, things were great. My son likewise, was a little bundle of joy, proper daddy's boy too. Slightly younger than his sister, he'd copy her actions, and what actions he could copy, it was funny like that. Such thoughts kept me happy and strong within. Comforted yet saddened by the thought of the reality of our situation, because of my actions, my family were also placed in a situation that they themselves would have never predicted. We were all paying for the choice I'd made. My lust got the best of me from time to time, and I believe that even up to today, it played an indirect role in me ending up behind bars. I had let down my beautiful little family I'd begun to establish in London, and now we were all paying the price. Yep, even the innocent. My Children and their mother in England had nothing to do with it, nor did they play a role in my situation, all they did was love me; and now they were paying for it. My son likewise in Jamaica was innocent, but his mother, well, that was another story, one that would indirectly hurt me. I will discuss this bizarre and crazy situation in more details later in this book, as it's not as straightforward as one might expect. I guess all my actions and doings stemmed from what I was exposed to and shown. Some things were down to my own desire to explore, but then that is also due to me having no guidance from a positive male role model showing me better. It is not unrealistic to say I kind of nurtured myself based on what I saw portrayed before me via whatever outlet. The key here is, if a child isn't taught what to do, then the child will teach his or herself what to do, and it may not always be the best of choices. Who's to judge, if you haven't tried guiding the individual yourself?

Chapter 23:
Painful Memories

There are so many contributing factors to why children or young people act out of character. In truth, I don't think enough energy and time is invested in understanding the issues that affect the future generations, some of whom will grow up to repeat a cycle, further bringing and creating division and pain on so many levels. Not only is the breakdown of family structure, social deprivation, and the lack of self-knowledge energetically devastating, it's also extremely problematic in so many *other* ways *too*. The universe mourns in agony as she works tirelessly to aid and turn mankind away from self-destruction. Mankind must also remember each individual has a role to play in the paramount shift necessary for equilibrium. Talking specifically about descendants of transatlantic slavery, and indirectly, to the nations of the world, as all mankind are connected in the mystics of life. Our past experience as bondmen and bondwomen and the true understanding of, and lack of understanding of what was experienced by my ancestors, has a global effect both physically and through vibrational shifting. This can play out for good or bad, in all reality having an impact on the planet. When power is misused and misplaced, the results are detrimental, hitting hard globally and causing a reaction on the universal energetic vibration. Our youths carry such powerful energy, what we send out is received globally, the world patterns off our very being. Just look around you, what *don't* we influence? In prison I realised we are our greatest assets and our enemy's most powerful weapon. What those in worldly powerful positions either failed to realise, or purposely planned was, setting mankind to function at a low-level vibration with the intention to reap havoc and confusion believing we would remain asleep, spiritually dead. Truly they have no understanding of how the spirit works, well, at least not the spirit world our foreparents understood. A plan put in place without spiritual hindsight and lack of foresight. DNA has always been the target and is the true key to unlocking both hindsight and foresight, but this is a whole different topic pulsating at a frequency beyond modern social and systematic comprehension. What is true and undeniable is, by keeping us focused on the external and not the internal, we continue to keep the emotions of a dying system alive. If a hamster no longer spins the wheel, it's only natural that the wheel comes to a halt. It's also true that what we are exposed to, also affects how sensitive or desensitised we become to what we have heard or seen; a not so clever way to keep mankind confused. The advertising of low-level vibration otherwise negativity through various outlets, the lack of care for humanity, over emphasised exposure of family breakdowns, promotion of social deprivation and lack of respect for life and all living things, when looking at it from a psychologist's point of view, would fit into two theories, learning and conditioning. We learn consciously or subconsciously what we are constantly fed, this conditions our minds and causes us to act, knowingly or unknowingly. On that note, all that I was exposed to as a youth, within the home, community, society and via various media platforms, had an effect on me. Therefore, it acted upon my wellbeing, and in turn affected others that encountered me; one big cycle of confusion.

I was exposed to a lot as a youth, thinking about all that I had seen while lying in my cell made me fear for the generations to come, as I knew I wasn't the only one who carried this pain and sadness inside. In a crazy way, I was thankful that I was there, incarcerated taking time to reflect. Nothing is without purpose. I came to that conclusion while reliving and facing sorrows of the past, travelling a journey I so needed to make, if I really wanted to move forward. Understanding became easy, reality became clear, the outcome was always on *me* and me alone. My mature outlook was nothing to do with age, nor was it to do with experience, rather my perception. Strength without perception is weakness, and so much is done to weaken us as people, even though we may feel strong, it's an illusion; perception is key.

When one begins to lose friends and family to the streets at a young age, it has an effect on you that one can't comprehend and may never until one reaches a level of maturity. This maturity isn't and can never be connected with age, but more aligned with mental awareness. Unfortunately, some never reach it. Many adults have lost their lives, gone crazy, or just can't seem to understand, or don't *want* to understand why they are the way they are, yet inside they know something isn't right with their behaviour. It's a matter of acceptance and perception. Early exposure to pre-planned social destruction is detrimental, this I relate to from first-hand experience. Psychological trauma can have a serious impact on the psyche and can manifest in so many ways. The channels used to release these emotions are none profitable and self-destructive in the long haul. Vicarious trauma, stemming from trauma is widespread throughout society, especially in the hood. Everyone, and I mean literally everyone, has experienced some form of vicarious trauma, and this exposure to trauma has a massive effect on the community, who are constantly exposed to all manner of pain, anger, sorrow, hurt and death. Such exposure creates psychological as well as physiological repercussions impacting on a truly devastating level, and who is there to heal these wounds, to comfort the hearts of those who don't know how to channel these emotions? Most times, if not all of the time, individuals are left to fend for themselves. Yet a community and society that has never been taught how to deal with their emotions, will naturally find a way to channel them, and the method used may develop problematic behaviours, worse, create a ticking human time bomb. The reality is, the choices made from the experience of trauma or exposure to trauma if left unaddressed, true healing is literally an illusion of thought that will never be attained. Pushing of emotions to a dark place in the mind hoping all is forgotten, while not addressed, always finds a way to manifest even in or through habits, or showing through characteristics that may not come across as appealing. The sad thing is when individuals can't see their own bad traits; or at times even believe it's someone else who has the problem, that in itself is problematic. Others truly may have problems, but in reality, those individuals are your mirrors, but one desires not to see, so to you the glass is broken, when in truth, *you* are broken and there's no healing from the pain without acceptance. Personally, it took me a long time, jail reflection time to really start analysing and see how much I carried from my youth.

During my childhood, I lost my cousin Squiggly (R.I.P) to violence in Kensal Green and began losing close friends to what today we call street culture, way before I had hit my teens. My cousin and I shared a very tight bond; I loved him so much, and used to look up to him. He wasn't my cousin by blood; out of respect, we would call each other's family that. This is how it was; we were close with many families like that. I guess back in the days, my old neighbourhood in South Kilburn was one big family. I had more aunties and uncles than one could imagine. We grew up like that; my mother would kill me if she heard me call an adult, especially someone she knew, by his or her first name; that was not accepted. My cousin was stabbed and killed outside Moonshine in Kensal Green. Looking back on it, we were told he had encouraged the youth to stab him if he's bad, and so he did. Whether the youth had done it out of fear or pride, he was conditioned on some level by what he had seen or heard prior to their final encounter, and likewise, my cousin was too. To tell a man to attack you is something straight out of a movie, or learnt from the local yardies back in the 80's who would act fearlessly, but even they learnt from and were conditioned by cowboy movies. Anyone who knows the history of Jamaican media, knows that cowboy shows hit the screen in the late 1960's, by the 70's crime was rising, and in 1980, Jamaica had its bloodiest election, many lives were lost. We can call it coincidence or low-level programming, that depends on you. In fact, movies, especially cowboy movies, had an impact on a lot of old-time gangsters from Jamaica, not to mention some legendary dancehall artists. Just research the origin of the names of some of the greatest 70's and 80's entertainers, and the names of some of the most renowned street warriors and criminal organisations from Jamaica, and you will understand my point. To add to that, after the uprising of violence in Jamaica in the 80's, the UK then had an outburst of Jamaican political fighters, aka gangsters flooding the streets of England. The question is, how did these so-called street warriors with known histories for violence make their way to the United Kingdom, or should I say who helped them leave the island and made way for them to enter the UK?

Politics, or should I say politricks and illusions working at their best! The destruction of Jamaica and Jamaicans has been their plan for a very long time. As a people, we just played blindly into it. As Garvey would say, "up, you mighty race," Jamaicans you have work to do.

When I heard the news that Squiggly had been murdered, it ripped into me; words can't even explain how I felt. I was young, sad and angry, and that misplaced energy took hold of me. As time passed and the anger disappeared (or did it really?), I got on with life as normal (or did I really?). It's amazing what we carry without even realising. I remember telling myself, "Nobody is going to kill me", as a youth, I must have told myself that numerous times. Now, I couldn't say if that was a part of my coping mechanism, or I just said it to myself sincerely with conviction, but I do know that when death comes knocking and takes someone close to you, there is a lot of emotional energy leaving you vulnerable while that door is open. The educational system taught many things, but never how to deal with emotions and trapped energy, hidden in one's body waiting to disperse by a trigger from a similar occurrence. This again can have a detrimental outcome affecting self and others. The more one is exposed to, the greater the build-up of low-level vibrations, which feeds the system, keeping the wheel spinning. Looking at social professions, most if not all are established on low-level vibrations and built on pain. Without wrongdoings and crime, many professionals have no job. Without sickness, suffering, death and physical harm of some sort, medical professions, including the pharmaceutical industry, which along with firearms and weapons of mass destruction are the largest capital spinners, could not exist. I could go on and on. Low-level vibration is welcomed, and is honoured in secret. Building schools and universities, graduating thieves and murders, oh I love Bob's perception. On numerous nights, while under lock, I would read my Bible and listen to the Legend raising my vibration. Like a vampire, the system was sucking the blood of the sufferers. Awakening to how much I was suffering inside was frightening. Losing so many friends to what I refer to as street culture, being that youths share the same dress code, speech, like for music and so much more, it is actually a culture and not a way of life. A culture fashioned from the streets and not ancestrally connected. Looking back on the effects of this culture on my life, it saddened my heart deeply. There were so many triggers in life all stemming from experiences; the question is who could have understood them all? During junior school, I was referred to speak to someone due to my behaviour. Reminiscing my mother coming into school and sitting with me while I spoke to this lady, today I understand it was a psychologist, as if that helped. The doctor made suggestions from time to time concerning the blackouts I used to get, but then medically they had no real diagnosis. I say it was a mixture of anger, sadness and maybe over thinking, because of everything I went through personally, and my surroundings. An individual's surroundings can have a serious affect, more than one even acknowledges.

I was on the verge of going to high school when I lost my good friend to the train tracks; he himself was a little boy when his life was taken. Gone but not forgotten, Evil (R.I.P). It might have been a year or so later, I lost another close friend Uni, (R.I.P) who also died in a similar way. Those were the days tagging was a big thing, myself personally I wasn't that deep into it. The news of their departure shook me up. However, years later, I would play an insane game. When looking back, it was senseless to the point that I'm wondering, was there a connection between the emotions and memories regarding the way my friends lost their lives, and the actions I would undertake. I used to play on the underground train tracks with a few school friends who were stupid enough to play chicken with me back then. The worst thing about it is, we didn't even need to take a train to go home, but we would get off the bus and go to Kilburn Park Station on the way from Hampstead School, just to see whom the bravest one of us was. Back then, I wouldn't refer to the game as stupid, being mature now, I see how careless I was at times with my own life. Looking back, I wonder if playing chicken was a way to fight my anger and fear of not wanting to die as well, although it seems illogical. Then, risking my life could have been me reaffirming to myself that I was not going to go out like that. Truly, I don't know what drove me to play such insane games; it may have just been the adrenaline junky within me, and loving the buzz of risk taking. Whatever the reason, it wasn't the wisest choice to make. After losing my friend Evil, I began hanging with his big brother nicknamed Sky (R.I.P.). We both lost two people we cared about to the train tracks, but for Sky, it was deeper, as one was his little brother. Many years later, I went on to lose the big brother too, but that was to street violence. When I heard the news of his death, it ripped me up. I'll never forget being in my cell on the phone talking to a friend in the UK who told me this original South Kilburn soldier had died. Water came to my eyes; I couldn't hold them back, just as I couldn't hold back the tears when Vino (R.I.P), another South Kilburn soldier died on the estate, as I was told. In the NW10 area of London, quite a few of my close associates were killed, others charged for murder, and so many escaped death. Hearing so many sad events made me think deeply about life. During my incarceration, so much death occurred not just in the UK, but in JA and America too; so many of my close friends and comrades have died. Memories are all I have to hold on to. I had to ask myself if being incarcerated was really the worst thing that could have happened to me. I remember asking myself if happy and sad memories set off the same natural chemicals the body produces during the different emotions. The reality is, if they are different, not to mention unseen, how do we know we have dispersed all that which isn't good for us when it arises. If happy thoughts lift us up, brightening our mood, and we all know sad ones make us feel low, then what is it that really lifts us up again? Is it having a positive outlook or another happy thought, or is it accepting the sadness and moving on therefore using pain as a driver? What I'm getting at is emotional energies don't always disperse the same way, therefore who knows if it leaves and how much of it really goes. I questioned myself a lot whilst in prison, to a point where I knew I was beginning and willing to analyse everything.

What really beat me down in prison wasn't the fact that I was locked up at the age of fifteen, but recalling the moment I was making a reverse call to my mother from the airport police station. I remember her asking me how comes I'm reversing a call to her; shouldn't I be on the plane. The sound of her voice as she burst out crying came flowing to mind as I laid there thinking, mind travelling back to my youth accompanied by tears. Within days, my mother had come to Jamaica and worked on my case. It had taken just over two weeks and I was free, young and still troubled. I remember my mother asking me if she should make my stepfather rot in prison. She was angry for the fact that she thought he knew what I was doing and allowed it. No matter how bad he treated me and I hated him, and believe me, I did, I couldn't allow him to remain in there under false accusations. So, I took the responsibility and told my mother he knew nothing of it, even though his cousin had told her different. But in all truth, he didn't know anything about it. Back then, that was also a very painful moment, I was in mixed emotions just thinking about it in my cell. There were seconds I'd wish I did let him rot because I hated him, but then I knew it was the right thing to do and not lie on him even though he would do it to me. I admit, I was in conflict, and that can be painful, even more painful than just hating. At least hate is a one-way feeling, whereas confusion on the other hand, is conflict tied with unsettled energy and emotional stress; it can never be good.

My mother, Janita Bathsheba Samuels transitioning in 1994 from this realm to the realm of the ancestors affected me badly. Even though I was seen as the strong one by close friends and family because I didn't cry initially when my mother passed and all her siblings were shedding tears, but I was hurting that bad and couldn't cry, as a million and one things ran through my head. I hadn't seen my mother since 1991. It was three years and some months, I was now nineteen and had missed so much time with my mother, and had caused her so much pain over the years as a youth. Not to mention things she would hear about me in Jamaica, every thought came to me at once, there were no moments to cry, mentally I felt bombarded. It was only recently in 2017, my sister Marie during a conversation told me to stop blaming myself for our mother's death. Deep down I used to think it was because of me, the stress I put her through. What led me to think like that was because my mother used to take medication for stress and anyone who understands the human body knows high levels of stress weakens the body's immune system, causing the body to be prone to infections and alien germs, creating all manner of physiological problems. Marie told me there were other health problems that contributed to her departing from us. Honestly, deep down, I still feel I contributed, but in all reality, even if I did, I needed to let go of this guilt. Speaking with my sister was the best action I'd taken for years concerning this issue that secretly troubled me. Deep down, I knew my mother wouldn't want me to carry such a weight; she was a light-being and would want me to walk in the same manner. In fact, during the few weeks spent with my mother when she came to Jamaica in April 1994 to return me to the UK, mummy to the rescue again as she did in 1990, we had some very interesting discussions, many of which I hold to my heart dearly. Hence, I dedicated the first documentary I produced and directed titled 'North East Africa: The Hidden Truth' to her memory. Little did I know or believe what she would say to me would begin to come to pass. Her spiritual insight was something out of the norm. Proudly I say, with all her imperfections, my mother was complete. I battled with myself to come to the understanding that time with her wasn't short. I may have missed a few years and saw my mother for only a few weeks when we returned to the UK, but I know she loved me. My mother fell sick; she was taken from the hospital ward to the ICU. She remained in a coma until she physically left this world. I didn't truly comprehend then, but I do now understand her life lessons; ancestral teachings live within me via her DNA, therefore she constantly equips me with all that I need. My father passed while I was incarcerated. He too likewise joined the realm of the ancestors. As for my father, I didn't see him much or know much about his ancestral family, but something deep inside tells me there was more to my father and his lineage than meets the eye, so on that note, may I rejoice even in my sorrow.

Thinking deeply about my trip to South Africa in 1998 also brought sadness to my heart on various occasions while behind bars. Reminiscing on my Rastafarian days, I was very keen on the development of Ethiopia and Africa, not that my feelings for Ethiopia and Africa have changed, just my perception and mindset towards culture and my journey. Ethiopia and Africa on a whole will always be an important figure to any awoken mind. Thinking back, a few elders and representatives from a South African camp of Rastafarians were in England, and my passion for the continent led me to attend a meeting they held at Bridge Park Complex in Stonebridge, North West London. Driven by passion, I made connections with these elders and representatives, who were accompanied by other elders and representatives from the Nyabinghi movement in Jamaica such as Bongo Time and his son Scooby, who on that day to my surprise wore T-shirts designed by me. In fact, there were quite a few people in my clothing line. I made them aware the T-Shirts were my designs, and we got speaking on all manner of things, which led to the topic of me going to South Africa to visit the Motherland for the first time. Excited on being welcomed, I travelled the following month. Filling an extra-large suitcase with garments I designed, jelly sandals, shoes for little children, colouring books and pencils, I headed for South Africa. On my arrival, there was no one to meet me as pre-arranged, disappointed I refused to turn back and went with a complete stranger who offered to help me find this Rasta elder as I had his number on me. He said he would call the number from his house. He was an airport taxi driver. I remember jumping into his minibus and thinking what if he sets me up, but then gripping hold of my fear I was on the continent and didn't want to leave, I was taking a risk and knew it. Deep emotions covered me like a blanket, while at the same time a thought in my mind said to turn around and return to the UK, but my determination and stubbornness wouldn't let me. There was tightness in my stomach as we drove through various communities. He made a call at which point I noticed he had a mobile phone and spoke in his language. At the end of the conversation he said "...meet me there." In English, and that bugged me out. Mixed emotions filled me; I was paranoid that it was a set-up, yet my eyes were saddened by the poverty I saw. He asked me if I was ok, guess he could feel the tension; I made known my feelings about the poverty, not my paranoia. I only felt fearful for a little while longer, and within seconds, I let all negative emotions go. His minibus came to a halt, a very attractive young lady came out of a house followed by another and an elder woman, and they greeted him. It was his family. Inside the house they gave me food and spoke with me, he called my contact that said they'd be with me by nightfall. His daughters took me into the community, where I received so much love and respect, I felt comfortable and to be honest, saddened to know I'd have to leave. When we returned to the house, I saw an unfamiliar Rasta sitting on the settee with a 3.8 revolver handgun hanging out of his waist. I could see the Taxi driver wasn't keen on me leaving with him, and said in front of the unfamiliar Rasta, I could stay. I asked the unfamiliar Rasta where the Rasta elder whom I had met in the UK was, he responded saying that he's making his way to Cape Town and sent him to get me. Again, that uncomfortable feeling came, but not wanting to bring trouble to the bus driver's home I left. Before I did, he gave me his card. The look in their faces as I left spoke volumes, I just knew I had made the wrong choice and time would tell. Later that night, the elder and another Rasta came and collected me from the walls of the South, a known ghetto in Cape Town, and took me to their community, which was at least six to eight hours drive away and up in the mountains. Everything went pear shaped once I got there. I presented them with all the gifts I'd brought, a hundred T-shirts, jelly sandals and shoes for young children, colouring books and pencils. There was no gratitude or showing of appreciation. Within days, all hell broke loose. I wanted to leave their community, and they refused to let me. It was a weird experience, quite hard to put into perspective even today. I wouldn't call it a kidnapping, because I went there voluntarily, but after arriving, I wasn't permitted to leave their area. Being up in a mountain with no transportation out of the community, where could I go. At that point, I realised I was being held captive. There was the odd member of the community who'd tell me how much I meant to them, then there was a very dislikeable energy the majority gave off, it was crazy. At night, they would beat drums, sing in their language, and at times in English speak out against me, man it was weird. They had a massive cauldron blazing under fire, big enough to fit me in; I swear I thought they were going to eat me. Looking back on my experience, as scary as it was, and trust, I wouldn't wish such a moment on my worst enemy, I had to ask myself why I thought they were going to cook me. Was it based on a subliminal preconceived idea planted in my mind by an old school movie implicating Africans as cannibals, or was it my own emotions running wild? All I do know was at that time I was undoubtedly afraid; it was truly one of the weirdest experiences in my life. I've been face to face with death on various occasions, but at no time was I so fearful. When fear is mixed with confusion, emotionally one can't truly register what is taking place. The following morning, I persuaded them to let me call my family, as they'd be worried not hearing from me and they know I needed some money. Pudding answered the phone, instantly I spoke to her in back slang, which is coded English. I quickly explained my position. She asked me if they could hear, I told her no but present in the room. To all her questions, I just said yes or no. She asked me where I was, and I responded in back slang giving her the address of the nearest location point I knew. That was good enough. The British Embassy got involved, who in turn involved the South African police. They found me in no time. That same evening, I was on my way back to the airport, with an immediate flight out of the country escorted by the embassy and police. Man, it felt good to be free from that moment of craziness. I still wonder why they treated me so badly, when the purpose of my trip, which they knew from the get go was to help and build with my people on the continent. I'm still puzzled by what happened and why, but they should be even more confused than me when I think about it; honour and integrity are both to be questioned when one welcomes a stranger into one's home and then abuses them.

Chapter 24:
Defining Words

Not everything in my life was unpleasant; there *were* pleasurable moments, in fact, many enjoyable memories. Neither to stray off topic, nor to overanalyse a situation, but depending on what's defined as enjoyable, and the mindset of the one benefiting from whatever creates this feeling of excitement, pleasure can even be considered an illness. To be totally honest, even some of the things I did unto others, the hurt, the pain inflicted upon them, in a weird and crazy way I considered pleasant at the time of the act, as it made me feel good. However, I have come to realise the pleasure I felt from inflicting pain on others was sadistic. Notice there is a heavy connotation of negativity placed upon the word *pleasant* when it's aligned to anti-social behaviour. Nevertheless, that's the emotion felt from such an act, and is a reality for some whose mentality is caught up in or addicted to energy gained from someone else's pain. The question is, are we to judge such individuals or help them? When a bunch of youths or even a single youth commits a serious violent act in broad daylight, during the midday sun and walks or runs off, are we to judge him or them negatively for the pleasure they received, because clearly, many look like they're having fun, and most times during the act they are. From first-hand experience, I know at times, personally *I* was; but knowing what you've read about my life and now understand about where I was coming from and what led me to the streets, what would your perception of me be? Would you have judged or reached out to help me? The relevance of me asking isn't for myself, but pertaining to individuals faced with emotional troubles today. The system has failed those with violent tendencies. Some parents either turn a blind eye, or just totally misunderstand what is truly occurring, and others, whether parents or just community members, are not worried unless it falls upon them in some way, shape or form. What is the correct approach? Is there a correct approach to take? Shouldn't understanding the root of such actions be the first priority, and if so, then having a judgemental mind can neither find the answers nor come up with solutions. There were and still are too many street judges, lining up to pass verdicts on members of our community regarding situations and circumstances they themselves are totally confused about how to deal with and why they occur. Note, the root of every solution should be based on the individual and not the masses. We must always bear in mind, it is the individuals that make up the masses, not the masses that make up the individuals. Indeed, it does take a community to raise a child, but it also takes a community that misinforms and has *been* misinformed to kill a child too. The purpose of me expressing the word *pleasant* attached with a negative connotation, is just to show that what is pleasant to one, can be not so nice to another, and how the dynamics surrounding a word can change its very meaning. Another example is *gang*. Today, 'gang', is associated with youth crime, based on two, three or more individuals involved in anti-social behaviour, which is also connected to the labelling theory. However, people working in a factory back in the days were known as a 'gang' of workers, two or three banks that 'gang' together, are known as a virtual bank. Both of these connotations are positive, however the label placed upon our youths isn't. The point I'm making is, when the standards of definitions change, so do the people, and when the people accept misinformation, it becomes the norm, which then becomes problematic. Everything is interconnected, it's not rocket science. We just need to take a step back from the fast pace we've been unfortunate to live at, and most importantly, meet people where they're at and not judge them.

Chapter 25:
Pleasant Memories

Relating from a happier place, filled with shining, extremely pleasant and pleasurable memories lifting my vibration, as I journeyed back, I found myself reflecting on my football skills. As a youth, I loved football. Talented from junior school through to high school, I'd always make the team and be a vital player on the pitch. I owe so much to my friends, many of whom I considered family back in South Kilburn. We would play football on the mound right outside where we lived. My next-door neighbours and the rest of the Back-Street Crew, plus a few of the guys from Blake Court, especially Paul, would be on our team. The whole community knew Paul to be my cousin, although he was white no questions were ever asked, but that was respect. South Kilburn people had a lot of respect for one another. We had a great football team; we would play Front Street and most of the times rip them up. Front Street was anyone who lived on the old podium side of South Kilburn Estate in Dickens House, Austen House, Wordsworth House and the small flats above the shops. Blake Court was also considered Front Street, but we had a few guys from Blake Court who were loyal to us, like my other cousin Size. It was funny back then as they had more youths to pick from but we had raw talent. My next-door neighbours were awesome ballers, both brothers were skilful especially Bash, my brother JT, Paul, Kevin, Junior and his brothers plus a few others. We had the dream team; well at least to us it felt like that. Those were the days way before I hit my teens and got into all manner of madness, in fact I hadn't even entered high school yet. As youths, we'd all meet up in Paul's house, his mother (my aunty) and my mother were best friends. She would give us the sitting room where the block, both Front and Back Street lads, would watch Sunday *Match of the Day*. In those days, I loved Liverpool, in the eighties they were my team, I could name all their players and knew everything about them. I loved QPR too; so, I was a bit of a two-team lover, which didn't sit well with some of the guys, but that was my choice.

Marion club had a local team back in the days, and of course, I was on it. We used to play competitions against other areas and in various cups, we didn't always win, but we were a force to be reckoned with. South Kilburn had some serious talent. Not only myself, but also quite a few of us had the ability and skill set to play for a professional academy but didn't take it seriously enough. I guess we lacked that drive and support. I believe it is so important that our youth's abilities aren't overlooked by parents and loved ones. You may just not only help a star to shine, but protect it from falling to the dust. So many lives when I look back had the ability to do such great things, but they were never pushed. That's not because parents never believed in their ability, they just didn't focus enough on what the child had passion for, and instead pursued education alone as priority. Not to offend, but we must realise how important passion is. Positive energy for a specific thing, whether it's sports or playing an instrument, should be nurtured and cultivated. Do not be mistaken, by overlooking a child's passion, you miss the child's strongest aspect of self and growth, which would cause the child to excel in so many other aspects of life.

After so many years of not playing ball, I'm glad to say I still have it in me. On my release from prison in 2006, after not playing ball for well over a decade, maybe even two, in 2007 I did the Goals Project which took place at Loftus Road Stadium. At the end of the course, we played against Queens Park Rangers' coaches and drew 2-2. They literally found it impossible to get past me, and long balls had to be used to overcome the truck that stood in their way. I was highly respected on that course, every course in fact, not even a full year out of prison, yet who could tell? My drive, determination and motivation shone before my peers and staff alike. I can say I'm super proud of myself as I was undertaking three courses at once, the Goals Project, Fitness Instructor and F.A football-coaching badge, and aced them all.

I can't deny my big brother Jay and his mates were my inspiration when it came to football, they had some A-class players; South Kilburn bred talent.

There is nothing for young people today. Government setbacks and cuts in all the wrong places make areas like South Kilburn a den for crime, but then is it in all the wrong places? It depends on through whose eyes one looks. By the time I began going to high school, all of the great community trips had faded away. As a youth, South Kilburn Adventure Playground was a hot spot back in the days, but nothing beats S.K.A.G, which stood for South Kilburn Action Group. We would go on trips every summer, and that highlights the problem today, youths don't have any of the excitement my generation had, nor the generation before us. You name the theme park we were there. Our holiday camps were amazing; we would visit loads of places with S.K.A.G, which local people from the community ran, S.K.A.G really catered to our needs. I can never forget, on one of our holidays to the Coast, one of the elder guys put toothpaste on the cheek of a local youth when he was sleeping, when he woke up it was all over his face. He also shaved off another guy's eyebrow while he was sleeping; in the morning, he looked in the mirror like a thousand times and still couldn't believe it. No one was going to sleep after that, I remember putting a chair behind our door with the intent that one of us sharing our room would hear and wake; we refused to be victims. The funny thing about it was, we all found it humorous at the time, not the victims of course, but even they would come around to see the funny side of it. We had crazy fun as youths.

Those days the love of reggae music and dancehall ruled. In the eighties, the big hype was who had access to the best yard sound clashes and artist mix tapes and of course, I was a leader in my field. Regularly, Vino and I would swap tapes and videocassettes. Lots of people would get cassette tapes from me, and whenever I got a new tape from someone that I didn't have in my collection, I'd copy it immediately. I used to love talking about 80's and 90's dancehall music, especially with Tickla (R.I.P), a close friend of mine, more like a brother; back then I loved dancehall and still do, although it's not the same vibes and energy.

In 1988, I visited New York and met some of my family from Dunkirk who'd migrated to the USA. My aunt's son owned a sound system from out of the Kingston area called Love Vibration. Before our encounter, I had video tapes of this sound system and cassette tapes with many of Kingston's popular dancehall entertainers presenting themselves on set, but didn't know I had ties to the owner. It wasn't until I was in the States that I found out. I believe this inspired me to begin writing tunes, although at that time I wasn't serious, but I believe it was where my desire to write lyrics first stemmed from.

Travelling, and entertaining some of Jamaica's hottest artists at the end of 1990 also had a massive impact on my love for the music, not to mention my personal experience; it was one of those memorable moments for a young reggae lover.

Hanging around Gilbert studio and Miami Vice studio brought great memories to mind. I would catch a vibe with Little Chris, Meekie, Needle Point, Turbo Belly (R.I.P), Conan, and many others. Those days, I loved being in Spanish Town, for me it was the place to be.

Early in 1994, a few friends of mine residing in St Ann, set up a group called Kush and we were deep into our music, but at the same time we weren't going to studio, it was more sharing of vibes on a spiritual level. These guys were very spiritual, something at that time I didn't know much about. We came from two different walks of life and I believe that drew me to them. We would sit on the Cove and sing and chant. I found it so uplifting. It's hard to explain the peace I felt amongst them, they carried a different kind of vibe and energy from the people I'd usually hang with and I loved it. One of the members of Kush was the son of a wealthy Caucasian family in St Ann, he had brought down a friend of his on a few occasions; believe when I say his friend Mr Miller, had a most unique energy to him. His warmth was soothing, yet radiated like the sun. I could feel him even when I was on the other side of the room, or if we were at the Cove, he could be sitting by himself mediating, and myself and the others reasoning at a distance, but I would still feel him, as if he was sitting right there amongst us. He seemed so relaxed and just calm; I used to marvel at him. One day, Mr Miller took me to Port Antonio where he lived, and introduced me to some other brothers with whom he shared a house. The little time with these brothers really touched me. The level of spirituality they introduced me to was shocking. I used to stare at them amazed by what they spoke. They told me they weren't Rastafarians but they were Israelites, which explained my question concerning why they ate meat and had dreadlocks. It was at this point I came to the understanding that the movement of wearing dreadlocks predated the crowning of Tafari Makonnen in 1930.

I remember introducing the humble Israelite brother to my mother when she came down to JA to bring me back to the UK. She was the first person to ever tell me about Israelites, not that I really took it in to be honest. The two of them would talk for hours; in fact, when I went to Port Antonio to Mr Miller's house, it was my mother that had sent me. On my return, she told me things that manifest up to this day, while comforting my heart. Although I experienced so much pain from 1994 up until now, it's comforting knowing that throughout all my trials and tribulations, there have been learning and strengthening processes along the way. On that note, mummy saw and predicted right.

One of the most beautiful moments in my life although the memory is accompanied by pain, was my mother's funeral, and the direction in which it went always makes me smile. Being a woman of the community, our friends, whether my brother's, sisters' or mine, were always welcomed at our home. Our door was always open and I literally mean always. Night and day, friends would come in and out; some stayed over, if and whenever they felt to do so. Mum would look after and out for everyone as if they were her own children, and the love she gave showed the day she was laid to rest. Anyone would have thought it was a young person's funeral. I am still smiling at the thought of how many young people came out to say his or her goodbyes. It was the whole community and beyond. Thinking back on it, it's kind of funny, it was more like spot the adult. There were adults there of course, and many too, but the youth and children outnumbered them like crazy, in fact she had a really big and beautiful send off. For me this is a memory of joy I carry.

After my mother's burial, I slipped back into the streets. Deep down, there was a level of guilt and anger I carried because of all the stress I'd caused. I was relating it to the thought of her transitioning to the realm of the ancestors, and as mentioned before, I blamed myself up until my sister made me more aware of the other health complications. Negativity has a way of latching on, especially when one opens the door and welcomes it in. Old habits don't die easily they say, in my case I guess it was true. A little while after my mother was physically laid to rest, I began to create problems for myself up and down the country. It was only a matter of time until the walls caved in on me, and I knew I had to get out of that house before they did. So, I focused on leaving the home of the streets behind and turned to the Rastafarian faith and music. In the very short time span of my music career, I focused hard and achieved a lot, which makes me proud when I think about it. Those days my recording artists name was Shadrock, and I made many connections in the business and was linking up with a lot of artists. I had voiced a few good tunes and had some playing on radio. I did a few local shows and began slowly getting exposure out there. Those days, I had started growing my locks. Being a go-getter, I established a Rasta fashion line. Initially, I began with designer T-shirts, and then expanded into sleeveless bomber jackets; the company was growing fast. Up and down the country, my T-shirts could be seen. Close friends from the Kick-off Head family supported me by buying my T-shirts, which helped promote the business too. Those days, I had a tune with my cousin Sparky Rugged, and a song with UK rap sensation at that time MC D that was getting a lot of play on pirate radio stations. The tune with MC D was being played on legal stations too. Together we did an interview on Choice FM at that time and therefore I was reaching different audiences. MC D and I were very close in those days. I had finished a crossover Hip Hop Reggae album that I titled 'Ancestral Blood,' unfortunately it didn't release due to my incarceration. As I stated, my career back then was very short, maybe just over a year or two if that. However, everything happens for a reason, and one and two of those tunes have been re-recorded and tailored to my current understanding of life.

Unlike my experience in South Africa, visits to Palestine, Israel, Jordan and other parts of North East Africa since my release from prison, have shed so much light on history pertaining to the indigenous melanated people of that region and life. It brings joy to others and me when I share my experiences and what I've learnt, via the documentaries I've made and distributed for all to see. These living memories not only comfort, but also lift my inner being. Describing the journey of my youth to where I'm at mentally today, and what I foresee for tomorrow, isn't quite easy, but it is a beautiful journey.

Chapter 26:
Increased Knowledge

Everything happens for a reason, both good and bad. Although bad experiences, also considered by many as negative occurrences, are always affiliated with low-level vibrations in the expression of pain, sorrow, fear or sadness to name a few. Energy is energy, and depending on how one perceives the energy received, it will affect the heart and mind. I was beginning to understand that everything happened only to make me stronger. I was seeing prison not just as a place of punishment, but where I was meant to be to allow myself time; this time away by myself was drawing me closer to me. Closer to a side of myself I never knew; from sorrow came about joy. If I hadn't been incarcerated, would I have ever studied as I did? I asked myself and comforted my heart with the notion that the very truth of my circumstance was, in prison is where I found myself, and prison was where I was supposed to begin this process and journey. In other words, I started to see and accept it as my destiny. Not saying that I was happy being in prison, but I knew I was there for a reason, and therefore understood there was more to me, and the path I was on. Life isn't complicated, mankind is. Everything understood in simplicity should be seen on source level I told myself, accepting what was happening and what I began to understand. Being human, things will knock me down and could create imbalance within my emotions, after all, I was in prison, but the key was to get right back up and look on the brighter side of things. Understand and learn from it, make the best of it, and this, I was doing. I knew I would and could still get angry, mad and even sad, but learning and acknowledging what caused it, comforted me; made me wiser. Reading the book of Ecclesiastes in the Bible over and over, was a real eye opener. Solomon had shed so much wisdom on folly and the errors of life, I could truly relate.

My knowledge of the Hebrew language had really begun to expand. Filled with excitement, I was more than making sentences out of words, I was reading from the Hebrew side of my Tanakh. Not perfectly, far from it, but I understood sentences and could speak out the odd verse of a scripture. What I delighted in was that I could recite the names of the whole thirty-nine books of the Old Testament in the Hebrew tongue, and recite the alphabet and numbers as if saying them in English. I was studying day and night, educating myself at any given time. The history and culture became more than just a need to know, as I reflected on things my mother used to tell me about Jerusalem. My mother was a very spiritual woman and had raised me the best she could, but as they say, you can take a horse to water, but you can't make him drink it. In a sense, I was that horse. Because I never really allowed anyone to know me, and my true feelings, no one really knew what I felt. It wasn't until I was older, my mother and I had a good discussion about me whilst I was still in Jamaica, just before she brought me back to England at the age of nineteen. I'm glad we did. Roughly, two weeks from the day of my return, my mother fell sick, was hospitalised and then went into a coma. She never came out. Studying this ancient culture made me wiser, along with the experience I was going through. What I was learning wasn't teaching me not to make further mistakes, what it was more showing me was how to deal with the situation appropriately. My mother had always told me mistakes are there to be made, but it's always up to the individual to gain something from the experience, and she was right. My mother referred to the Bible on numerous occasions, but reading the scriptures for myself with an opened eye, I saw this same philosophy take place time after time.

I began to refer to God in Hebrew, and it felt powerful when doing so. I was putting words together and begun making my own prayers. I was praying three times a day as written in the Book of Daniel. Genesis 1:14 gave me my understanding, and Psalms 55:17 my three prayer times. The first prayer was early morning when the sun begun to rise, at noon when the sun was at its highest point, and late evening any time after sunset. I was truly using the heavens for signs; I had never felt so strong in myself. There were days I would pray more than three times, but that was my daily obligation. Meditation was something I did a lot too. I loved to be still and allow myself to journey, allow the spirit within me to travel; knowledge would come flowing and it felt amazing. We live in a society where self-reflection is rarely ever taught, if at all, but there I was in prison, using time wisely, and it was paying off.

After Malcolm X, its commonly highlighted that when many black males are incarcerated, they find God, which really isn't a bad thing when you think about it. Then there are those that say we turn to God because it's an easy way out from the corruption that takes place within prison walls. Personally, for me it was totally different from the above scenarios. I was not running away from what was going on around me, in fact I was embracing it all. As for the concept of finding God in prison, it's as silly as the concept of racial hatred. The idea is none profitable. Racial hatred is flesh based, yet flesh withers after death, therefore the hatred is based upon an illusion that's momentary when you put it against mother earth's endless existence. If one is an atheist, and doesn't believe in the concept of God, it can be hard to understand what I'm about to say, but then, even an atheist I'm sure can grasp this concept. Malcolm X, like any other individual first learnt to identify with self, before taking on the knowledge of God. What I'm saying is, through embracing self, anything is possible at any time or in any given place, it just so happens that many young melanated males take that step back to reflect on themselves whilst incarcerated. With so much time on one's hands and being away from the speed and pace at which society works, anything's possible when one stops chasing everything outside of self, chills and looks within. So realistically, it's not really a prison thing it's a time thing, the hand of time is key. Individuals have also come to believe strongly in God through the gain or loss of a loved one. This thought pattern can also relate to a psychology model based on time; time of action and time response; accompanied through circumstances and situations allowing self-reflection, this understanding being shared isn't based on books learnt in a classroom but via experience. In fact, many, even those who have never seen inside the walls of a prison, I'm sure can recall a time when they have thought deeply about a situation without haste, and allowed the heart to lead, and were satisfied with the outcome. That is also reflection based on time. The point I'm making is, God is more than universal and one can connect to the inner God in man at any time; acceptance of source existence comes with and at no specification.

Chapter 27:
History & Childhood

I didn't grow up studying black history nor was I interested as a youth. Not that I wasn't proud of my African roots because I was, from a young age I had known my ancestors were black Jews. Having a better understanding of the etymology of the word Jew, unlike when I was growing up, I'd prefer to say my ancestors were the original Israelites. Nevertheless, the bottom line is, as a youth I had other things on my mind and studying or thinking about culture was the furthest thing from the direction I was going in. In fact, it wasn't until my teens when I returned from Jamaica in 1994 at the age of nineteen, that I took a real interest in history and learnt so much. After experiencing such an amazing energy amongst the group Kush and some Israelite brothers in Port Antonio, I came back to England a new man, well, at least I *thought* I did. Pain can hit hard and uncontrolled emotions are a man's worst enemy. My mother's transition saw me return to the road and streets. I became caught up in all manner of foolishness, negativity had found an opening once again, low-level vibration found a way to project itself and I became a self-destructive tool. But even in the madness that occurred, I now understand it was a part of my further development. Not saying my lessons in life really had to be so hard, but I was a stubborn, hard-headed child, it was just the way I learned. I see it now, and have begun implementing ways to help my personality and character traits to aid my decision making and awakening. However, stubbornness isn't always a bad thing, sometimes being difficult to move, especially when one knows they are correct and on the straight path can be a blessing, and an energy force that drives determination.

I experienced something so beautiful when I met those humble Israelite brothers, but looking back on it now, I was like a child tasting a tantalising favourable sweet, only to be told you'd have it when all the homework was done. Hard-headed and troubled, I journeyed through the learning process, making errors and re-learning to finally finish and be given back the sweet taste of life that remained memorably deep within. Satisfied by the reward, I was able to rejoice, this was the feeling, reflecting on my tribulations and journey.

As a youth although we all knew our grandfather was a true proud melanated Judean, the concept of studying and understanding black history or even looking at the Bible, wasn't something really forced on us. Mum would send us to church, but I found no interest in going and tried my best to leave the house at the last minute or would walk slowly so I would be late for the service. Regarding any kind of history, my mother never really pushed it in the home; I guess she saw there was no real interest in it. It just wasn't of much importance in my life as a youth.

Today, the teaching of history is far more represented in the home then it was back then, with this generation more open to learn and speak on it, this plays an important part. Youths of all races intermix more today culturally than before, as street culture plays a paramount role in their lives. Some say we live in the age of information, the age of technology; but then that depends on how one sees information and what one calls technology. Are man's inventions really going forward or backwards, when we really take history and its effect on the universe into account? I'd prefer to look at today as neither the age of information nor technology, but as a universal shift of energy causing the desire to seek insight. The study of the planet's indigenous people has become meaningful to many, including non-melanated people. Growing up in South Kilburn back then, black, white, and a few Indian youths on the estate all hung out, living in our own little bubble world there was no discrimination. Not saying that racism didn't exist in South Kilburn, I'm sure it did, but it wasn't something that I can say I experienced. Our parents kept friends with people of different races; my mother's best friend was a white woman with whom I'd stay as a child on many occasions when my mother was abroad. Football and other things both good and naughty were more of interest than the study of history to be plainly honest. There wasn't as much information out in the media regarding Black history back then in the early 80's as there is today, it just wasn't there or maybe I wasn't looking. But with the creation of the World Wide Web, the times have definitely changed, and the reason and purpose for the shift to open access to information is questionable. With so much information easily at hand, not to add confusion to the present reality, but in which direction do and will we shift to from here? But doesn't that depend on the mind to interpret what the objective is behind the abundance of information; surely not all information is good information. The truth is, at this time there is an undeniable shift taking place both positive and negative, and the masses of information accessible, are *only* tools. A wrench cannot do the job of a screwdriver and vice versa, they both may be necessary tools to fix the same appliance, but at different points and parts of the appliance they become useful. Understanding what you are fixing first is of most importance, and then the right tools for the appropriate job can be used. Look at self as the appliance and the information as tools accessible to aid you to run efficiently. Information is great, but history has taught me understanding self is the true key, aligning self with truth, and that must be sought within self, and not in a book. The information should be in your heart, not your heart in the information. Meaning, if any book has to tell you how to live, to love, then you still haven't found yourself, or self-worth. Find self; this is not only an ancestral path, but also a universal connection. For me the study of the Hebrew Text didn't tell me how to live, instead it projected what I began to feel about life and the universe around me. After all, the scriptures confirm that the universal laws shall no longer be on tablets, but will be written upon the hearts and minds. Truth must come from within, there lies true power. My journey within self, whilst incarcerated brought me to see humanity, humility, simplicity and love. Although the Holy Scriptures and other books reflected these attributes, they were first sought after within myself and reconfirmed in what I read. I was not perfect behind bars and still I am not today, however, black history or should I say an ancestral connection and journey within has taught me that my DNA is alive.

Chapter 28:
Charged with Manslaughter

I had been going back and forth to circuit court since 1998, it was now the end of 2001. Three years on the circuit, nine, ten trips to St Ann, I'd lost count. Not to mention additional months in holding before being placed on the circuit. I was becoming pretty fed up of going back and forth to Kangaroo court. A few of my old circuit buddies had been sentenced over the last two appearances. National had dropped out and was now in the realm of the ancestors and as for me, I was in limbo watching new inmates acting shy, testing the waters and hyping up themselves because they were now located amongst us circuit inmates. No one bothered me and I kept away from the bullshit, apart from when anyone came to my cell and talked shit; that was stamped out immediately. They knew to take it elsewhere. I wanted peace in my surroundings, well as much of it as I could establish based on the circumstances and environment; problems and trouble in my cell I didn't need. Reading my Hebrew text, I meditated on scriptures and prayed for road. Though I knew my son's family were going to be there to give their testimonies, they wouldn't miss it for the world, I still hoped for my trial to start. I was just tired of going back and forth, looking at the judge and twelve jury members who had my fate in their hands. Twelve people were always used on a murder trial if I remember correctly.

I remember being in the bullpen and my cowboy barrister coming to me and saying we are going on trial today. As much as I prayed for it, I remember asking him if he had prepared himself for the trial. Believe me I had little, in fact no faith in him. I had pointed out to him how conflicting their statements were and of course gave my account of what occurred around the domino table. As for my son's mother's statement, which she withdrew, it had nothing to do with the charge I was on. Therefore, it was irrelevant from the beginning, and was never considered a fright, but *was* relevant in expressing that there was more to this case than met the eye. Her statement was really all about my youth and personal feelings, nevertheless she'd withdrawn her statement but the cowboy representative still had a copy. I really disliked him and saw him as a useless bum. I always had to direct him and analyse the statements for him, I really wished I could represent myself, but I didn't think that would be wise. I asked him about my plea; he said it's best to go guilty to murder, and they will argue that mentally I'm not in the best of health, and after a few years then they can petition for my discharge on compassionate leave. The look I gave him told him exactly how I felt about his plan, his aim and him. Believe me, if the police or grille hadn't kept us apart, I'd have been charged for him too, that's how much he angered me at that moment. Maintaining composure, I controlled my emotions and spoke to him. Making him know if that didn't work, I may end up riding a massive sentence and I wasn't going to take the risk. We discussed the different statements again and I firmly expressed that he *must* aim to get my case dropped to manslaughter from murder, and get my remand time taken into account, as it would be if I were in England, based on the notion that Jamaica although an independent country, is still bound to the British judicial system. I was fully aware and frightened by what inmates told me about the amount of time some of them ran on remand, and were sentenced without it being taken into account. He said he would see what he could do and left. I watched inmates go up and down, back and forth and waited for this puppy show of a barrister to return. Deep down I was so furious at him but kept that bottled up, or should I say I channelled the energy; being angry wasn't going to change anything. I had to trust and believe in destiny. I wanted to portray calmness, and not anger, so I did; I wanted something to come out of this circuit court appearance. I didn't want to run remand anymore, but knew any form of negative excitement and I would fry myself. They would throw the book at me, and for how the system is set, the size of the book is unpredictable. I didn't and wouldn't want to experience the worst of the kangaroo court.

It was my turn to face the judge, my heart was beating, I didn't know what to expect as the police led me upstairs. Finally, I thought, today's my day. I wasn't scared but felt an unusual feeling deep within; everything and nothing ran through my mind, I wasn't myself. As I stepped into the courtroom and walked towards the dock, I noticed the jury of twelve no longer existed and the three witnesses weren't there as in previous times when I was remanded. My barrister came over to me and quietly stated, "We are going to plead guilty to manslaughter correct." I agreed still thinking about what I don't even remember. I just wanted it over.

The judge asked me for my plea to manslaughter, which I stood and pleaded guilty to, and was sentenced there and then. I was sentenced to fifteen years, of which I'd do half behind bars. My three years on remand were taken into account, therefore I was to serve a little less than five years. It was like a dark cloud had just disappeared. I knew I was going on road; I knew Freedom Street was seeing me soon. Leaving the dock, I kept my head straight and didn't turn to look at the judge, I just wanted out of that courtroom. Downstairs in the bullpen my cowboy barrister came and spoke with me; I didn't even listen to him, whether I nodded or said yes it was all spontaneously done, nothing was in relation to his words. He knew it too. I was in my own world, preparing my mind now to run a sentence. I was used to Spanish Town prison as a remand prisoner but it dawned on me, I'm now sentenced. It shouldn't really have made a difference but it did. I started thinking about going back and was like damn, I'm going to be running time. I comforted myself with thoughts of everyone I knew in Spanish Town prison and the years I'd done there. Now it was just to run off some more, and all is well, get with the programme I thought. Looking back, it was crazy how I wanted to be free from limbo and then couldn't relate to what had just transpired for a brief second.

Back at the station, I learnt I wasn't going back to Spanish Town aka St Catherine Adult Correctional Centre, but was going to be transferred to GP, General Penitentiary otherwise known as Tower Street Correctional Centre. I was pissed. That was an understatement. On the block, I gave trouble. I began to make the last few days miserable for everyone. Why I reacted so poorly only was a testimony to myself, I had much work to do on myself, the change of environment, which I was unable to control, I didn't like, and this wasn't a good sign. During my tantrums, I disrespected inmates for less than nothing, and argued over everything with any police officer who came on the block. From the day I returned from court, I had not picked up my Bible, especially after finding out I was going to GP, but that was a mistake. I allowed anger to feed itself on my disapproval of something I had no power to change. I could no longer just look at it, I sat down and picked up my Bible and began to read. Reading through the night, I fell asleep at some point, if I was to say when I would be lying. All I know is I woke up and felt better; General Penitentiary it was. I was only doing just under five years; it was much better than twenty-five or more and charged for murder. God was good to me; I was getting a second chance. I knew I still had a lot of anger in me. I was reflecting on my life choices and experiences and there was a lot to correct about myself; and I knew that wouldn't be done in a day or two. I was heading to unfamiliar territory. I knew I would know people in GP who had transferred from Spanish Town prison, plus I had friends in there from road, so I knew I'd see them. However, I had built up a certain respect and routine at Spanish Town prison Oval and it would've been easier to re-adapt and formulate myself for the next five years there. Life had thrown another curve ball at me and I had to change path and start from scratch again. What worried me was my temperament, knowing it could go at any time I was pushed over the edge, believing and thinking about being tested, thoughts of how much I could take before snapping, or if I reacted instantly to anyone, how far it would go before ending. Numerous thoughts ran through my mind. Spanish Town prison is dangerous, but GP is a war zone. There were too many factions and I wasn't looking to get caught up, but then I knew linking up with certain people could make my life easier, yet depending on how they themselves lived, it just might bring more trouble my way. I knew if I didn't just chill and let whatever transpired manifest, I'd set myself up for a downfall and be defeated before the battle even began, so I did. I just let the direction set before me take me and went with the flow, knowing in my heart the Almighty Yah is guide and protector.

Chapter 29:
General Penitentiary

A chain of thoughts ran through my mind as I arrived at Tower Street Adult Correctional Centre. As the prison gate shut behind the truck, it was time to get with the programme. Just go with the flow I told myself, so like water I travelled along the course set before me. When they brought me downstairs after processing, Waynie-Bones called out to me as I walked towards the arch next to Remand Block and said he would come check me before lockdown. Just like Spanish Town, I could tell the system ran without real rules, especially when it came to locating inmates. I had seen a few associates that I knew were sentenced yet were on Remand Block, particularly a good friend of mine from Waterhouse, he'd been sentenced years ago. Remand Block was in front of the processing block where warders could be seen going to and fro; lawlessness was the order set, and the prison was chaotic. While the officer escorted me to my location, my friends walked alongside us and spoke with me until we reached the stairs before exiting under the arch to head off to the front. Seeing Waynie-Bones again didn't bring a good feeling, he'd been rearrested on another murder charge. I'd known this from when I was in Spanish Town and was upset about it. As Eddie Fitzroy sang, "Prison life it no sweet," and believe me I didn't want to be there, neither did I want it for him.

New prison, new start. I will never forget my conversation or better should I say my exchange of words with the warder who brought me to E North Block to locate. He had asked me if it's true that I had come to Jamaica to kill people. I looked at him as we walked. He could tell by the way that I stared at him; I wasn't there to entertain him. "I'm charged with manslaughter, not murder," I uttered. He then went on about how I came to Jamaica and killed a Jamaican, how much he believes I'm a hit man, I'm a bad man and all the rest of that shit I just didn't want to hear. The only thing on my mind was who the hell was I going to locate with. I was so used to locating alone, the thought of locating with other inmates, not to mention strangers disturbed me deeply. When I saw the size of the cells on E North Block, and to make it worse, some of the cells had two hammocks, I thought fuck that shit; I don't want to locate in any of them. The warder called out to the orderly on the block. Before he could locate me, from nowhere Gunmout's younger brother Duffus came and said he's going in my cell, he told me to come and then walked off. I didn't even wait until the orderly and warder agreed, I handed my big bag of clothing to One-Two, another thug I knew from St Ann and bounced. I wasn't waiting to hear anything. Although I know sometimes familiarity breeds contempt, and later down the line we'd fall out, but there and then, I wasn't feeling the vibe to locate with any and anyone. My desire was to feel out my surroundings and this I began to do.

Duffus sorted me out; I didn't even need to buy a sponge. He had a new one in the cell and gave it to me, keeping the old one for himself. I was happy to see there were no two hammocks in his cell; the cells were just way too small. I hated to be cramped up coming from Spanish Town Remand Block GB where the cells were a tad bigger. Not to mention I located by myself for a very long time, it just felt weird sharing a toilet size room with three other grown men, but it had to be done. E North didn't have one single cell; it was like sardines in a can up and down the block. Quite a few cells as mentioned before had more than one hammock hanging; it definitely wasn't Spanish Town and believe me I wanted to go back to Prison Oval Rock.

Later that evening, I found out that one of those cells with two hammocks that caught my attention when I first arrived belonged to a set of Jungle youths. I found out days later via conversation with a few of them that they were close to my cousin who'd done me wrong on a visit back in Spanish Town prison. They knew her father and the rest of my family who lived in the section of Jungle known as Angola. Whether our encounter on the block was really just an introduction or they were sizing me up seeing if they could intimidate me was yet unknown. Neutral respect was given, everything was cool, plus they saw I knew a few of the older Junglists located on the block right underneath us downstairs on F North. On E North Block, there were loads of guys from Jungle, not to mention throughout the prison from different sections of Arnett Gardens, but on E North, most of them chilled together. Strength in numbers was definitely their motto.

Within days of my arrival, two well respect warrior inmates Tommy Troubles and Jerry Guts took on one of the most notorious cliques in a block known as Building. Building's reputation and structural appearance was similar to New Hall aka the Ship in Spanish Town prison. Standing by the top of E North steps with my cellmates and a few other inmates from various garrisons, we watched, as all hell broke loose. Back and forth inmates ran, the weapons some of them brandished you would swear they were on road and not prison. I told myself one thing I needed was a little jammer of my own. I knew like Spanish Town; Tower Street Adult Correctional Centre could get crazy at times and I refused to be a victim.

For a good few months I hardly left E North Block, I would shower there, eat there and chilled there. Leaving the block was something my cellmates hardly would do; it wasn't out of fear it was just the way Duffus and the others moved and I just went with the programme. Most of the times under lock even when listening to music with my cellmates I'd read my Hebrew Bible and look over the King James Version, sometimes just comparing sentences and the meanings of words. The etymology of a word can have a big impact on the true meaning, and that I found interesting.

Like within the walls of St Catherine Adult Correctional Centre, many acknowledged my love for reading, especially for the fact that I had a Hebrew Text, it was different and caught the masses attention. Due to peoples' reactions and as far as I knew, not one warder I encountered not to mention inmate, had ever seen a Hebrew Text or the written Hebrew before. Well, not to my knowledge, and therefore all manner of questions were asked. Sometimes questions were asked on various occasions. During search time on the block, whichever warder or warders searched our cell, I was guaranteed a conversation, sometimes leading to them not even completing their search thoroughly, but hey, no complaints there. Like everyone else, I just wanted it over and to be locked back down again. The quicker the better; I appreciated time. The name Hebrew spread around the prison like wildfire, as like previously in Spanish Town prison even the few inmates who knew me from Road, stopped calling me Tata, and joined the masses referring to me as Hebrew.

In those early months as mentioned, I would hardly leave E North Block. Sometimes I'd walk downstairs to F North Block to see a few friends; Waynie-Bones would come from around the front to check me from time to time. Foreigner, the inmate who defended me when I first arrived on Remand Block at Spanish Town prison when Alton drew an allegation on me in the cell and punched me in my face while holding his knife, he'd checked me a few times. Max had come up to check me on various occasions. I recall him telling me Chuku (R.I.P) was no longer with us, and explained to me what he knew. Listening to Max explaining Chuku's experience made me think briefly about Al Capone and my own experience in jailhouse. Police custody is no joke, Al Capone and Chuku weren't the first to be murdered in police custody and won't be the last, I'm just thankful I'm still here. Max had taken me over to G North block. G North was a block that I had never visited, not even once since I landed in GP, yet it was directly opposite the block I located on. In fact, only a short passage separated the two blocks. I wasn't the kind of guy to make loose movements, carelessness can cost you your life and I wasn't about to wander around prison for the fun of it. Prison was no tourist attraction, and if I had no reason for being somewhere, believe me, I wasn't going to be there. Wherever I believed I had no association, I wasn't going; well at least I thought I didn't. Max had introduced me to some inmates on G North that were from Kingston 8, and knew my family. A few of them were from White Hall Avenue, the others from Manning's Hill. It was good to have new connects; but I was just doing my own thing, my mind was thinking about road as well as being in my book. I could fixate my desires now limbo was a thing of the past. What I did realise though, was now that I was sentenced I yearned even more deep down to be free. It's like knowing I'd be free didn't really ease my mind, it made me think more about road, be on edge at times and desire Freedom Street more and more. Emotions played me; I believed humbling myself more was the best way to deal with it. What I didn't need was to be on edge or deep in thought and someone pisses me off and I'm unable to control myself and lose sight of the bigger picture, which was my freedom. The result could be disastrous. I still knew I had anger to deal with, I guess I was going through another transformational stage. I just needed to align myself, accept and deal with it the best I could. So time alone, not that it was always possible, but time to reflect, harness and channel positive energy was definitely something I needed.

More months passed and I witnessed so many arguments, fights and a few stabbings; prison life was no joke. I definitely needed space. It was a readjustment period I believe I was going through, and with so much on my mind, having a dislike for the environment I was in didn't help. I needed to control my emotions and tried to trap out all the negativity that surrounded me, trust that was hard, but it had to be done. I went into my own world, a world that existed within me. The more I tried to focus on myself, I found my cellmates and I, especially Duffus, getting into some silly little arguments over foolishness, which pissed me off. I was escaping problems on the block but from time to time we would cross words under lock over things that meant nothing at all to me, deep down I'm sure it meant nothing to him either. Different spirits have different purposes, and some latch on to the flesh only to create mischief. I felt the temptation, and tried my best to ignore the energy he presented to me. I was definitely going through a spiritual battle, but it wasn't about whatever Duffus was doing or how he was acting, he had to deal with his own demons. My battle was about my demons and I, and whether I was willing to allow low-level vibrations to penetrate and affect me. A prime example that played on my mind when Duffus and I were going through our emotions, was the biblical story of King Saul and David. I came to understand good and evil spirits, how they affect individuals, and how and what the individual did or didn't do would affect the outcome. Therefore, the outcome was always on the individual. I came to understand the outcome was on me, and didn't want to harness low-level vibrations, anger and hatred in my heart for Duffus or even anyone else. David was a great warrior and had won many physical battles, and lost some spiritual ones; but the *spiritual war* he never lost. Why, because a battle is a single event but the war continues and therefore David being a man forever repentant for his sins, overcame all his trials and tribulations making him victorious. Being human, I'm far from perfect, I may not have always won the battle but the spiritual war, I guaranteed myself to see it out to the end.

Once in a while, I'd go down to H North for a mature conversation and visit the elder Zion Train (R.I.P) and Indian from Tivoli. We'd been introduced via Jaro when she told me to let him know we were family, and from there the connection began. Reasoning with Zion Train was always positive. Once, he told me if ever I needed anything to ask. I appreciated it, although I can't remember myself ever taking him up on his kind gesture. I wasn't a man to really like asking for anything, I personally had problems with that, I still was very stubborn, but that was just I.

On my rare visits to H North, I would encounter Tommy Troubles and Jerry Guts. Tommy Troubles, Jerry Guts and I would hail one another. Jerry and I showed mutual respect, but Tommy Troubles and I built a healthy positive connection about a year or so later, one that confused many inmates, especially because of how many saw him. Tommy Troubles could be a wild man when ready, but he had a good heart and that made us click the way we did, and created a level of understanding and trust that I showed him and in return he showed me.

My big brother from my father's side had sent his niece nicknamed Jan (R.I.P) to visit me. During that first visit she told me, her uncle sent her and she'd be visiting me from time to time, which made me feel really good. My big brother and I were very close; as mentioned earlier in the book, it was from his house in East London that I left as teenager to go to Jamaica. My big brother and I related very well, he understood the issues I faced as a youth, and to me, feeling someone could relate to my struggles felt good. Like my mother, he was also from Dunkirk, had grown up in the UK, and experienced his own struggles in life. His wisdom and expressions comforted me as a youth, so I looked up to him. Jan's visits came as a treat. When she visited me, I felt like a fat boy receiving his favourite candy, her cooking was sweet; my cellmates and I enjoyed every basin of food she brought. Sometimes I'd send on some munchies to my friends down on F North, especially Starkey. I had maximum respect for the Junglist; Starkey and I were very close. We had come from far and he showed me nothing but love, if I needed anything, he had me and wanted nothing in return. Through him, I got to know Benbow and Ninie, two real brothers from the same ends. When Benbow came from around the front to where we were, he would make bear jokes. Moments of laughter made prison vibes just feel a little lighter. One thing I realised was the majority of real serious men didn't really hype in prison they were just mellow and would run their time unless need be.

I remember one day, King-Kong came to tell me, the big man was around the back on Remand Block. King-Kong knew of my mother's family and also knew via conversation, that the big man was my brother's first cousin on his mother's side and had told him I was there. One day the big man on his way to the Kitchen shouted King-Kong and told him to bring me down, so he did. At the Kitchen, Stumpy (R.I.P) and I spoke. We briefly discussed family and prison. He made it clear if I needed anything to just come check him round the front. On occasions, I visited him at Remand Block when I'd link Waynie-Bones and a few others, but didn't need or ask for anything; it was just my character. Stumpy and I would reason more often when he came around to the kitchen or out on the front. He would also tell me he respected the way I moved in GP, and from his observation, a lot of inmates respected me. It was something I'd heard several times and being observant of my surroundings, it was pretty well known to me too. The reality that confronts us is, what does one do when power or respect is given, do you abuse it or use it? Personally, I did neither. The key for me was to respect all and treat everyone I encountered the same way. This was something I'd never known and never did, but I was rediscovering myself and saw how much respect really goes a long way.

Even though I had connections with lots of popular inmates, I was a man about my own business; my greatest companion was I. I was determined to get into myself more and needed space to do so.

I'd experienced a lot in life and knew that I couldn't continue living like that. I was seeing and valuing myself. I believe inmates saw it too, hence I got a lot of respect for it, but never ever acted as if it meant anything to me. Humility won me favour with many. Troubled and broken due to my youth and experiences throughout my life, I needed to be humble and take that step back to analyse myself. I was seeing my likes and dislikes, and a lot that affected me, which I didn't know was there. This was scary, because I understood there was so much that I had buried and put to one side, and they were key issues never dealt with, not resolvable in a day; I wondered if some ever would be. It got really conflicting when I thought, if that's the trigger for this action, then what triggered that action, and is there something even deeper than this to be understood. Going through a self-analysing process made it easier for me to look at other inmates and understand where they were coming from regarding their own behaviours and actions. It was not that I pardoned or gave excuses for their actions, but they like myself were troubled via their own experiences. The only difference was, I no longer accepted this lifestyle was who I was, or was destined to live as, while many of my peers did, and believed as if it was fate or destiny. When in truth, this wasn't and isn't who we were born to be, but who we became through circumstances and situations, over which many had no control. There are so many factors as to why our lives had gone in this direction, having spoken with numerous inmates, sometimes the mindset even predated one's birth, and the spiritual realm isn't to be underestimated or overlooked. Exposed to an unproductive environment from the womb, who's to judge why we do what we do. What was clear is that a better lifestyle was never sold to many, so they made their own paths to happiness, even though it brought more sorrow. Not to mention being stripped from history and culture meant losing ancestral traditions and spirituality. There are many spirits desiring to latch on to flesh; without knowledge of self and ancestral understanding, it isn't easy *not* to fall victim to the unknown, for how can one fight *against* what was never taught to them. Seeing and coming to acceptance of my own experiences, I knew there was no better way to explain that we are not born and destined to be nothing, so I *chose* to lead by example, and *I* did. Not saying I never rose to anger, got caught up in conflict or even allowed the mad head, as Jamaican's would say, to take me from time to time, but I'd always reflect on the consequences when some of my peers wouldn't. I also knew how to relay my feelings and express myself, which made some check themselves too, and that was a positive thing.

Chapter 30:
Location Building

Almost a year had gone by since being sentenced, and one day I just got fed up with the petty arguments with Duffus and decided I'm leaving E North. On a few occasions, he mentioned some weird, illogical things. He was definitely fighting his own demons and I refused to allow that energy to latch onto me. Some spiritual battles are just unnecessary to take on; shake off confusion and keep it moving I say. Apart from the few people I knew from road, I made a lot of associates, but that was just due to the way I carried myself; people took to me. He would get paranoid thinking I'm going to switch on him and all manner of madness, which to me didn't make sense. Trying to rationalise his actions, I assumed it was about his nose rather than him thinking I couldn't be trusted anymore. But then he always had weed, and that was the only logical reason I could think of on the surface level. After all, at no time did I ever show him any dislike or disrespect. He'd say things I didn't agree with, whether it was directed at me or someone else, it could be no one in particular, but if I didn't agree I wouldn't act as if I did. Being the man I am, I was outspoken and expressed my views, sometimes causing arguments, but in my eyes that was petty, as everyman is entitled to their opinion. I've always believed a man doesn't have to agree with me, so there was no way I was always going to agree with him if I didn't think he was right. I myself am not perfect, and when I was wrong, he'd make me know I was wrong and I'd agree, but at times it escalated over nothing and we'd end up arguing. Even though we had no real vibes there was clearly an underlying issue affecting our friendship. This was a shame because we both knew deep down when push came to shove we had one another on E North. He'd shown me that loyalty as much as I'd shown him the same regarding defending one another. Cell loyalty was a big thing, if a man came to your cell and violated someone within, it didn't only affect the person who got disrespected, but looked bad on you too. On that note, knowing one another before Tower Street Adult Correctional Centre, we were down for each other. I remember when I had an exchange of words with a youth from Back Bush, during second fly-up, he began moving shady on the block whilst I was on the toilet. Even though I noticed him and had a jammer in my hand thinking if he comes over towards me it's on, Duffus, clocking the play, stood at the cell door watching him with bloodshot eyes and a smile that said try and die. Earlier that very same day Duffus and I had a big argument, but he clearly showed me he had me always. On numerous occasions, we dealt with one another's situations without the other being present, but a point arrived where one of us had to draw away before we pushed the other's button beyond the point of control, and words became blows and friends became foes. One-Two had stepped between us one too many times, and for me the moment we both smiled at one another during an argument, it was time to leave. I knew what was going through my mind, not proud at all of the thoughts that were comforting me, and I knew the same thoughts ran through his, as he once said to me, "You think I'm going to sleep with one eye open?" Our friendship was turning sour, and my love for him deep down was strong, so it was time to jump ship. I know deep down he still had mad respect and love for me and would prove this once again over time. A visiting bag came to me, but for some reason the orderly took it to the cell we once shared on E North, Duffus sent One-Two to Building to give it to me. In return, I sent on some munchies and a little smoke money just to show the respect was still there. Another occasion, some guys on E North plotted to get me at the gym, word not only reached me about what they'd said, but I was also told that Duffus confronted them too. Prison life was crazy like that; in fact, life itself is crazy, some friendships are unreadable, and you may find some families' bonds are toxic like that too. The connection is strong but polluted. Sometimes there are deeper issues at hand than the eye can see, spiritual conflicts; yet equally as deep, are the powerful emotions keeping individuals bonded through a connection; one has to wonder if it's a sickness. But it was life and a part of my reality, a reality I didn't want to waste too much energy on so I left the cell. It wasn't a spiritual battle I needed to keep facing, some we bring unnecessarily to ourselves; I knew this one wasn't worth fighting and chose to shake off the confusion and keep it moving.

Like yesterday, I remember the green suit warder's face when I approached him asking if I can transfer over to Building. The look on his face asked me if I was crazy. At that time no foreigner had ever located beyond E and G North, out on grass was out of bounds. It was either one of those two blocks I just mentioned or round the front on Remand Block. A grey suit warder asked me if I was not afraid, and went on to talk about how the block is a bad man block, and they'll kill me over there, and I must find another cell on the block and relocate. Ignoring his statement, I asked the green suit again and explained I'm good, I don't want to locate on E or G North. We stood there debating for a few minutes when the green suit raised his voice and said to the other warder, "Locate him on Building!" as if to say who can't hear will feel, and so I was allowed to relocate.

I had been going to Building to use the toilet at that time, as E North only had a few toilets for a ridiculous number of prisoners and after a while I got fed up with the waiting or pushing in line and the petty arguments it caused. But when a man has to defecate, he *has* to do it, or soil himself, and that's not advisable believe me, your life would be forever miserable behind bars after that. During those days I was going to Building to use the toilet before I transferred and located there, I would also check my friends over there whenever I passed through. Max located on Building, as well as Buju, the Kirkist had been transferred to GP from Spanish Town prison. By this time, I had made a few connections of my own with other inmates, and being me knew how to manoeuvre around to survive, after all man is a survivor. I have been through so much in my life and could adapt to any situation, I had proved it time after time since my youth. Adapting to the way Building functioned wasn't going to be hard at all; it was just going to be another experience that would only make me stronger.

I was located in a cell upstairs. I wasn't happy to locate with anyone in truth, but the likelihood of getting a single cell in

Building as a new arrival was as unrealistic as a camel going through the eye of a needle. Max came up to hail me and exchanged words with my cellmates; they were his friends. Buju did likewise. Max also introduced me to a long-standing prisoner known as Drummer, he was a friend of my family from Kingston 8, and was to be released within the next year or so. He'd served way over a decade and was respected by many. Drummer and I got taking about road and family, and he gave me encouragement to just keep my head down, run my sentence and leave. I could see he was a man who'd come to grips with his past and learnt from it, and maybe I guess he did a lot of reflecting and soul searching himself just by our brief conversation. It was over time I came to realise he did just that, soul searched and wanted better for his life than what he had known as a youth.

Gone but never forgotten Tubby T (R.I.P) had called me a few times whilst I was in Building. I can't recall how he got the number I was working with or from whom, but it was a joy to hear from my brother. He told me about his music that it was popping off and I told him to stay focused on it. His phone calls came as a joy to me; it was always good hearing from the outside world and being brought up to speed with what's good. As youths we were cool, we had a lot of respect for one another. There were brothers in NW10 that I was much closer to but didn't hear from, so that made Tubby's calls that much more special. Not that Tubby and I weren't close, because we were from our youth, but some of the other guys and I had history, but then it only showed that out of sight, out of mind, was real. One thing I knew and accepted even before I came to prison, was that even the most loved man on road can be forgotten to the world once behind bars. This knowledge was shared with me as a youth by a few of Jamaica's notorious residing in the UK back then. So, knowing that lesson, it didn't come as a surprise when I never heard from certain close friends from NW10 or NW6. As I was taught, so-called friends would pick you back up when you're free, which to me didn't make sense, because when I'm free who needs your help then; but that was the streets. It wasn't disloyalty, that's the wrong perspective, I saw it as people were caught in their own world and situations, the kind of out of sight, out of mind connection. I've heard friends talk many times about similar situations, I've witnessed it with others, and it was just my time to experience this strange love.

I knew certain brothers were there for me even if they weren't sending money or calls, but had my family's back, due to occurrences that took place on road that they handled without question. Therefore, I knew love was there. It was that strange love associated with the streets.

I'll never forget receiving packages from Size, he would send CD's and martial arts magazines. Believe me when I say this, receiving mail behind bars at times feels better than receiving money. It's the excitement of opening that package and holding something tangible, something someone has taken timeout to send for you; the feeling is so uplifting. I'll never forget listening to 'The Senior' Ginuwine's album for the first time. As I lay there, eyes closed, thinking about road and life, the tune 'Locked Down' came on, I remember playing it at least 10 times. I put it on repeat and wouldn't stop listening to it. When I did finally continue listening to the album, I became emotional and brought to tears when I heard the song 'Our First Born'. Lele, Nazerine and Ezekiel, especially my daughter, as she was our firstborn, ran through my mind. To be honest, I journeyed back to every wonderful experience and moment we shared, and every pleasant thought that came flowing to the forefront of my memory bank, was accompanied by pain and sadness. I truly missed my children so much, but in the same thought I thanked Size for being there for me, and supporting me in the way he did.

My cellmates and I were cooking. I was now allowing myself to trust others. We were buying food and cooking all manner of dishes. Sometimes re-cooking the rice that came on the tray and making our own meat, things were different on a daily basis.

Months passed; Jan was visiting me regularly thanks to my big bro. Jaro would come sometimes via my mother's siblings. I had the odd spell where I had neither money nor visits, but was grateful for how I was living compared to what I went through earlier in my incarceration. I had the latest clothes, not that it really mattered, who gave a shit about what prisoners thought of my clothes, after all, it was only them seeing it, or anyone who came on a five-minute visit who observed me through a dirty see-through plastic window. Designers were pointless, but not to sound ungrateful, much appreciated. Raymond would still visit me popping out of nowhere; sometimes without warning from my family that he was coming. Bearing gifts like a Black Santa. I had maximum respect for his aid. He was truly there for me. Got nothing but love for Raymond, and all those that gave him things to give me that weren't my biological family; truly appreciated them then, and appreciate them still.

I felt loved from beyond the prison walls; close friends and family made sure I wasn't forgotten and I felt remembered too. Believe me, knowing you're not neglected can have a massive impact on one's psyche. After experiencing so much struggle and hardship during the early period of my incarceration, I undoubtedly knew what it felt like to feel hardship behind the rusty bars of confinement. Yet I also knew what it felt like to find self-love within the prison system too. I'd found love in the form of self-worth; I was seeing and feeling a priceless comfort within myself and within the scriptures too. My love for biblical Text had me in another dimension mentally. I was constantly reading and comparing words from the Bible and Hebrew Text, the deeper understanding of words and their meaning made a big difference at times. I loved the scriptures and was in love with the knowledge of being an Israelite, cleaving to my ancestors, to what my grandfather said and my mother confirmed was of importance. I took that understanding to a whole other level. I had learnt so much and was learning more and more every day. I composed songs, small ones from words that I formulated, and would sing at the shower pipes behind Building after I used the gym, and at the washtub when I was washing my clothes. Inmates would listen to me and stare, some would nod and hail and others just hailed me. Believe me none of it was for attention, I was in my own zone and the best thing anyone could do was allow me to be me, which they did.

A year later, I jumped ship and went into a cell with Drummer, someone had moved out of his cell and he wanted me in so I went. We had many positive conversations but at the same time, he and the other cellmate liked their quietness too, so it was perfect for me as I adored silence and loved to think, read and write. Hence, their desire, and how they ran their cell sat well with my spirit. Not that the block was ever really silent anyway, but a cell with less noise made a big difference when it came to meditating and getting some work done. Right opposite my cell located an inmate nicknamed Fire-Links; he was the leader at that time of one of Building's strongest cliques. I came to know him over time whilst being there; I never mingled with his crew but showed respect and they did likewise. I remembered them from when I first arrived and watched them from E North warring with Tommy Troubles and Jerry Guts. He'd told me on numerous occasions, "If you ever need anything, come to me and I'll hook you up." To be honest, the only support was using a phone. Their connection helped me interact with the outside world from time to time and I would run a credit on them for allowing me access, but that was standard procedure in prison. I didn't want to get close, and over time it would frustrate some of his crew causing conflict between them and myself, especially because I'd do and live my way, not always following orders, particularly when it affected the less fortune inmates, I just couldn't do it.

Gym was a regular for me; I'd train daily and felt amazing within. I was as strong as a lion, and was becoming as wise as a serpent and believe me I wasn't slivering through the block, I walked proud with my head high. It's surprising how knowledge and love for self can lift one's spirit. Whilst at gym I got to know the real Don of that notorious little clique located upstairs in Building. Shotback and I would work out from time to time. Shotback was a humble but serious guy, he had relocated out of the block for whatever reason but still ran things amongst his peers. Unlike his peers, he never asked me about my crime, nor did he ever try to hold a conversation with me about violence or badness, just gym and daily life experiences. He had nothing to prove, but whatever was his driving force to live for, he seemed focused on it, and I saw that from the get go. Gym had made numerous men from different areas and cliques intermix, and everyone knew they were there for one reason and one reason only, and that was to workout. Gym was a safe haven; it was no man's territory.

Chapter 31:
Security & Protection

A year or so after leaving E North Block the warders must have thought he's still alive why not send more foreigners to Building to locate and stop packing them up on the E and G North. I began seeing new faces, and you could always tell a foreigner in the midst of yardies no matter how hard they tried to blend in, especially the white inmates. It was the opposite of being a fly in milk. As for the new black foreign inmates, they just had a whole different energy and way about themselves. But what the warders didn't know or maybe they did, was that the revenue in Building was about to increase, not drastically, well, not to my knowledge, but it was evident from where I stood, it meant a better lifestyle for more Jamaican inmates. A lot of foreigners paid dues, and I'm not talking the standard procedure where if you use a man's phone you pay a credit or so, that's natural. Individuals were giving money to their cellmates or those who their cellmates looked up to, or they would buy the daily meal for the cell, meaning they were eating well and not off the tray and still got the protection from their cell. The latter scenario was always the best option, because at least then the inmate felt kind of secure and got the satisfaction of having his belly full at the same time. The downside was when they did both, look after the cell and gave handouts to their cellmate's friends or just those who'd approach them.

The odd foreigner would say, "Hebrew, you don't give cellmate's money, do you?" and I'd reply, "No, but I do help out in my cell, we all do." I can tell they had been observing my interactions in prison. As conversation would go on, I would never speak to undermine a foreign inmate's decision to pay out, making them feel like they were fools for doing so, I understood their position. Strategically, I say it was wise. Most were only there for months, maximum a year or so, prison wasn't the be all or end all of their lives, it was a strategy to survive and have an easy run, it was a move necessary for some. A few inmates I knew who personally paid out to prisoners, those same individuals if this bullying or dictating tactics was on road, would kick the shit out of those Jamaican inmates that took the piss. Not that all inmates did, but those that did, if they were on road or even in a place where it was the two Jamaican inmates and specific foreigners who I could tell deep down weren't fools, they'd get a free face lift. Some inmates played it smart, it wasn't worth the hassle and changing cells could cause you problems, especially if you didn't have links, you just may fall into their friend's cell and the situation could then become even worse.

The humorous side of it was, after a while you had some Jamaican inmates looking a foreigner to locate in their cell. There were the odd arguments when a new foreigner came on the block. These walking, talking, hot meals were in high demand. Some foreigners became human food banks, they were considered able to provide typical basic provision and edible goods, free of charge.

The cosy joy that came to the odd foreigner was when he hit jackpot and entered the right cell where he was treated with respect, or landed in a cell whose friends were well respected. Even if he gave out money, he had it good. You could always tell him apart from the others. There was swagger in his walk, sometimes accompanied with a voice. Don't get me wrong a few inmates would stand up for themselves when shit got too much, but there were some that did it only because they were under protection. It was funny when Jamaican inmates would tell them they are only running their mouths because of so and so. It was hilarious at times; Jamaicans and foreign inmates seemed to get a dose of the same thing. You had yard inmates taking the piss at times and then the foreigner who had run up their mouths to some Jamaicans and the problem would always get pacified because of their connections. This irritated some Jamaican inmates, not to mention the jealousy shown from other foreigners who could never speak or say what they really felt, the only voice they had was the murmuring they did to themselves, while some didn't even do that and suffered in silence. On the flip side, I understood the protection game, but never played it for money, well not in prison anyway. I had helped and looked out for the odd inmate who'd give me or make me collect his money for him and only come to me once in a while for a specific amount. At least if inmates went through his belongings when he wasn't there or he didn't want the hassle of being bullied and losing it all, they'd only get a portion.

Looking back on road, the protection game had put thousands in my pocket, not that our connection started out as me being their protector, but when people don't understand the foundation of establishing friendship, they use all manner of unnecessary things to keep people close. Such actions always end disastrously. Never help someone and look for something in return, always give to bless others, nor ever assume material wealth creates loyalty. I was linked to a well-known individual from West London, it was genuine respect to begin with, well, that was my intention and it didn't come with a price, but I guess we had different ideas around friendship, and when money was thrown around wrongly, it created all manner of problems. It just became a regular thing and a part of our journey. I was a very calculated guy; I was doing nothing but getting something. Between him and another individual, neither of them really getting themselves into trouble, both giving me a little something here and there on a weekly basis, and if I ever needed a specific amount, I could always get it, that regular income was good side-money. It wasn't bad. It didn't last forever, as me and one of them fell out. The funny thing is, I didn't initiate for this specific individual from West London to give me money, that was never the mindset I had in the beginning of our interaction, but I played along with him. Over the time we interacted, there were two altercations. One where he witnessed my ability to take care of business, the other was me pacifying a moment he thought he would be taken away by some guys never to be seen again. All ended well for him. As for the other individual he never ever got into any problems, but was just happy to know I was an associate of his he could call upon. On the flip side I wasn't as calculated as I believed. If something occurred that was out of my reach or connections, I would have had to extend my arm into the unknown, and who knows what could have been waiting on the other side. Nothing is worth your life or freedom; materials can be replaced but you can't be.

Chapter 32:
Coincidence or Fate

W as it fate, coincidence, luck or bad luck? I always seemed to find myself at places and during moments when shit was about to go down. One day I was standing at the shower pipes and suddenly a big explosion went off. The few inmates who stood there looked at one another including myself and then at the wall, which was meters away from us and separated the prison from Rae Town community. Before our eyes was a massive indent in the wall on our side but a small hole exposing the outside world. The hole made was big enough for a baby to go through but not big enough for an adult. Everyone looked up at the sentry box (warder tower) and then back at one another. What was going through inmates' minds at that time is another thing, what I do know was loads of inmates began running over, warders were coming, and I was bleeding from the blocks that flew in my direction. I wasn't the only inmate bleeding, but I sure didn't want any part of an inquiry so I stepped, not wishing to be charged or accused of anything. In my cell, Drummer put cigarette ashes on my cuts to stop the bleeding and hide the wounds. Prison lockdown began immediately. Not that it happened quickly, inmates were so excited and all over the place at the thought of dynamite being planted and blowing up the wall, it was kind of chaotic. In everyone's mind there was the thought of a prison breakout, an escape was attempted and that hyped the whole prison. By the time the prisoners had all been put under lock the rattling of the chain and keys said it all. A search was about to take place and it wasn't for drugs or weapons but for inmates who had any marks on their body from the explosion, they wanted them for questioning. With the ash settled on my wounds and replaced over and over again, being as black as I am it was a perfect cover up. Warders searched me and to be honest because so many of them had respect for me because of the way I carried myself, they didn't thoroughly inspect my body so I stepped back in my cell and smiled to myself. No way did I want to be questioned about the incident. I know it would have been some mad interrogation. The last thing I wanted was to be interrogated on something I knew nothing at all about, not that they would have believed me if I said that. I thought to myself, an attempted jail breakout at Ocho Rios police station and now this, was it a sign of early release, or was it temptation, would I have taken the opportunity. All I do know was I always seemed to find myself present when craziness was about to happen and that in itself was questionable, but only God really knows why.

Chapter 33:
Hunger Strike

A s normal, situations would rise and word would spread on the block that no inmate was to eat off the tray, so the orderlies for the block knew the drill. Go get the food as usual and inmates would take it upon themselves not to eat, and the food then would be returned untouched. Strikes always got the authorities attention, but what it also did was pressure the poor amongst the prison population who weren't getting visits. Worst those who had no friends that they could get a biscuit or piece of bulla cake from, and those inmates suffered *extremely* badly in the process. Personally, I know, I'd experienced the suffering in the early part of my remand in Spanish Town prison, it was a dreadful feeling and depending on how long the strike was, could have a negative impact on one's mood, not to mention body. So, what I did when I heard a strike was about to take place was buy extra biscuit, bulla cake and bread as much as I could, and give to the few guys I knew located on the block that didn't have anything, while keeping what little I needed. Those where the moments a lot of inmates weren't hasty to sell because a strike was about to take place, but some would, for some inmates something to smoke was more important than having extra food. My actions caught the attention of a few top men on the block including Fire-Links and some of his crew. Nothing was said about what I did but then I noticed after that some of the other big men on the block who didn't run with Fire-Links, nor would he or his crew cross them, would reason with me. Although some would hail me up from before, now conversations were taking place. Acknowledging this transformation of communication, on a serious note, it meant nothing to me, I knew why I did it and what I'd experienced myself in the past, and honestly, I've always had a soft touch for people despite my childhood struggles, frustration and temper, I guess it is in my nature. I hated seeing people go through struggles, not to mention if they're ones I can relate to, my heart wouldn't allow me to feel comfortable just letting people face hardship if I could help. Plus reading the Bible and seeing that not only was it law, but humane to treat strangers well, even though these inmates weren't strangers but my fellow brothers, it was impossible to just sit and watch them suffer. Kindness is natural law; historically it is custom to show compassion for life always. How was I not to help if I could? So, I did. The strike only lasted two days, well not even two full days, at the last fly up inmates were told they could take food off the tray, and so everyone went for their portion when food was served just before second lockdown, including me. There were many occasions where I also ate off the tray even though we would cook too. I was never too proud to eat off the tray; it was just not me. Reheating prison food could also be nice at times, depending on what it was, a little added seasoning or something else to it would spice it up and make it more desirable. Sometimes eating it just as it came could also be desirable. Prison food wasn't perfect by a long shot, but I was training hard and eating was necessary, not to mention under lock, a comfort too.

Repeatedly, strikes occurred whilst I was located upstairs. There was one specific strike wherein I pissed off a few inmates by my actions. Whether Fire-Links was one of the inmates that were really pissed with me is yet to be known, because he never said anything to me about it and of course, we had numerous conversations after it occurred. Without hesitation he'd helped me out various times after this specific strike, but I recall him shaking his head as if to say *seriously?* But then myself and Fire-Links always had mutual respect for one another, it was members of his crew who would say or hint the odd indirect disrespectful phrase or word, to which I would either smile, return similar utterance, or pay it no mind, word is wind. Inmates were told not to take food out of the blue, I don't even remember if this was a whole prison strike or just our building, but looking on the faces on some inmates, I didn't wait to find out. I grabbed my basin and walked to the tray, on seeing me doing that, Jo Monkey, a big man from East Kingston did likewise, and Dallas, another East man grabbed some rice, before you know it all inmates who were living off the tray and relied on it for their daily survival made haste for their portions. Other big men on the block watched and said nothing. I recall one or two respected inmates smiling, it was a mad moment; I just felt driven to do it. Thinking about it, I knew I had taken a big risk there, being the first to grab food. It could have got me disciplined or worst-case scenario killed, but I felt compelled to do it, and acted on impulse more than rationalising what was taking place. Strikes are serious things and are not to be looked at as a joke, prisoners say prisoners do, on that day and that moment I just couldn't and thank God nothing came out of it, well not directly anyway.

Chapter 34:
Overcome Obstacles

As time went on, daily life continued as normal, reading, studying, emptying my piss-bottle, refilling my drinking bottles at last lockdown, talking to family and friends on the phone. One morning I was studying so much when the cell doors opened for inmates to carry out their piss-bottles, I remained behind and kept my head in my books. This wasn't something new, on many occasions I had done this. However, this specific morning Mac-11, a member of Fire-Links crew was eating something at his cell when I passed, an exchange of words took place and I continued on to empty my bottle. At that time, I was no longer sharing a cell with Drummer, he'd been freed, and due to myself and another inmate who'd jumped in the cell not getting along, I relocated and went into a cell with Richie Badness and Talles from Jungle. Talles became man's link through reasoning, Chucky had made it known to Talles that I was Bragga's (R.I.P) close friend and the friendship developed from there. On my return from emptying my piss-bottle, Richie Badness was in the cell and we began speaking, before I knew it, Mac-11 was at our cell with his entourage. Words exchanged between us; during the exchange of words Fire-Links was asking me what happened. It's pretty difficult to have a reasonable conversation with one person when others are speaking and shouting. Myself not making it any better I arose to their voices and it got heated. Mac-11 pulled out a bread knife. I was looking at the same weapon I'd used previously which landed me in this hell whole. Bush also pulled a knife; Richie Badness stepped in front of Bush. Mac-11 went to slap me, I leaned back and it skimmed my face. Richie Badness stood

244

between us shouting for it to stop, Fire-Links told them all to chill in an angry tone and everyone calmed down.

Word spread on the block about what happened. At that moment I was in two minds, do I retaliate or think of Freedom Street. My logical mind reminded me I was due to leave prison in a few years. I'd escaped twenty-five to life, at this point was I going to throw away everything over my pride. I had found a side of me I didn't know existed. I was learning to love me and see the true me that shone bright. I had a future ahead of me, and it wasn't in crime. Over a period of years, many inmates serving serious lengths of time, including Leppo, accused of murdering legendary reggae musician Peter Tosh, had spoken words of wisdom to me. I wasn't about to let myself down. Honestly, it's never easy biting pride and restraining anger, especially when one knows what they're capable of, but it was and is important that I did and do swallow my pride and just stay focused. The fact that they came to my cell, technically with the whole crew and tooled out too, told me they did not intend to underestimate me, and neither did I intend to underestimate myself. I found no reason to prove anything, although a few friends of mine wanted blood, I wanted freedom; this was one war I didn't need. I could see how destructive it could become, and the consequences and casualties on both sides would be high. Plus, their leadership never came at me on a disrespectful tip, I'd witnessed his approach to war when I first landed in GP, and his approach to me wasn't in any shape or form similar. A few elders on the block had talked to me about it, and told me don't worry about anything, just easy. I explained I had no intention of retaliating and left it there, although I could tell some never believed me. Fire-links and I spoke as his friends watched from a distance. Whatever they told him we didn't discuss, neither did I tell him my side of the story; I just left it there. Within a month the inmate who'd slapped me, also got slapped hard in his face by a top man on the block who didn't run with their crew. I watched as Fire-Links spoke with Blacks, Mac-11 stood there angry but unable to do anything for fear of reprisal from the Junglist himself, or his friends and connects in prison.

As time went by Fire-Links and a few other members of their crew found Freedom Street, Mac-11 and I exchanged words on the odd occasion, but the communication was never as before. This occurred before Fire-Links left, he had set it that no tension remained between us; though we both knew things would never be the same. The weight they'd had on the block disappeared, like the leadership they once had. Characters and attitudes changed; it was fascinating to me. Not that I wasn't used to seeing it from my own experience of road life, but with my new developing mindset I was seriously understanding the way people acted in front of others, walking in false strength and pride. From my youth I'd always been a lone soldier, although I'd been around street warriors and teams of warriors from different areas and they'd been around me, never did I show face, and I was always me. Back then, I wasn't always a positive person, definitely not the guy writing this book. I saw life very differently, I was where they were but had different issues at that time, but confidence in self and my capabilities was never one of my weaknesses. In fact, my overconfidence could get me into lots of problems, but then I had the mindset and ability to handle situations too. I could understand they had their own issues to deal with; likewise, I had mine; different issues affected different people. Nevertheless, we all had the same root issue, which was a poor understanding of life, but then who really does know it all. We were a product of our environment, and in prison, being or acting hard was the difference between being bullied and having an easier time, though this wasn't always the case, it was the vibe highly projected. Then there were those who acknowledged life a little bit deeper, realising that you neither had to be nor act hard, you could just be confident in what you set out to achieve and achieve it. Such a mindset made a prisoner even stronger and was why I looked up to Buck-Wheel, Zion Train and others, who didn't act hard or weak, but just focused on what they wanted and what was before them. The reality of it was to run their time and get out, nothing more nothing less.

Prisoners, like many people in society run from reality. Reality is so hard to deal with, yet is spoken of so easily. Facing reality, I realised, was and is the hardest thing anyone can do. It's not easy to live in the present, but it is to live in the past or the future. Acknowledging what one wants to achieve whether good or bad and accepting where one is coming from, whether an easy life or hardship, carries less burden, but to remain focused on the current position of life can drive one crazy. As much as I spent time reading history, looking at my personal experiences, studying biblical Hebrew with the intention of what I'd do tomorrow with the knowledge, and how I hoped family and love would be on the outside, the reality of where I was at became more and more visual. The importance of not creating false strength based on the unknown nor comforting myself with the past, but living in the present, accepting daily and momentary experiences in prison and learning from them, made me wiser and stronger. I was living the here and now. Thinking and dealing with my every experience, it taught me a lot and built me while breaking me down too; only to re-grow into something and someone that was always there but dormant. I was finding myself, on a journey of rediscovery. I was telling myself that reality begins with my perception, and that I am my greatest obstacle. In real time, I truly stood in my own way. I had so many triggers and emotional baggage, lightening the load was easier said than done, but the greatest thing is, I was not only aware of it but was in acceptance of many things, and had much to work on. I wasn't looking at prisoners or prison, well at least trying my best not to see them as part of my issue; instead, I was looking at myself. Watching and analysing how I conducted myself and acted within those parameters. My challenge was to re-educate and re-connect, to learn about the true me. I realised, even though while incarcerated I wasn't perfect and wouldn't always act correctly, the outcome for every circumstance faced both behind bars and from my youth had always been on me from day one, I was just too blind to see.

Chapter 35:
Gifts & Blessings

Besides my studying and reading, my artistic side began to shine. In fact, I didn't even know I could draw and paint so well. It all began with me drawing pictures from magazines. Because everyone knew I loved scriptures, an inmate had left two religious magazines for me to read. I had them for weeks before I thought about picking one up to read, for me it was all about my Hebrew Text, dictionary, studying and looking at the Bible. Because of my studying, I had a few pens, pencils, and books, which I used to take notes and write out Hebrew words and scriptures. One day I was just messing around drawing things in my cell; a drinking bottle, biscuits, literally anything, they looked ok. I decided to pick up one of the magazines and started to read. I found the stories of the people's lives interesting, their struggles in Palestine; to be honest I was taken by the head covering the women wore, it reflected beauty and elegance. I had knowledge of Islam back then, not as much as I do now, due to embracing all the Abrahamic books. Back then, I was fully focused on the Hebrew Text, otherwise known as Tanakh and the Bible only. But as a youth, I'd been to a few Nation of Islam meetings, and during my time in Spanish Town prison, Moses, my friend from America, spoke with me on Orthodox Islam about the prophets and the Children of Israel in the Quran. We agreed on many things, but honestly, I wasn't aiming back then to really search into any other studying. We both agreed Children of Israel were the most talked about nation in the Quran and their history and prophets were the most mentioned. Their foundation played an important role, therefore to me it was wise to truly understand the foundation of my ancestors before reading anything else. This is why, after reading the Bible from front to back, I asked my family to get me a Hebrew Text, which they did. I felt it was wise to start with the foundation. Since being free, my love for the Quran has grown, what people teach and say isn't always what is written, and so I embrace all Abrahamic books.

Drawing the sisters from the magazine wearing their hijabs, which I can't deny I found very appealing to the eye, as well as Jerusalem and landscapes in the Holy Land, I felt uplifted. This practise became a part of my daily routine; it went on for a while. The more I drew, the better I became, as with anything, practice makes perfect. Although my artwork was not perfect, I was shocking my cellmates, others and myself. People would call me Israeli for the fun of it, and ask me if I was going to Israel when freed and I would say yes, I'm going to Israel and Palestine.

But them calling me Israeli would bring up a massive conversation, about identity and race, I knew enough due to scriptures and Kemetic history prior to my incarceration, plus my mother's father would say he was a true Jew. I had more than enough evidence to prove originally Israelites were black, but it was limited knowledge to what I now know. Most of what we saw was on TV, broadcasted on Jamaican news, which at that time covered the conflict between European Jews and fair skinned Arabs, and that was a catalyst sparking conversations. I'd never stepped foot on the Holy Land back then and knew nothing of what I know now, believe me I wish I did. I'd have had so much to educate inmates on, especially on the origins of the black tribes and people indigenous to the Holy Land that never left and who still live there, including Canaanites, Ishmaelites, and some ancient Israelites. Prisoners used to say to me they've driven out all the black people, that there are no more blacks in the land based on what they saw on TV. I'd tell them we are still there but not as much; I believe God won't move us all out of the land. We'd speak on the Ethiopian Jews, who I knew about, but even prisoners who had never left Jamaica had the sense to know that the Ethiopian Jews were following European teachings. Inmates' argument was that the original way wasn't being practised, because no black people were there practising it. Truly, I had no proof, just gut feeling, for some inmates that wasn't enough, and I couldn't blame them either. Word is wind; tangible evidence of their existence was needed. I had none, scriptural content wasn't enough, and to be totally truthful, for me it wouldn't be either if I were them; I would need to see we were still there physically. The odd few inmates believed some indigenous black people were still there but the majority didn't. It was very clear, media coverage of the Israeli-Palestinian conflict never showing a black face on TV, helped to keep the very thought of our connection to the land as a thing of the past, even non-existent.

Having made more than ten documentaries on the indigenous peoples to that region known as the Middle East, rightfully North East Africa since my release from prison, has been a dream come true. I've been able to evidence all that my gut felt during those rough times in my life behind prison walls, where nothing but deep emotions comforted me. The unshakable feeling of our presence in the land, spiritually driven to accept and believe, it was nothing less than faith. I do hope that the work that I have been blessed and fortunate to carry out touches the hearts of many.

From drawing pictures in the magazine, I went on to draw family members who were amazed by my artwork. One of my best drawings was that of Minnie and Lele, which I sent to them. I'd drawn a picture of Jan and loved it so much, I put it over my bedside and decided I'd paint her the very same picture. She brought me all the paints that I needed on a visit, and then I began my venture. Blown away by what I'd done, I was channelling the deeper part of me that displayed the reality that gifts are given to all but they must be nurtured, like all things. We are multi-talented beings, nothing is one-dimensional, all living things have depth, and there is always more than one aspect to any natural thing. My artistic ability was developing rapidly, especially for someone who didn't really draw, that was more my brother JT's field, but I was seeing I had it in me too.

For one and two inmates, I drew pictures of their loved ones, which they framed and sent out. Most that asked me I turned down; for as much as I loved the newfound skill, ability and the attention it brought, my research and studies were my priority.

Drawing was something I'd do in between times. It was a talent I learnt I had.

The pride of all my artwork would definitely be the painting I did of Disney cartoon characters for Jan's little princess, not only did I personally love the painting, but so did Jan and her daughter too, which meant the world to me, because Jan meant the world to me. I truly loved and appreciated her support, love and kindness.

Not only was I reading the Holy Scriptures, but comprehending them too. Seeing each page, chapter and book in a way I had never before, all because I removed every preconceived idea and teaching and started afresh. Drawing and painting were skill sets I didn't know I had and could easily do, the fact of the matter is, I'd never given it time before, so how would I have known. As all things in life, nothing is ever known unless one seeks to invest time into finding out, to understand, to nurture and truly do it from the heart, everything must come from within. As a youth, I allowed too much to stand before me, creating my own obstacles. I was my own enemy, as mentioned before, the outcome for every circumstance and trouble faced from my youth was always on me. Controlling the outcome was my duty, one I wasn't taught about, a principle many aren't taught how to control nor shown. Young and old face this same problem all over the globe; not understanding the outcome is on them; looking for external influences and guidance, never really trusting one's own heart, not always following one's instincts. How sad, always needing that validation and acceptance from others to tell me I'm right; today I know that was wrong. So many of us seek that from others, looking for people's approval, their recognition and other acknowledgements, but neither of these really allows the true inner being to live. In society, we live to please bosses, friends, family, loved ones and so many other things, but not ourselves. Never taught to seek and love what's written on one's own heart, only to love what we see and not truly feel. I came to the realisation I needed to trust in only me, no preconceived ideas or reassurances but to seek after my passion and what makes me feel truly alive. To love what makes me happy, that uplifts my soul and do them regardless of who likes or dislikes it. In time, I told myself I would spiritually draw those necessary to aid me on my path, via the vibrational frequency I sent out. There are levels to energetic frequencies, some exchange to build, others polarize on a different spectrum only to cancel, or to stagnate the inevitable. This is the law of nature, a universal principle, many see it as the law of attraction, it can be seen like that also, but the spiritual connection that binds the universe isn't just an attraction. The more I thought about it behind the walls of confinement, I realised it had binding elements to it, as mankind are living, energetic beings and affect universal equilibrium. The power of energy, matter and vibration all send frequencies seen and unseen. The body's locomotion, the emotions we give off and the force that's felt, some call it feelings, all have their role. People are attracted to and not attracted to all of the abovementioned. From a social perspective, physical attraction limits the eye. Where freedom is expressed, meaning energy sent forth from within not taken in from the world, the attraction of spirit and energy is deeper than what meets the eye.

I understood more that by changing my actions and thought processes, consciously and unconsciously I was changing my environment and the way in which people dealt with and saw me. Reflecting on situations and issues that had taken place in my life, my youth and while in prison, I could see how my energetic levels at those particular times played a role. How warders and some prisoners treated me, the respect they showed, it was all down to the energy I gave out. I wasn't always projecting the best of me, I was still in transformational stages, so errors were expected and each error caused my physical entanglement in situations I'd have preferred not to be in. The greatest thing was that even if I didn't see my part and role at that specific moment, I did when I reflected, and understood the level of frequency I was pulsating at the time. Truly looking at the situation, I was able to comprehend what took place and was then in a position to change it, even if it was in the past. I understood from reading the Bible that even though past and future wasn't the here and now, but their energies were here in the present and therefore history could be changed and the future fashioned. All is energy and energy is power. To be the best I could be, pride and ego needed suppressing; stubbornness, depending on where I was or what I didn't want to do, could enhance or inhibit the flow or energy, weakening my frequency, I was seeing life through different eyes.

252

I was beginning to use my gifts, the ability to reason with one's own heart, to understand my errors whether they resurfaced regularly or came occasionally, I accepted them and knew they were mine. Reading scriptures daily had led me to the understanding of acceptance. Even in my sorrow, I felt blessed. Display of talent isn't just doing things such as getting better at drawing, literature, painting or even physical activity, talent was the recognition of my natural aptitude and skill that came from within. We are all born talented, we just need to seek to find. As stated before, I was channelling the deeper part of me that displayed the reality that gifts are given to all but they must be nurtured, like all things. We are multi-talented beings, nothing is one-dimensional, all living things have depth, and there's always more than one aspect to any natural thing.

Chapter 36:
Unpredictable Friendship

The struggles of Spanish Town prison were not the struggles experienced while incarcerated in GP. I had been through so much in St Catherine Adult Correctional Centre and established myself to the point that even though it wasn't done intentionally or for recognition, more people knew of me in Tower Street Adult Correctional Centre than I even realised, and many more quickly got to know who I was. Well, not *really* know me, but were familiar with who I was. The name Hebrew and my face were known to a lot of inmates. I was a lone soldier, even though I had connects that I would deal with frequently. But then there were some acquaintances or associates with whom I would connect, and many onlookers seeing how we interacted would find it weird. For me, gym was a place I'd hang out mostly during fly up and workout. Quite a few inmates did. Occasionally, I'd be working out or would have just finished and be at the shower standing soaped up, and Tommy Troubles would come over and he might ask me for $25 or $50 worth of ticket (food booklet). I'd tell him to go get it from my pocket, and the look on inmates' faces was as if to say, are you crazy? But there was a level of trust or should I say respect between us. The fear or lack of trust other inmates saw, I didn't see, nor do I assume did he sense that coming from me. Sometimes, I had at least four to five booklets each containing $500 dollars plus cash amounting to a few thousand. Nearly every inmate knew I had money when I had it, not that I would boast and show off, but I never hid money or acted like I didn't have it if I did. I didn't see a reason why I should, what was mine was mine. If an inmate asked me for something and I didn't know when I was getting money again or for whatever reason I felt I wasn't going to give or lend, my answer was no and that was it. Not that an inmate asked me regularly either, to be honest, it's something I didn't get bothered with, inmates constantly asking for money. I witnessed other foreigners and even Jamaican residents themselves going through this money issue, but not me. Until now I'd not thought about it, there were many factors I could think of as to why this wasn't my experience behind bars. I personally don't believe it had anything to do with people seeing me being a tough figure or hard man, I believe it was more principle, a level of respect for me, from where I came from and how I carried myself. I believe that played a major role in a lot of things that worked in my favour whilst incarcerated. I feel people grew to respect me as an individual and appreciated my principles. Keeping real was one thing I did. I believe prisoners appreciated that, and believe me prisoners can be the weirdest of people, unpredictable at times, but I had my way and it worked for me. I had no reason to hide what I had, nor did I feel obligated to share and I assume prisoners knew that and respected it. I never faced that situation in prison of being bullied for my own. Even from the early days, when I think about it, I had a lot of fights due to arguments. Some fights stemmed from me not having anything to give, and was therefore looked down upon, others from me not liking an inmate's tone of voice or whatever, but even when I started to get visits, no one ever tried to tell me how to spend mine. Although many inmates had gone through whatever, it wasn't my experience, so I didn't live by that fear. As I stated previously, neither did I live by the notion of showing off on the least fortunate. For I was once in that position and definitely delighted to help those in need and was very careful not to give money on the basis of buying friends, the poor were my targets. The less fortunate brought me blessings; this is what I felt.

What caused Tommy Troubles and me to interact the way we did, stemmed from Tommy Troubles previously asking me for a small thing, which I gave him. By that time, we were now no longer hailing one another as previously when I visited H North to link Zion Train, we were reasoning on the odd occasion. One day, I decided to test the waters, he asked me for a little something and I sent him to get a ticket, each ticket was $25 dollars in a $500 dollar booklet. I didn't check how much he had taken until I went back to the cell, I felt no reason to, after all I wanted to trust him and I wasn't wrong. When I counted my booklets, everything was there plus my cash too, only the $25 gone. I recall smiling to myself; it was a test and Tommy Troubles had passed, not proving to me but proving to himself, he was trustworthy. The reality is, if he had dealt with me wrong, he would have only let himself down and not me, but then he undoubtedly showed me that what I preconceived regarding him was right. I'd always felt a genuine vibe from him. Although I'd seen him mistreat others and heard of wild things he'd get up to, I never believed in judging someone based on another man's experience, it was just something I didn't and couldn't do. I had always believed in learning for myself whether good or bad, I needed my own experience; this was my character, I wanted to understand and feel for myself.

Believe me when I say this isn't always the best way to live or attitude to have, there's a saying, the wise learns from a fool. No doubt, I could be foolish at times and didn't always need to experience things. Strong character channelled wrongly had gotten me into some serious trouble on numerous occasions, and I participated in and got up to things because of wanting my own experiences that could have landed me behind bars a long time ago, or worse dead. In fact, so many things have happened in my life before and even during prison I wouldn't speak about, just based on the fact I wouldn't incriminate others and myself, but all relate to personal experiences that I desired and needed to encounter. Some experiences are based on cravings stemming from negative emotions. No matter how strong a person's character is, strength without perception is *destruction*, and I'd been chipping away at myself for a very long time. Some of us don't realise that its cravings based on emotions we're having, why we want to experience some things. What I mean by *crave*, is that sometimes things aren't about the experience, it's the emotional buzz that comes with the thought of doing it or participating that drives us. Some stimulus arrives from more than the physical experience itself; we need to think deeper. Satisfying the unscen is overlooked. Caught in mortal perceptions, dumbfounded to what kind of energies we attract, when that is mixed and confused with a strong character, a very determined soul, which is what many young people are, then it's a dangerous ride. A rollercoaster with an unpredictable drop, when reality kicks in, one can even scare oneself. Always desiring to experience for oneself isn't always the best thing. Learning from others can be just as beneficial.

Reflecting on numerous conversations with inmates close to me, I believe I was hard to read and predict, but then who wants to be predictable. I made associates and friends with some people that inmates wouldn't expect, depending on whose eyes I was viewed by, they saw me differently. In a positive way, that in principle carried a level of respect. I was unpredictable in more ways than one. I could be speaking and chilling with the most famous and known inmates, then you will see me spending time with someone no one even knows exists, and such actions I knew threw a lot of inmates off. As I said, I was unreadable and genuinely enjoyed interacting with whomever I did, when I did. For me, everyone had a story or something to say that was beneficial. Bear in mind, I'm a loner; I'd been that way from when I first entered prison. In fact, anyone who *genuinely* knew me or knows me from *road* knows that more often than not you would find me on my jack jones, (walking alone), so spending time alone behind bars was naturally a part of my character. I made a few friends early out but still had and loved my own company and sharing time with self. As mentioned before, over time I became more known throughout the prison but still remained to myself as much as possible. After all, I loved to study and think, yet when engaging, I interacted with whomsoever my spirit pleased. Whether it was some of the most respected or least respected inmates was neither here nor there, I was following my heart and emotions at that given moment. What I couldn't do was display an unstable personality to someone, switching from friendly to unfriendly, it was just something I couldn't and wouldn't do. For *me* to change the way I dealt with an inmate, there'd have to be a reason, but this kind of off-key interaction was common in others for whatever the material reason. Whether it was to gain something or when an inmate had something others didn't have or wanted, this messed up personality appeared, unveiling a disharmonised character. Witnessing personalities and companionships totally change due to material gain or benefits, was sad, it showed and displayed weakness and disloyalty too. Whereas myself, I remained loyal to me while behind bars, which made me loyal to my truth and in the way I dealt with others. Indeed, my loyalty was to my heart, my pure emotions; to myself is where my priorities lay. I learnt to love me whether I had things or not and be respectful to myself, which enabled me to respect others. Prison taught me a lot, educated me as I journeyed within. I was able to manifest my inner man. Feeling a sense of self-worth, I promised myself in life on this path of inner peace I would always aim to be loyal to my heart. This bugged lots of inmates; the fact that I dealt with all manner of people and then had moments where I'd be by myself a lot, even though most times they'd see me reading or studying, it still bugged some, because I was so unpredictable. I used to be told by inmates that they couldn't study me and my response was "Why do you need to?" Some would smile, others responded with a further question or state an accusation in a calm tone not really meaning to offend, just looking a response, one of the weirdest sentences was, "Man waan kno whose side yuh deh pon?" Even that was said with a smile and joke to follow the curiosity. My response was always do I look like I'm taking side, which usually ended it there.

Everyone knew, although many of the people close to me were from Jungle and Dunkirk, it was evident I dealt with inmates from all over the island; I wasn't about joining mass confusion.

I was very close to certain individuals from Kirk, such as Buddah and his brother Screw, as well as Likkle man, King-Kong, Jet Lee (R.I.P) and others, but then I was close with Starky, Ninie and Benbow too.

On Building block itself, I had close associates, some of my friends might consider others enemies, or incorrect associates because they lived in areas that had issues with close comrades of mine or had a problem with them in the prison before I came. My philosophy was very simple, I dealt with people, how they dealt with me, and it was never something I hid. Not that I would go around and not care about how my close comrades felt about my interaction with someone who they had problems with, and sometimes people had to be cut off, it was inevitable, but not all the time. My communication was very open, there was nothing done in secret or on the sly, everything was there to be seen. Whenever a friend of mine brought up something about a specific inmate or inmates, I'd state my point, not that this happened regularly. But it got to a stage where no one even mentioned anything about who I did or didn't deal with, and I think that also showed respect and played a role in the level of respect inmates showed me.

I had always been a man that saw life in a different way, even when I was on road, interacting with different cliques and crews. However, living and being myself doing this behind bars was another thing, and taught me that I definitely have communication skills and could interact with people as and when needed. It was a valuable lesson, truly a priceless one.

Chapter 37:
Unpredictable Showers

The showers behind Building where I located I'd say were no ones and on no-man's-land, although Building inmates claimed it as theirs even though there were a few showers built inside the block. The showers were situated right behind Building, opposite the gym with a nice piece of open land leading back to the other blocks. But this also made it no man's land, and prisoners from all over the prison would come and shower there. Its location and popularity at times caused tension although words weren't always said, however, individuals like Tommy Troubles would openly shout, "Yuh tink yuh can kill mi?" Not that he was saying it to anyone specifically, it was more of a message to everyone, or "Mi dayah, mi no trust nobody." Sometimes an inmate might respond making him know no one is planning for him, in the process breaking the tension, other times no one replied. He wasn't the only one to pass a remark; quite a few inmates made their general statements or knew whom they were throwing word at. Weapons were present on certain inmates, others wrapped theirs in their towel or just had a friend or friends watch as they shower, some did it slyly others very blatantly. The watch and swop routine was the norm for some, even the odd Building gangs, especially when specific members came out they were never alone. This was prison life, the unpredictable could occur; I guess it's better to be safe than sorry. Believe me; I've witnessed those that were sorry, not a pretty look regarding the aftermath. Seeing someone being blooded up is never pleasant, not that it happened regularly at the shower pipes, not even daily punch-ups or stabbings. Individuals and cliques moved smart and tight, eyes opened always, but when problems occurred and tension got too much, it was guaranteed action.

It was the last-minute rush that always caused most of the problems. As inmates who lived further away needed to get back to their block and those who located close by, for example within Building believed the showers belonged to Building and this would and could cause inmates to buck heads. Sometimes inmates from around the front, referring to Remand section or on any of the North blocks, may start something. Some inmates just wanted to prove on others and that caused arguments, or an individual being slapped or punched in the face leading to a fight if not stopped, or something worse.

Last minute showering was hardly ever done by the so-called simple inmates; it was always the roughnecks, footballers and us gym guys. Many of the footballers were located in Building, then there were us gym guys, individuals like Ticker, Gunmout, Sappa da Bull, Gorilla and Shotback who also was a big footballer too, and trust, none of them were pushovers. Sometimes, so many dangerous men all looking to shower last minute could be rough. But as always, it was noticeable even when tension was high, when the most serious inmates were all in one place, the desire to war and fight is less than when a few hotheads with something to prove step in the midst. Personally, I really had no problems when I showered. The only occasion when I was hurt at the shower pipes was when the pieces of the prison wall hit me during the attempted breakout, but then that wasn't done purposely. Whoever planted the dynamite did not intend to hurt the few inmates that were there; I believe it was a job gone wrong.

Chapter 38:
St Ann & I

Word came to me on the block, a friend from St Ann told me that a mutual friend of ours from Runaway Bay had just been processed and located around the front. Whilst locked up in jail during the early stages of my remand, I'd heard Crack-Star (R.I.P), wanted me dead because of the incident that occurred down at St Ann, leading to my incarceration. Believe me when I say I was confused as hell at the thought of him wanting me dead, as we were tight from the moment I landed in Jamaica as a youth Crack-Star and the other scheme men had maximum respect for me and the feeling was mutual. If I'm not mistaken, I was one of the only Derry youth at that time that scheme men respected, moved with and showed that honour to. Here we were in prison, Crack-Star and I, truth was definitely going to come out or shit was going to go down. Whichever way, I was going to know what was really up. With us both behind bars, there was no need to rush around front and seek to find out if there was any truth in what I'd heard. He had never taken side against me, even when his cousin and I had an altercation in front of Brampton's bar. Not proud of my actions, as his cousin Mr Jump aka Bad-Indian had once saved my life on the beach, but when liquor and too much weed is absorbed, unusual characteristics sometimes unfold, and I'd wounded him with my friends three-star ratchet. Even with the altercation between his cousin Bad-Indian and I, Crack-Star and myself were still cool, so I wondered if it was true or just people creating rumours. Nevertheless, he was a youth not to take lightly and now we were both behind bars, locked away in GP, it was only a matter of time until we ran into one another.

Within days, I saw him out on the grass. I had left Building and gone to F North to visit friends and there he was stepping through the arches. I watched him as he walked down the pathway, he had not noticed me standing there in the midst of my friends, and neither did he look in my direction as he walked on about his business. For me timing was everything and to approach him or to call him to come over to where I was when I was with my people would send the wrong message. I knew he knew I was there in GP and not Spanish Town prison, and he also knew I had a lot of connections too. If he had no intentions to ever start anything and still saw me as a close friend, it could be problematic or cause feelings if I approached him now, as my people would hear the conversation too, and they might respond unpredictably. There was no predicting what their response could be. They may say nothing, but then if they start sizing him up, looking at him in any off-key way, or worst-case scenario, say something to him on the strength of my questions or our conversation, it could cause him to react or get paranoid and I didn't need any of that. Clarity was what I needed; there was no room for error. Knowing street mentality, especially when friends have one another's back, misunderstood loyalty from friends can escalate situations making them worse. Even though they have your best interest at heart, their actions or reactions can trigger or cause the unpredictable, and I wasn't looking to put my friends or myself in problems. My loyalty towards my friends aligned my heart on a straight path, a path that would keep them out of problems. I wanted for them what I wanted for myself. I was far more conscious of my actions than my youthful days, I was moving more wisely. Clarity is always the best way; to me it was essential. As Crack-Star walked about his business and out of sight, I wondered if he heard different things regarding myself too. I had been told he wanted me *dead*, what could *others* of said to him about *me*, and my feelings towards *him*, not that I had any, but people can be very mixed up. Over the years, I've seen, witnessed and heard the passa passa (gossip and confusion) between some prisoners and people with whom they had contact on road, and it was something I didn't really want a part of. However, this was my life at question, whether I hated or loved contention, it was something that needed to be dealt with and I planned to, but I was growing wiser, no longer young and hotheaded. Well, trying not to be, my intention was to tread wisely and smartly.

Crack-Star and I met as he was returning from wherever he had come from. I approached him on my own. "Rudy wha gwaan," he smiled and laughed. Anyone who knows Crack-Star knows he had a funny laugh. Responding back, I laughed too and we began to speak. He filled in the missing pieces, as he spoke, in my mind I thought about how much people love confusion, or was he withholding his true feelings and intention, or maybe it had changed now that we were face to face, both knowing my capabilities. Additionally, I was in a position where anything I wanted to do could be done; so was he just acting wisely. Whichever way, no expression of dislike was displayed; it was as if we were still youths on the scheme reasoning as one family. To be honest, that suited me well. He expressed no acknowledgment of the claim that he wanted me dead or was going to try to take my life. That whole topic ended right there and we discussed further about St Ann and what was happening down in the Garden Parish. He told me a few things that made me laugh, if they were true or not it put a smile on my face nevertheless, jokes were needed and are a valuable treasure in a place full of so much tension. Even Crack-Star referred to me as Hebrew during our conversation. He'd heard and knew of the transformation I had begun from beyond the prison walls, and showed respect for it, not that we'd discussed scriptures or anything about God really, although I brought up the Most High once or twice. Our conversation was a lot about St Ann, both past and present, in fact, speaking with him caused me to do some serious thinking about my life as a youth in the Garden Parish of Jamaica.

During lockdown I lay there in my cell. Deep in thought, my mind travelled from experience to experience. Looking back, I tried to understand the drivers of my actions in specific circumstances encountered during visits to my mother's birth land. Self-reflection was something I did a lot under lock. As I lay there allowing thoughts to come and go, while holding on to the thought of the man I now felt growing from within, where I wanted to be mentally, even though I knew this was only the beginning of the journey, it felt good. I had so much to learn about myself and looked forward to it. I had come from a troubled and dark place, I was now seeing a brighter me, a happier me. This joy didn't come without pain. I had so much to face, but every time I did reflect, accept and move upon my feelings, it felt good, but it was never easy, not an easy task at all. As I stated earlier, the countless things that occurred down in St Ann are enough to write a book about in itself. On numerous occasions I've come face to face with death, been caught up in problems and even hurt the people I cared for. I was a troubled child, no excuses, but I had issues and didn't have the greatest outlook on life, nor did I have the knowledge to know within me existed the tools to aid me. I was too busy looking outside or hoping for someone else to do it for me. But then who could help me if I didn't express myself? Could anyone really give help to someone who wasn't in the right frame of mind to receive, it's quite simple, the answer is no. You can bring a horse to water but you can't make him drink. If I were not mentally ready to intake because I was not ready to give, there would be no aid for me at all; change would begin with me, and me alone. The key was to help or get me to the right frame of mind, and that itself was a challenge. I first had to accept and know the root of the problem. There were many factors to take into account, which played a role in my actions and life choices. Numerous contributing factors that caused me to do things that the average child wouldn't do, well least I hope not the child next door. I wouldn't wish my life choices on anyone, but then anyone next door can be experiencing similar hurt as myself and distribute their emotions in the same way or even worse. There is so much that goes on behind closed doors, whether physical doors pertaining to family life or mental doors regarding one's thought patterns, it can be quite scary. Truth is, it's better to express oneself; try finding someone to open up to. Believe me; taking certain kinds of wrong approaches to deal with problems only creates more problems. It's far better to find a more positive outlet to channel such energy, unfortunately, I never had that, and my reality is as such.

I'd just reached Jamaica for the first time. It was 1989 and within weeks, I had problems with a youth from a very wealthy, powerful family in Brown's Town, St Ann. The altercation with this youth occurred outside a bar in Runaway Bay over a girl, well, indirectly over a girl. Those days Patrick Ewing basketball boots were in fashion and I had various pairs in all different colours. Believe me, on my initial visit to the island I travelled looking the part, I had a few sovereigns on my fingers, my little chain on my neck and my British accent, I was good to go.

I'd met the local shop and bar owner's daughter and we began talking. I'd seen her a few times in the morning on her way to school and in no time we were friends, close friends, I was cool with both her and her big sister. One night, this well-established man's son from Brown's Town came to visit a friend of his who lived across the road from the bar where people usually hung out. On seeing me talking with her, he just greeted her and went back to dealing with his friend. He had known her from school, at that time I didn't know they were school friends, but then there was no reason to want to know anything about him. I promised her earlier that evening like various other nights I'd escort her up from the shop premises to the house. The hour came for her to go home, I stood there waiting for her as she spoke with people and said her goodbyes, when he approached her again. Words were exchanged between them but she kind of blew him off, it was then he bruised my ego and hurt my pride. I most definitely wasn't in the right state of mind as he didn't come up close in my face, neither did he remain in our presence after saying what he said, instead he walked off. Nevertheless, my ego and state of mind was troubled, I felt disrespected and he was going to pay for it. He had called me, "Eidat foreign bwoy!" and that was enough for me to start premeditating on him, to desire to hurt him. I was filled with false pride, ego and believed I had something to prove, so plot for him I did.

I walked her home and marched down the hill, hoping to see him still outside the shop. My ego told me not only that she'd heard him, but also others out there too, and I wasn't to let him get away with words, that's right just words, how ignorant. On seeing him still there I picked up a bottle. Without saying a word to him I slapped him in the face with it. As he backed off I threw it at him and all hell broke loose. One of my stepfather's nephews got involved, not that I needed the help, as I punched and kicked the hell out of him. It didn't last long as people broke us up, but he was clearly wounded. I know for sure he'd never felt so many punches and kicks in his life. When they told me who he was, in my rage I swore I didn't care, and I didn't, in fact, I wanted his blood. I was a young, troubled and very angry child. I guess I'd been hurt so much as a youth, at times, it would come out in my reactions to situations.

Trouble never sets like rain and I knew I would have to deal with him again. Late 1989 all the way through to late 1990 was a very crazy year for me. I mean, 1990 was a true nightmare. I visited Jamaica three times between the period of 1989 to 1990 costing my mother serious money in flights and expenses because I couldn't get my act together. I can never forget the year 1990. I had left England early that year due to problems with the law and streets, headed for Jamaica for a fresh start. Knowing the altercation I had with this top man's son from Brown's Town on my previous visit, I convinced myself all would be good, although I knew I'd have to deal with him again. My mother and I spoke and I promised I'd make a go of it, which honestly, I wanted too, but trouble also seemed to follow me, or should I say, I carried trouble as an accomplice, whichever way, trouble was present. Therefore, I left the UK with trouble by my side.

In Jamaica, I was in constant disputes with some of my stepfather's nephews and wasn't at ease with my surroundings. But this wasn't all down to me and my troubles, they were doing things and acting in ways that I wasn't going to let slide. Being the strong character I was, I was very verbal even physical when need be. Not to mention I had arguments and problems with a few local youths, and I experienced another encounter with the son of Brown's Town's elite. I knew it was bound to happen, although I did my best to avoid it.

Months had passed since our first encounter; in fact, it was a new year, 1990. That saying, 'out with the old and in with the new' wasn't always true, well not in my case it wasn't, hell no, he was carrying 1989 in his heart and made it known.

One day I was on the beach with one of my stepfather's cousins and a bunch of guys from Runaway Bay. I had walked up to the shower pipe with a few friends; can't remember why I was going to wash off, but all I know is I heard someone say, "See him there." When I looked at them, I froze mentally for a second but didn't make them any the wiser, so I stared at them as they stared at me. There he was with a few of his friends, they were on motorbikes and two cars were parked up beside them. They weren't there because of me but just to chill, nevertheless, we were all at the public beach in Runaway Bay and shit was about to go down. We turned back and walked down to the beach. When I told my stepfather's cousin and the others, and the guys who were with me explained who was up there with this man's son, their reaction weakened my soul and even got me frightened. I learnt a powerful thing then, not that I didn't know it before, but when accompanied by anyone who shows fear in battle or in anything one's aiming to do positive or negative, it can also have a very bad impact on one's own mindset. Hence, from a youth I loved and delighted in accompanying myself and counting on my own emotions and not the energy of others, yet I didn't know why I was like that and still am today. Nothing do I love more than my own company. I have always felt that I am my strongest asset. Many years later in prison I would see when reading the Torah this was universal law, not to mention global logic. What I had experienced on the beach was genetic emotion; it was something that ran in my DNA. Historically my ancestors believed in the very same principle. The book of Deuteronomy Chapter 20 talks of the faint-hearted to return home lest his brethren's heart faint as well as his heart. Without trying to make them sound worse than they were, every man but one of the guys who came with me to Runaway Bay public beach, decided to swim out to sea instead of walking back up with me. I had taken a Rambo knife off a youth who considered himself a so-called friend. Friends don't take to the sea when problems are at hand on dry land I thought. One of them tried to encourage me to swim and stay down on the beach as if that would help the situation; they were scared, that was the plain reality, and they opted for the sea. I mean realistically how long could I stay in the water before I had to face them. Gripping the Rambo knife, I looked at it as all manner of thoughts ran through my mind. The knife was one of those fisher knives with a compass on the top. Staring at the knife, I told myself there was no other way home apart from going past the youth and the guys that were with him. I had strengthened myself and told myself it was time for war. I couldn't believe it, every man with me was faint hearted, I was alone. From nowhere a Jamaican Indian walked over and began

268

speaking to the fool that stood talking to me trying to convince me not to go up there, as if they were really going to leave knowing I was on the beach swimming, yeah right. Others started to come out of the water wherein they ran for refuge and began explaining to this tall slim Indian man what was going on. At that time, I didn't know it was Crack-Star's cousin, Bad-Indian. Bad-Indian had heard enough, he picked up a big thick piece of wood and said come, without hesitation I walked with him swearing to myself I will never go beach with those *bitches* again, and if it's war it's war, his actions lifted my spirit and strengthened my heart, I felt totally confident again.

As we walked up to where they were, he made sure to walk as close to them as possible, he was smart and strategic; he walked directly at them instead of walking past them on the beachfront. "You're his bodyguard?" One of them asked, the way Bad-Indian replied neither of them said anything. I held the Rambo knife tight in my hand with blood in my eyes as we both walked through the valley of the shadow of death. That day I swore I was a dead man. Well, I told myself I was going out fighting and one of them was coming with me. The sigh of relief I made when we'd reached way across the road heading towards the stables as if heading back to Centre. I felt an instant release of tension. I thanked him and brought him a drink that evening, in fact we drank a lot that evening and many times after that, as we became good friends.

I had found myself in other problems, mainly within the surroundings of the stepfamily. Half the times they couldn't find me, I would do my own thing and come back in the evening or at night; I didn't like to hang around much. There were many uncomfortable moments, not all were their fault or started by them, but things weren't pleasant for me and I was never really settled, so I found myself back in the UK after begging and pleading with my mother.

Repeating my errors of my past, I got into more trouble with the law and had to leave again, this time I jumped out of the frying pan into the fire. I got myself into more problems and fights in Jamaica, and worse, I was held at the airport and locked up in Central for intent to export weed from the island. I'd skipped bail in the UK, as previously mentioned, on a robbery charge, before getting locked up for trying to export cannabis. That whole year was just a back and forth, back and forth cycle that benefited me nothing and only brought more problems to my family.

When I really look back on it, I was truly in a confused place mentally. My mother had taken me away from the drama in the UK, only to go Jamaica and repeat the cycle not once, not twice but three times. I was arrested and charged with robbery on my second return to the UK, only to skip bail, which made it my third trip. Whilst in Jamaica I was told I needed to return to face court but only returned due to my mother coming to get me out of custody, and not only me but my stepfather too. Wow, how costly and unnecessary, all that back and forth says the man I am today, but looking at it from the mind of the youth I was back then says another thing. I was crying out, for what, I still don't have all the answers for, but I know I was hurting inside, confused, and had a lot of misplaced anger that led to me making poor choices regarding my morals.

As I stated previously, I hated St Ann and used to think the Garden Parish was bad luck for me, but now in my maturity I understand it was my energy, vibe and lack of self-control that brought all the troubles I'm about to explain that occurred in my life there. Believe when I say there are so many things I wouldn't even think to talk of because of the repercussions it could have on me and others, not to mention hurting reputations, destroying lives and legacies of some still living today and those who have transitioned to the realm of the ancestors.

As a youth, I found it hard to deal with some of my stepfather's family, I guess they didn't always agree with my company and I didn't always agree with their methods and lifestyle. Word came back to me several times that people would say I would end up dead one day in Town. Those days I would leave St Ann and head to Kingston, Portmore or Spanish Town by myself and loved doing it. To be frank, the only thing that kept me coming back to St Ann was my little sister Minnie and my partner who later became my son's mother. I really didn't care what my stepfather's family or anyone thought about me. I didn't give a shit if they wished me dead or not, I was in my own world mentally and was doing me. One day I left Kingston and returned to St Ann only later that night to receive a message that my friend Panhead (God rest his soul) had just been killed. It hurt me deeply, only a few days before I'd seen him in Drewsland and we had a really good conversation about life. Anyone who knew the artist on a personal level knew his reasoning ability and insight to life had expanded joyfully and reflected in his later music, and not even his music truly showed the highest consciousness Panhead was really on. One would have to had reasoned with him to understand truly. My brethren who had told me of Panhead's transition to the realm of the ancestors walked up the road with me, where we linked a few other friends, and chilled for a bit. The demise of the artist hit us both hard I would say. Returning to the house later that night didn't help my feelings, I was told that it was said that if I kept going to Kingston, I would be next. The following morning, I kissed my sister and girlfriend and was off, I headed straight to Drewsland and Waterhouse. At times I really disliked my surroundings in St Ann. Looking back on it now, although my little sister knew I loved her and would do anything for her, I believe I neglected Minnie to a degree and my duty as a big brother; because I was unable to handle my situation and surroundings, I ran a lot. But when we were together which was much more than I was away, we truly loved and had one another's back.

I had so many altercations in St Ann, whether it occurred in Runaway Bay, Brown's Town or St Ann's Bay where I'd hang out in the ghetto, at times it would work to my favour. I had won a lot of respect on the streets with the people, that name Rudy was respected by a lot of people in St Ann. It also made a lot of serious enemies too. A very famous police officer swore to kill me, after I slapped someone related to him. I remember him telling me he's going to kill and send me back to England in a box. My response to his threat was a warm smile. I knew how dangerous he was, he was known to pour Pepsi Cola over his victims; by the grace of God, I wasn't one of them.

Late one evening a man was being pulled down Runaway Bay, led by an angry crowd of people coming from Mt Olivet. They were heading with him to the police station. He was battered and bruised, with blood coming off his face and body. Every bus that passed the people would ask what he did, even a bus driver came out of his seat to slap him with a stick when he heard that the man was caught having sexual intercourse with an animal. A lot of people hit him with all manner of things, but a few people were saying my friend and I had butted him with our ratchet knives. To me, I didn't know why people loved my name so much in their mix up. I had no knowledge of what they were talking about. Even if it was true, so many people had hit him, why was there a need to focus on us, but I guess that was their personality, they just liked to talk. There was a time when that side scheme behind Brampton's bar in Runaway Bay was uninhabited; it was in the process of being built so all the houses that were put there were under security protection. Some of the security guards and myself began to link, and so some of the locals started to say we had guns that weren't legal but the police paid them no mind as the security were licensed firearms carriers. I guess they saw a few of us were too close with them and didn't feel comfortable with the situation. Us being over there at night and they not knowing what we were doing, as it was off limits to the public, made some people most sceptical, but this was the foolishness man had to put up with.

I had non-stop problems at Brown's Town College; forget about high school in St Ann, I couldn't even focus on that, my mind was elsewhere. College I hoped would be different, but I just couldn't settle anywhere. My college problems and distractions stemmed from when I bucked heads with a few guys from a place called Salem, which was known for its go-go club, drugs and rude boys and we got on, as they say in England, like peas in a pod. We got up to all manner of mischief when I should have been at college, I was too busy enjoying girls giving me private dances and doing non-productive things. Well, that's how I see it today, back then it was a whole other story. Those days I made a few extra dollars at times, and got a lot of respect from the owner of Salem's local sound system and their close followers, some of whom were friends of mine. If I remember correctly, the sound system was named Conqueror. They would give me some money, and I'd go to the studio and get them dub plates, from up and coming artists to Jamaica's hottest in those days, which undoubtedly was the Prophet, Capleton.

One of my not so pleasant moments in St Ann was when Bad-Indian and I clashed. He was someone I had a lot of respect for, he had saved my life on the beach and we became really close, but one night he made problems with one of my close friends from Drewsland. Hothead was a dangerous individual, known to have a few screws missing; even in his local area, people didn't know how to take him. But to me back then he was the most loyal soldier a man could have, along with his cousin from Jungle, and a few others. Hothead had family that had moved down to Runaway Bay St Ann, so all of us down in the country together were a mad force of love and strength. With them, I felt family love, even when Hothead and some of the others went back to Kingston, Minnie and I would still chill out with their family, which made it nicer then to be in Runaway Bay. His niece was Minnie's best friend, and someone I cared for very dearly.

Alcohol and weed in excess can cause so many problems, I witnessed this on many occasions, and one night sadly it contributed to my incident with Bad-Indian. We were all outside the bar drinking and talking when Bad-Indian came over and started speaking with me. The conversation turned sour quick. I knew Bad-Indian was drunk; he would never behave like that towards me if he were sober. Myself, I was high and drunk too, but still conscious enough to humble myself. My friends weren't and Hothead started to tell him to leave and go away, after all, they weren't friends and never knew one another. He began to get abusive and told me to tell my friends how dangerous he was. Bad-Indian himself was no pushover, I knew that, but his attitude wasn't doing him any favours, nor were my friends feeling him. At this point, I was trying to calm him down, but the more I'm telling Bad-Indian to chill, the more he's getting louder and abusive. Hothead whispered something to his cousin and they started to move in separate directions. I clocked the play, Bad-Indian did also, but his eyes were on the cousin whose ratchet was in his hand, with only the butt showing. Those day's youths, especially town youths, used to cut off the top of the case wherein the blade of the three-star ratchets was, so the point of the knife was always accessible making it easy to butt someone with it. But Hothead had his three-star wide open, drunk and high but conscious enough for me to assume he wanted to stab him and kill him there and then. Not that a man can't die if he gets butted in his head a good few times, but Hothead's knife was always glazed with garlic and I knew he wanted the distraction. Bad-Indian would have never felt those stabs if the play had worked due to the garlic. Instantly I stepped between them, everything happened fast after that. I pushed Bad-Indian aside and we got into an altercation. Grabbing his long hair pulling him downwards I took the three-star from Hothead and sliced him a few times in his back. There I was warring with the very man who'd once saved my life. Looking back, it was a moment I wish had never happened. Same time I'd attacked Bad-Indian, I was moving him out of the direction of Hothead's cousin who tried to butt him. It all happened fast and I told my friends let's leave. I remember people screaming my name as I lifted up my arm, I know they thought I was going to stab him, but that wasn't my intention, as drunk and high as I was, I loved Bad-Indian. That night everything went too far. The following day people told me they thought I was going to kill him, and all manner of foolishness came out of some of their mouths about my friends and I. We weren't all to blame; Bad-Indian had played his role in it too. I really didn't even want it to reach where it had, Bad-Indian was someone I loved dearly, but things got out of hand. Liquor and weed in excess had allowed unfamiliar characteristics to manifest both in Bad-Indian and myself. He was never usually like that, nor was I, well, not towards him anyway, but it was a crazy night. Later the next evening he showed me his back under the light of the lamppost outside the bar, all I could do was bite my lip. We reasoned and he told me so many people wanted him to press charges against me, but he swore to me he wouldn't do that, and he knew I was returning to England and my mother was coming to Jamaica to get me. In fact, he was one of the only people that knew my mother was coming for me in 1994 the year my mother died after bringing me back to the UK. That's how close Bad-Indian and I were. Over a period, I'd told Bad-Indian a lot about my life, we had many heart-felt conversations. But when word got out that I was heading back to the UK, I'm talking weeks after the altercation, some people tried urging him to get me locked up, but what they didn't know was that I knew their wicked and bad-minded intentions, Bad-Indian hid nothing from me. There were a lot of bad-minded people around me, but divine mercy and grace was never far away. I'd made many errors in my life, some I have to live with forever, but the underlying fact is, even during my troubled days, I had compassion and love within me, it took a similar heart to see that and Bad-Indian did. Sadly, certain people down in St Ann judged and saw me wrongly.

One of my craziest and scariest moments was in 1997. Again, drunk and high, but this time I was leaving Kingston 8 to visit my son in the country. Accompanied by two friends, we were heading to St Ann; an ex-soldier was driving the rental, with me in the front passenger seat, and our other friend behind me. Only God alone knows why, but as we passed Ocho Rios and headed toward Priory, the car just lost control and flipped over. No doubt, God loves me why I'm still here. I wasn't wearing a seatbelt and I was heading through the front windscreen. The driver braced me with his arm, and my friend who sat behind me held my clothing I was told. Poor me, I was too out of my head to even know what the hell was going on, to be honest I don't even remember bracing myself but I did they told me, clearly it wasn't enough as they had to hold me too. If I had come out of the car when it flipped over, I may have been crushed by it when it turned over again. "St Ann is a curse." My friends told me I was saying. We headed straight back for town leaving the rental I'd taken out where it was.

The worst situation that happened down in the garden parish, well the worst of what I'm willing speak of, has to be what led to my incarceration. That was in 1998, and knowing my son who was only three at that time witnessed it, which I didn't know he even saw until recently in his adulthood, he told me things that only saddened my heart and brought tears to my eyes. To know he saw so much and carried that in his mind isn't healthy. I'm just thankful to the Most High he's come out a good man and it hasn't affected him negatively. To the Greatest, I give praises. Nevertheless, truth of what led to it, directly and indirectly had never been explained. So many rumours regarding my actions, what led to it and why, the story in itself is trouble. Nothing is never ever as clear-cut as people make it out to be; there's always more than meets the eye. As I stated before, today I see St Ann in a completely different light from when I was young. Not that good never happened there, because I have some good memories, but a huge amount of bad things happened to and with me. The problem was, I never saw my contributing elements to the situation and that was my downfall. Not on all occasions was I to blame, but when I did play a role, I didn't see it, or at times overlooked it. This is how I dealt with things over and over again. I overlooked my actions and it indirectly played a role in leading me to hell behind bars.

Chapter 39:
Facts from Fiction

The rumour in the beginning that had reached many ears as to why I was incarcerated, was that I had killed the youth over my son's mother, which made no sense. After all, we had separated back then for almost four years and I was in a relationship with the mother of my children in England. Even though we were going through our ups and downs, we were still together and strongly in love. I mentioned before, Lele had forgiven me for my inability to be faithful back then, not that I always cheated. However, my son's mother in Jamaica, well that was another story. We were not together, however, she still wanted me, and I'd taken advantage of it. A man's greatest downfall is thinking from between his legs and not from his heart and head.

The main purpose of me leaving London for Jamaica in 1998 was to pursue a career in music. Back then, I was an artist and heavily into music, the streets were something I was really determined to put behind me even though I still made errors, plus I was on the search for self via the Rastafarian faith. I also intended to get my name signed on my son's birth certificate. By the time he was born, late in 1994, I'd already returned to the UK with my mother. As I stated before, a short time after my return, my mother had fallen sick pretty quickly and everything went downhill from there. My son's mother in Jamaica and I were having problems. Truly, it was minor, but I believe the distance between us didn't help. My mother had just passed, and the pressure and arguments that followed were too much for me, so I ended the relationship. I had reunited with Lele my childhood sweetheart who stood beside me through the rough times that I was facing. At that time, we had no children together.

Not being present when my son was born in Jamaica was something I regret, but there were reasons why I didn't return later that year, particularly my mother's transition. My son's mother had put my name down at the registry office in Jamaica, but my acceptance as father through the form of a signature wasn't there. I knew if I really wanted my son in England with me, for legal purposes my signature was essential on his birth certificate. It was early days and I wasn't going to ask his mother for him, he needed his mother's care and I needed to get my life back together where I was now resettling in the UK.

Although there were past problems with members of my stepfather's family and we didn't always see eye to eye, we were bound together for life. My son's mother in Jamaica was related to my stepfather. She had come from Portmore to live in St Ann where we met. We were friends at first, in fact when we started to date, no one knew, we clicked and a relationship developed in secret. She was slightly older than I was and very athletic at that time. In fact, she was really different and sweet in the beginning. I guess problems and people can change one's character, not that everything is or was all down to her, it most definitely wasn't. I played a major role in changing her and not for the best either; my actions would affect me very badly in the long term. I must admit, what I did when I returned to Jamaica for the first time since my mother transitioned in 1994, didn't help the situation between her family, her and myself. I had fooled around with my son's mother in Jamaica the night I landed in 1997. Purposely I had booked my ticket for Montego Bay and asked my family from Kingston 8 to pick me up at the airport. Knowing we had to pass St Ann when leaving Montego Bay in order to reach Manning's Hill in Kingston; I planned to surprise her and show up, which I did. That night, I gave her clothes, sneakers, jewellery and money for my son, and also gave her a little piece of me for old time sake, before heading into Kingston. I also promised to come spend a night or two with her and my son. My son's mother in Jamaica held onto my every word and I knew she would, even though it was my plan to go back there and sleep with her, things didn't quite go as planned. Nevertheless, I was stupid, totally stupid. It's really crazy

278

how a man can literally be in love and still cheat. I loved my children's mother back in England, we were together from early teens and had broken up when I left the country and then got back when I returned years later. We had a long history and a strong relationship, yet I still had the desire to have my cake and eat it. I acknowledge now that even though I may have loved her, I didn't truly love and honour myself. It wasn't about Lele it was about me. I didn't love me, if I really did, I would have loved myself enough to treat her and love her how she loved me. Looking back, I didn't comprehend love. I was lacking true respect for self; reflective image and the attributes love brings; faithfulness sits at its core. They say *hell hath no fury like a woman scorned;* and to my son's mother in Jamaica, I had embarrassed her, and honestly, looking back on my actions, I'm in total agreement. However, how I think she dealt with me; I don't agree with. The wrath of an angry woman isn't to be taken lightly. As I stated, the night I returned to Jam-Down for my first visit since my mother transitioned and my son was born, I had intercourse with my son's mother after giving her things for my little one, and left her hanging onto my every word. I made three major mistakes in the one night. The first, was the lack of self-honour and respect, the second was betraying Lele's trust and having sex with my son's mother, and the third was promising my son's mother I would stay with her a night or two, which I didn't even do after all. I know it wasn't just the fact I said I would come back and spend time and didn't, which led my son's mother to carry such anger for me, but it was what happened when I returned to St Ann the day I was leaving the country to return to the UK. That was the catalyst for the problem to occur in the future, and contribute to me ending up behind bars.

In truth, my initial trip to Jamaica in 1997 wasn't to see my son or his mother but was a business trip, street related and was only for a week, plus I was meeting two friends from London to do a little *sporting* as Jamaican's would say. But of course, I knew if I was going back to Jamaica, I had to see my son for the first time in person and his mother, as stated, hence why I came in via Mo Bay.

During that week, whilst in Kingston I did attempt to visit St Ann. Two of my friends journeyed with me down to country, so in truth, my promise was broken from the get go, the universe knew I had no intention to stay. I didn't even get a chance to see my son. The car ended up flipping over, if it wasn't for my soldier brethren the driver of the vehicle, and my friend Jumbo, who sat right behind my seat, I may not be here right now. Instantly we turned back and headed to Kingston on a bus.

The day before the crash, I'd met one of Jaro's friends from West Kingston. We'd made a trip to Tivoli to visit a few people, where my lustful eye beheld this beautiful browning and the rest was history. She'd come back up to Kingston 8 with us; in fact, she was also staying up those sides too. Temptation always makes the path easy, with her being on the ends, what was there to stop me? Truth is, my love for my partner in the UK should have been enough to stop me, but it wasn't, and I didn't respect myself enough to respect her, so I delighted in entertaining greed, exploring the emotions of lust. The thing about emotions is, any kind of emotional feeling an individual has is based on a powerful energy. Emotions are just forces of energy that only last for a moment in time, until another emotion comes along. Experiencing emotions is not bad, but it's what kind of emotions, where they stem from, and how we chose to use them, when taking all that into account, it can affect us for good or bad. In this situation, well, mine got the better of me and not for the best reason either.

The day I was leaving Jamaica the female from Tivoli had told me she wanted to come to the airport, caught up in my emotions I didn't hesitate to say yes. Wrong move, I was thinking from below not above, too much sexual energy. I knew I was going to pass by my son, his mother was at work but I was passing there nevertheless, lust and confusion should have been the last thing on my mind.

My aunt's boyfriend brought the car to a halt outside my son's mother's home. We all got out and I began speaking to her people. I had introduced my son to his family. Although I hardly knew him, we seemed to bond just like that, genetics I guess. My son and the woman from Tivoli got talking and he seemed to like her too. Because I had told the browning the truth that my son's mother and I were finished, naturally she felt no reason to hide the fact that we were having a sexual relationship when one of my son's mother's cousins tried to give her sweet talk, thinking she was family to me. What made it worse was at one point the browning was all over me.

When I returned to England, I spoke to my son's mother from Jamaica. She cursed me over the phone, telling me she had told her family I was coming back to spend time and spoke highly of me to them, and this is how I repaid her. In my ignorance I played wrong and strong and started to throw out into the universe what she already knew; which was, we weren't together and other things, but she also threw back into the universe the principle of what I promised and what I did to offend her. On the phone that day, she promised to get me back. I laughed at her, but damn, if I had even the slightest thought such a level of wickedness was in the pipeline, I'd have found another method of reaching my son instead of going to St Ann when I visited Jamaica in 1998, the following year.

Lele also found out about the lady from Tivoli, it hurt her deeply and at that time, in that moment I realised how much of a fool I was. She was devoted to me, but in my lack of understanding of love, I had wounded her. It would take time to heal and was an unnecessary blow to an innocent soul. As time went by since my return from JA in 1997, being the loving and supportive queen Lele was, we began discussing sending for my son. She'd forgiven me for my errors and we were really making a go of it. Lele and I talked about bringing my son to England on numerous occasions to live with us, but I knew that just having my name on his birth certificate without it being signed by myself for legal purposes wasn't going to work. It would need to be dealt with, so I would have to return to Jamaica and deal with it. 1998 I had touched Jamaica; as mentioned before, this trip was about music and my son, as well as avoiding a situation that lingered in the air like a bad scent. Believe me, at that time I was more focused on positivity, but things happen, the past isn't always easy to shake, nor does the street want to release its captives, and trust, I wanted nothing to mess up what my children's mother and I were building, so going to JA was perfect timing. My partner at that time and I were both musicians, Lele was and is an amazing singer. We invested together to make things happen, so I went while she stayed with the children, handled work commitments and everything else that comes with the upkeep of family life. We were not only partners in relationship, but in business too.

Unable to cry, yet tears came to my eyes as I thought about myself leaving Kingston city to visit my son, who was at that time and still is, living in the parish of St Ann. The journey was meant to be a trip that would bring me and my firstborn closer, instead it became the disaster that led to my incarceration. My journey to the parish of St Ann was only supposed to be a day trip or two so I only had a few garments with me. I called his mother and made her aware of why I was coming. The objective was to get my signature on my son's birth certificate. It's funny because I didn't quite fancy visiting St Ann, it was a parish I disliked at the time, and the worst things that occurred in my life in Jamaica were connected with that parish as a youth, so returning there wasn't a pleasant thought, yet it had to be done. What also got me bugged out was when I told my son's mother I was coming to St Ann to sort out my name on my son's birth certificate, it was the way she went quiet and said OK. I still remember how calm her tone of voice was. I remember thinking about it, but me being stubborn I overlooked my feelings and left Kingston for St Ann the following day. Knowing my dislike at that time for the parish, my friends from the area offered to come, but I turned them down. They even offered to drop me; and I turned that down too. Whatever was going through my mind, the cosmos knew, because this wasn't me; turning down a comfortable ride and companionship, heading into territory I didn't like, but I did it nevertheless and took a bus by myself. I guess if my people were with me, things wouldn't have happened how they did and maybe I wouldn't have gone to prison. However, when I look at the man I've become and everything that occurred on the outside while I was incarcerated, I say jail time saved my life and was a part of the deal I'd made with the universe in my subconscious.

I was in St Ann longer than I desired or planned to be. I had not seen my son's mother at all. We'd spoken on the phone the evening before I'd left to come the following morning, she knew I was coming but didn't return home from work that day or the days to follow. My son was in the family home, which was located on family land, surrounded by many aunties, uncles and cousins, but there was no mum, no mother to be seen. This pissed me off, and every time I asked them for her, they said they couldn't reach her and that she no longer worked at the work place I knew she used to work at, so like a duck I just had to sit and wait. Again, I felt that urge to leave St Ann, but being stubborn and determined in the wrong way, I stayed hoping to see her and sort out my child's birth certificate. As days went by, some youths and I verbally clashed. A few indirect remarks were thrown my way, but my responses were direct, and very straightforward. If I wasn't so stubborn and determined to get my name on my son's birth certificate at that time I may have avoided all that awaited me, but I guess that was an experience written to unfold, truly God *alone* knows why. These characteristics that make up my personality are who I am. I came to earth with them, and now understand that being stubborn and determined are two powerful mindsets in the universe, they are forces and energy that can be used to make my journey in life easier or harder. An uncalculated mind can misplace and misuse any force, whether it be passion, will or devotion, even the force of love can be used incorrectly if one's perception is blinded. The point I'm making is, where I was then mentally, manifested what was to occur, I knew trouble lurked but I was unable to remove myself, stubborn and determined to do as I desired, blinded to everything else. Today, I am equally as stubborn and determined, but I use these energies to keep me on the path of truth, wherein I seek and share information on history and current affairs via the multi formats and platforms I use to manifest the works for humanity, history and culture. I mean how many success stories have we heard where someone has been told not to do something or to give up on something and ends up achieving and accomplishing far beyond the expectations of others, even shocking their selves. Wouldn't such individuals have been considered in their early days as stubborn and determined by those who knew them and that aimed to sway them off course? Most definitely, the underlying fact is every force and feeling has a purpose, it's the way we channel it upon which the outcome depends. One's perception of life is very important; in fact, it is key. Stubbornness and determination are forces that manifest, both which crossover and are deeply entwined when you look at their core attributes.

Spending more time than expected in St Ann and not following my gut feeling to leave, members of her family, their friends and I got into a verbal confrontation which was followed by a physical altercation and a life was lost. What is so crazy about this whole situation was that I'd got clear away from the scene and only returned due to my passport, which I'd left down at Runaway Bay. I'd brought it to St Ann with me to show as proof that I was my son's father to enable me to get my name signed on his birth certificate. There were other means of getting out the country without a passport legally, such as a letter from the embassy; this approach is quicker than applying for a new passport. I knew such methods worked, a friend of mine had done so before plus, it was also how I'd returned to the UK after I was released from prison in 2006. Then there is the illegal way to leave the country, which need not be discussed.

They say a killer always returns to the scene of a crime, well this was no movie, I wasn't drawn back there to know who saw or if any witnesses were around, as I already knew many people had seen what happened and there were those that were involved. I returned for my passport or was it really, as I stated, other ways were options but something led me to return to where it all went down. As I say the universe knew better, the Most High had his own plan. Returning to the scene created further verbal dispute with the locals followed by a police chase. The police had shot at me twice; luckily for me neither shot hit me. I was arrested in one of my son's cousin's houses. When they brought me out, the community had a field day beating me while the police tried to keep them off. It was something they didn't try or dare attempt until I was in handcuffs, which angered me even more at the time. A police officer told me he should have let them kill me when I shouted to the community: "Watch and see!", after they had beaten me. I was fuming that moment after receiving many hits from the public. I remember one of the officers saying, "If we leave you to the community, they will kill you", and in truth, he was right. They may not have had the initial courage to come at me when it happened or when I'd just returned to the scene, but they would have. It would have been only a matter of time until those who were fuelled with anger reacted. Not everyone was against me, but those who were would have been far too many for me alone to handle. So on that note my life was saved and for a reason.

That evening I can never forget seeing my son's mother in the station giving a statement. My eyes felt heavy with tears and my heart filled with anger, I can never forget the look as we stared at one another. I can't remember why the police took me out of the cells, but there she was. She couldn't find her way home at no time from the day I'd come down to St Ann, but the moment I'm locked up, she finds herself at Runaway Bay police station. She was suddenly available and accessible to give a statement about something she wasn't a witness to or present at. I had a very uncomfortable night, all night I thought to myself, did she set me up. I told myself, even if she didn't want a life to be lost, she definitely wanted to stress me out, to place pressure on me by staying away all these days causing me to stay in a place we both knew I didn't like at that time. To show your face now I'm arrested for murder, I wasn't feeling it. The truth of the matter is; she was accessible and reachable, just not to me. She purposely didn't want me to see her. A lot ran through my head that night and on many more occasions. For days I was in constant thought about a lot of things, from my family back in the UK to my freedom, which I had just lost. I thought about so much, and every thought was interrupted or led back to one painful memory, no matter how hard I thought, I couldn't get the sight of my son's mother sitting around the table giving a statement out of my mind. But over time, I came to grips with reality. I needed to be slowed down, there were other situations in my past that could have affected my future and there was a future to unfold that may not have been aligned with what, where and the direction I walk towards today. The Most High God saw, and the universe knew what I didn't. So many times in history, we see from bad situations good can arise, incarceration can build you like Brother Malcolm, Mandela and so many others, or it can break you. Like Brother Malcolm X, I found myself through faith. Not until I started reading the Bible and Hebrew, did I realise the similarity between our journeys. Not to put myself in the same league or category as our beloved ancestor, but what makes it more of a spiritual awakening for me and easily relatable, is that he was my favourite hero when I began studying black history in my late teens. I admired his transition, but didn't have the slightest idea I would live it myself. To be honest, as a youth I was cool with prison and accepted it as part of my journey, but since trying to refrain from street life and growing my dreadlocks, I wanted different, but as I said, I had a past, and a few issues that may or may not have left me if I didn't go prison.

With time to consider the errors of my youth, I found a reason and purpose for closure on what led to my incarceration, and why I returned to the scene, which was far *deeper* than just to get my passport. That is what I saw on a physical level, but the universe and spirit realm is wiser, much wiser. Imprisonment was a journey I was destined to travel, not that I knew it then. No man wishes to be in prison, but I can honestly say it saved my life in more ways than one. Between the time I was locked up until the day I was released so much had happened in so many ways to close people around me. In some way or another, if I'd been on road, I wouldn't be the man I am today, doing what I'm doing to help youths and our community the way I do, but would be dead or in prison, that goes without question. I had too much over my head and was walking down too many dark tunnels, if light was ever at the end on those paths I cannot say, and luckily, I don't need to know.

Sadly, it took a human life and a moment in time to indirectly trigger a change. Through the documentaries, books and music I've made and the global, youth and community work I do, I'm also triggering a change in a moment in time. I pray to continue to inspire and touch more lives on my journey, on this new path of self-discovery.

Chapter 40:
Slow Down

Within the walls of confinement, inmates can act like working ants, always on the go. Their movements are a reflection of life on the outside world. Those who think, their locomotion is generally slow, they're laidback in their stride, in truth, mentally they're always on the move. Mankind is systematically designed to over think, period. In all reality, the system is just way too fast, and in no way, shape or form is it in harmony with the true nature of the rhythm of man's heartbeat, universal laws and principles. I remember coming out my cell and watching inmates act like they were on road, always in a hurry, speeding off to empty their piss-bottles, running around doing this and that, thinking to myself damn, slow down. I mean you're in prison where is there to go, there is only that much one can do or needs to do before being locked back up in that shithole of a bird cage. That's how I felt at times, like a caged bird, physically chained, but it's when I relaxed in myself and realised whether on road or behind bars I can move fast mentally that is, or slow myself all the way down. Freethinking, asking myself, who am I, what am I, and what is my purpose in life? As a youth, I was never asked these questions and even if I was asked, how to answer them was surely never explained. The reality is society and our daily lives just don't offer these simple solutions to life. In school, it was just something we were not taught to allow ourselves to do; to listen to and communicate with our true selves. Nothing we learned came from inside, everything we were taught was external information, we learnt to absorb and not to channel. At home I learnt to pray, the odd time I was told to be still and quiet but that was when I was in trouble, not much of a timeout to look into one's self and ask who am I, what am I, and what is my purpose, the energy and moment were just too conflicting. The masses aren't taught to excel, to excel truly by mastery of self, it's just something we are not taught, and great people and civilisations were never built without a steady flow of self-development. Even in stillness there is movement, just because our eyes don't comprehend doesn't mean movement isn't taking place. Society physically and mentally teaches us to speed consciously or subconsciously, but never to slow down and consider one's true purpose in life. Inside exists greatness; to really allow one time to think, is a priceless gift society will not afford us the luxury to have. Placing mental conditions to keep us constantly ticking and never feeling anything is enough. Thank sorcery for that, pumping imagery, sounds, direct and subliminal messages via media, and then there's the social ladder, which doesn't really exist or should I say exists because we give life to it, but hey, again that's sorcery. The power of illusions is man's best friend and we chase after it faster than we chase after life itself. Now, if that isn't the power of sorcery at work then please tell me what is. Many nights and days, I thought of this in my cell, reflecting on my life choices and actions, and the actions of others. I came to the conclusion that society puts values on everything accept us, which in turns makes us agree with sayings such as time is money, but time is endless is it not, so time isn't money, people represent money. The very foundation of the modern banking system is people, and to every being physically in this world, there is an end. Then I considered that the soul is endless, spirit never dies, yet we live not to connect and understand the endless existence of ourselves, but rather to that, which has no value. Again, we're never taught to look within and value ourselves, such privileges we are not rewarded. Therefore, we haste to process our environment, while our environment processes us. Programmed to always be on the move, a system designed to keep us outside of ourselves and never looking within.

My reprogramming took place in prison, not saying everyone should be a part of the prison slave trade, what I'm saying is slow down *wherever* you are and reflect. Many of us don't see the bigger picture. I know I didn't, in fact, in many aspects of my past life I chose to cleave to illusions. Running down what I couldn't control and fighting for what I had no power or authority to keep. Wow! I'm truly amazed at what I'd faced. Thoughts of many of my friends, family and even enemies, the similarity in pattern was evident, we all sharing the same thing in common, we were moving too fast and to a beat that wasn't in time with one's own heart. Out of rhythm out of tune, everybody I thought about was dancing but no one was really and truly enjoying themselves, not even the government puppets, only those at the top, the true orchestrators who spin corruption on the twin decks of manipulation; spiritual musicians whose expertise lies in building instruments of destruction, especially self-destruction. I had to jump off that train whilst behind bars and so began my long journey back to reality, to the real world, starting with the world that existed within me, connecting to the Creator and creation from which I was made. I realised it wasn't only about getting out of the Western World as everyone usually states Babylon is going down, that is true, but leaving the West alone isn't enough. I knew I had to leave that mindset of my youth behind, embrace the universe within me, and my ancestral path. Anyone and everyone who understands will have to do the same, a journey harder than it sounds.

Those days in prison I was still only reading my Hebrew Text, I was very determined to grasp biblical Hebrew. Prior to my studies, I read the King James Version (KJV) from front to back and memorised most of it. I can never forget the moment when thinking about the speedy system of illusions and self-mastery, the words in the Book of John jumped right out at me, 'Greater in he that is in me than he that is in the world.' I couldn't remember which book of John it was and went skim reading through the Gospels and then headed straight to the back of the KJV and there it was. I remember reading 1 John 4:4 repeatedly, then reading it right to the last verse of that chapter, only to come back to the conclusion of mastery of self. Even though it was based on the acknowledgement of Jesus, the messiah's principle was universal and directed one to begin the journey within and not as we are taught to look and attain everything from outside of us first. Something inside told me to read the beginning of that chapter because I'd started to read properly and not skim once I'd found the verse I was looking for, so I did. The two verses before the very verse I was looking for clarified it all; there it was the confirmation of self-mastery in the opening of the chapter. It spoke of Jesus coming in flesh and anyone who confirms him not in flesh is of antichrist. I thought what a blow to modern Christianity that doesn't accept or focus on the physical presence of the Messiah, if they did, they wouldn't say colour doesn't matter and it's about the spirit, but doesn't spirit need a vessel to manifest through. The message I was getting summarising the chapter was, the Messiah's purpose was displaying the journey of self-mastery, love begins within, trusting the God within; after all, we were created in his image and therefore have a natural connection to the Creator. To overcome the sorcery of man, which at Jesus' time was no different from now, one must remember the truth, that nothing is new under the sun. Things just appear to be different, and man is subjected to illusions.

I was seeing clearly, that it wasn't just I myself and others locked up behind bars in prison. Society itself was a big prison, one that kept mankind spinning on their hamster wheel, running at another man's pace. The streets are told we're the worst, as if the working class was any better. Then I thought, so Mr Man may have never stolen or robbed but if his only purpose is to live and fulfil another man's dream through his work and his daily interaction, how much more better off is he than me who's locked behind these bars. The notion was clear that he gets to go home night and day and has the freedom to move when he wants, but I had started to see the false sense of freedom that came with not only spiritual but physical chains. People were chained to conditions that they consciously or subconsciously knew held them such as work, school runs, meetings, juggling, and hustling. Everything kept and keeps one busy from doing the one thing we were all born to do, and that's to truly love and master self. Time is endless and priceless, but we aren't systematically designed to afford it. I mean can you really love someone else if you can't love self, and how can you truly love self if you don't know self.

I ran scenarios through my mind time after time. There are families doing their best and I was thinking of couples and not single parents, trying to paint the picture as beautifully as I could and the answer was always the same for the masses. There was never time for self-mastery and true greatness, everything that came to mind showed systematic sorcery being pumped into our minds and displayed in our actions, caught in their spider's web of illusions.

One of my scenarios were a beautiful family leaves for work, one rushes in the evening to the school to receive the child, the other may cook dinner, by the time they eat and all settle down, where is the time to reflect on self before it's time to go sleep? That's if the television hasn't absorbed the rest of the evening leaving no time to look into and question self, much less to even know your child. Then who teaches the child self-mastery when homework or something else is there to do? The reality is self-mastery isn't something encouraged by society and limitedly understood at home, if at all. Are we to blame, of course not, when has blaming anyone ever really solved anything, but self-acknowledgement, now there resides true power. We are to take responsibility for change; applying change must start with self and that isn't easy in such a speedy world.

Chapter 41:
Dodge & Avoid

At Tower Street Adult Correctional Centre, who could predict the outcome of any single day. Mission impossible is what it was, no two days were ever the same, and every moment changed with prisoners moods. Even when you hadn't seen any action nor heard any arguments for weeks, it didn't mean there was total peace on the block. What it did mean is someone was plotting and scheming or a lot of acts were being kept under the quiet. I think my speciality in prison was avoiding problems, not that it was always possible. I had my fair share of confrontation and physical altercations throughout my sentence, but at the same time, I dodged a lot too. Bear in mind, I served almost eight full years, so to not have had any problems with inmates, especially the way in which I held mine from the moment I was locked up, would have been highly unlikely; conflict was inevitable, however, it won me my respect. The way I saw it, getting into shit with prisoners over foolishness wasn't worth it, nor was it my business to get involved in other people's problems. Not that I didn't stand up for the odd person, or break the odd rule; but I wasn't one for creating my own entertainment, that just wasn't me, but believe me, many never saw life the same way I did. Some inmates went out of their way to create problems and contention with other prisoners, it was like boredom or haughtiness of spirit drove them, or they were just downright troublesome due to personal issues. The more I observed prisoners; I saw some individuals were where I was before, when I was in my teens. It's not that they haven't grown up, that wasn't the case at all, it was that they were still manifesting trauma, or better acknowledged as transformation of energy via anger from their childhood. Understanding the signs made it easy for some of them to communicate with me. I say some, because certain inmates were too far gone to come back ever. When one refers to tipping over the edge, there's a thin line between gone and really gone, and believe when I say some inmates were too far-gone, they were racing to the unrecognisable. I remember a few of us talking with an inmate who threatened to take another's life, my friend asked him, "Why you staring in the sky while I'm talking with you?" His super slow response showed he clearly wasn't with us but had zoned out. His reply when he did come back to the conversation was that he was looking in the sky for a spot for the inmate whose life he desired to take. For me it was time to go, my cell was calling me. It was moments like that; I felt man's too far gone. He was imagining his victim in the heavens, not only was he clearly thinking of killing him but also looking for where he would rest. There are various extreme accounts and remarks certain inmates made which just told you they were over the tipping edge, or could be pushed there at any given time. This made them really dangerous, not just to others but even themselves, because they'd lost all manner of insight and had a truly disturbed view of life.

Using myself as an example, I'd gone so far but was able to see my errors even though I still did wrong from time to time. In the back of my mind, a level of consciousness still existed, part acceptance and responsibility, but I denied myself the will or desire to take control and change. There were individuals on the other hand, who had no level of consciousness, or part acceptance. It was like their past experiences and the pain had taken over; totally empty, all their sorrows, frustration and anger overflowed in their actions, no responsibility was ever theirs, they refused acceptance for anything they did even when they started it. It was as if their youth had killed all logical thinking. At times, my heart cried for them, others judged them and some were beaten by warders. Believe me, there were inmates warders thought twice about lifting their baton to unless they were in serious numbers, but even inmates that they did beat from time to time or even regularly, did they ever wonder why these inmates acted or responded in such a negative manner and tone over whatever it was that caused the situation. The system definitely needs a shake up; warders either don't understand psychological trauma and therefore need further training or just refuse to care. But then with minimal rehabilitation programmes offered and no psychological support available, what hope do they have. To me, most warders didn't have a clue how to deal with inmates and the ones that did love the badness themselves, which reflected that they had been or were going through their own mental issues too. Whether a warder's problem was family related issues, social or connected to his or her youth days, the reality is they had also suffered or were suffering from some sort of psychological trauma and fed it right back into and at prisoners. Therefore, the penal system is a traumatic pool of destruction where everyone seemed to be psychologically drowning; some just swam a little longer than others before going under. It's like it was designed for both inmates and warders alike to sink. I would term it destruction by reflection. What some warders truly needed was counselling to help them with their own issues and pain, which would allow them to not only be more empathetic and caring towards inmates, but to help them get over or deal with whatever bothered them in their personal lives. Inmates also needed that support from a specialist, someone professional to help individuals traumatised by their experiences. Whether it was things that were done to them, what they'd seen or did to others, they were suffering from trauma and by reasoning with some of them, I could tell. To be honest, I avoided a lot and chose my moments wisely. Most times, I'd leave it until the following day or so and reason with an individual because I knew when I was really mad as a youth no one dare come and try to talk to me or calm me down, in fact that can make it worse.

Looking back on my life, I would have reacted in one of two ways if someone tried to calm me down, whichever way you look at it, both would have made it worse, resulting negatively. Prison for me gave me time to really analyse the actions of others and myself. The power of self-reflection, wow, it's undeniable.

The first negative would be the attention, personally I wanted and needed that in my life, absent fatherhood, lack of male role model, feeling of neglect and the list goes on, which is the same for so many. Not knowing how to really deal with attention, it would have exacerbated me, causing me to act out reacting to the attention. Whether I knew it or not, I wanted to hold on to this attention, and therefore act out more and become even more confrontational with the individual. This is commonly seen when two people are having a dispute, it may just be verbal and then you notice it gets worse when other people step in and actually try stopping it. Not that they are doing it for show, in some cases it may be, but in others it can be that lack of attention reflecting from their childhood, subconsciously they react, grasping this attention.

Then there's the second negative that can lead to victimisation due to lack of trust. As a youth, I wasn't big on trust because of all I'd been through and this is the same for many. Your kindness just may have made you my victim. Believe I would and have attacked the innocent in the past, if not physically definitely verbally. In prison if exchanges of words aren't controlled that too can lead to big problems, no doubt war, so it was about being smart. There were the odd times I got involved in people's problems for various reasons, from the day I was arrested to the very last moments in prison, but after a period, my actions and reactions became calculated. I wasn't young anymore nor did I project the mentality where I would stick my mouth or fist in a situation and just deal with whatever the outcome, I was becoming more empathic, rationalising, using wisdom, prison had definitely made me wiser. Plus, I'd come to the realisation that the outcomes of any situation concerning my life and my actions were always on me and therefore my perception of any situation could only be made clear if my mind was also clear. True strength could never manifest through blurred vision.

There are some incidents that are unavoidable, sadly the reality is, by association one can get dragged in, this almost happened to me on a few occasions, one of which I thought more deeply on. The big man Stumpy had found freedom and of course, I was happy for him, as I would be for any man that did. Only a few people knew there was a connection between the big man and I that stemmed from beyond the prison walls, nevertheless association within the institution is enough to get a man dragged into the mix. Everyone who knows about the Jamaican prison system knows when a person is remanded or sentenced to time behind bars, that inmate is referred to as a body and not a person. The notion is man is a body and not a person because death can come at any time and mix up and war was something I didn't want anything to do with, I wanted Freedom Street and not to be considered a body, but a person, a person with a destiny. In Jamaican prisons, inmates aren't given numbers like in the movies, or in the UK or American prison system, but they do have access to weapons, some that you definitely won't find in UK and American prisons. As for a number, when you first enter the prison and are processed you definitely get one. However, it is never shared with you, nor do you need to remember it as no warder is ever going to refer to you by any number or your name, unless there's a reason for familiarity and then you just might get called by your name. Most inmates are referred to plainly as just *inmate* or *you*. Life can seem meaningless behind bars, but I would no more allow my anger and lack of insight to rule me as if I was no one, neither was I willing to throw my life away anymore, and therefore mix up and war was the last thing on my mind in this corrupted traumatic system.

There's a common saying in prison, which is death by association, especially if people live by the Jamaican saying, 'If yuh cyaah katch Quaku, yuh katch him shut' (if you cannot catch Quaku, then grab his shirt). Hence why I walked alone most times, but then there were times due to unpredictability it was necessary to take a side, but on this occasion, it was one that I didn't and wasn't going to get involved in. Thank God, nothing came out of it. Madness had taken place out on the road according to inmates, bear in mind they're hearing it, not me and it's circulating around the prison that these two areas may have problems, well, sets of individuals in these two garrisons of Kingston. I was connected to not only the area but also the individual who had found his freedom so I was told to watch out. That was all I needed. To be honest, I prayed that day and at second fly up I left my block and headed round to the front where I knew most of the guys from the other area known as Southside located. A few of them were good friends with my friends who resided in their area in Central Kingston. We spoke and they made it clear it's their problem out on road not ours, and expressed it definitely wasn't my problem, which made me smile within. I knew anyhow they were going to attack anyone who was close to the big man it would have been serious. Things would have escalated both on road and in prison.

Certain inmates were known as strikers behind the bars, meaning killers, they had and would put in work and everyone knew it. But this goes for all garrisons, everyone had their strikers too, but war in prison was something I didn't want to hear about, I wanted none of it. Road I was looking towards, I had just less than two years left or maybe just a little over a year and a half, freedom was around the corner and I wanted to see my children and family again. I wanted to achieve all that individuals said and believed I was capable of achieving, most of all I wanted to explore the unknown and I also felt that greater was written in heaven for me.

Older and more experienced men from the streets had imparted wisdom to me. A lot respected the Hebrew understanding of the Bible I was bringing; most of all, people just respected me as an individual. The Rastas that transferred to Tower Street Adult Correctional Centre that knew me from before as a Rasta in the early days of my incarceration, and those who had heard me say I used to follow and believe Tafari to be Christ, knew how I now saw the scriptures. Nonetheless, they showed respect and encouraged me to keep on my path. G-Go my cousin had been transferred to General Penitentiary and also expressed a lot of love towards the trod. I was being myself, the way I loved gym and was getting ripped in prison they'd told me to go road and make this my career. I had heard that numerous times, and to keep up the martial arts. The odd person who knew I used to be a musician would try to encourage me to take the microphone, and tell me to join the prison programme that was running called Reverence for Life. This programme was very positive, what inmates were doing was good, but it wasn't for me. I had listened to Singy-Singy, Jah Cure and others do their thing, and was tempted to hold the microphone, but not once did I even approach them on that tip. Not that I was shy, but to be honest holding a microphone wasn't on my mind, I was so caught up in reading and studying and this really helped me avoid trouble and people, well most of the times, as I said, sometimes it was unavoidable but I did my best.

Chapter 42:
Prison Madness

It was the year 2005 when an insane madness took place at the Tower Street Adult Correctional Centre causing the transfer of many inmates, both Jamaican and all foreigners to Horizon Adult Remand Centre, on Spanish Town Road, in Kingston. I had just over a year left in prison, counting down the time and thinking how much I was looking forward to going home. Over the years, I'd tried my best not to become institutionalised and caught up with the madness, I didn't always succeed, but I was alive and had gone through the worst, I'd say to myself. I had established myself so that I could manoeuvre around prison when needed, but honestly, as time drew near, I was questioning everything, even asking myself: "Am I slightly institutionalised, why am I worried about going home?" Although I couldn't wait, I'd gotten used to my environment and that was frightening to me. It felt like a love hate relationship, on one hand I couldn't wait to get the hell out of there and as crazy as it sounds, I felt a slight feeling of belonging. Numerous times, I suppressed that feeling, reasoning with my inner man, I told myself not to fight it but embrace it; this was my reality. I'm here and have been behind these walls for a while now, there's nothing to fear, just know it's not home, and the outside world has so much to offer me, most of all, my children are waiting for me.

It's not always that when one seeks trouble it comes, sometimes it can come in the form of a blessing. As I've stated, I'd established myself in General Penitentiary and was used to my environment, but then tension could get high just like that and escaping problems wasn't always the easiest thing to do. Although

I walked alone a lot, if the companionship had problems it could filter or directly affect you too. Prison had its mad moments, sometimes too many, some on the quiet, as individuals may lay down terms to solve situations before they escalated. Being on the inside and knowing what caused this dialogue to begin, and hearing what one side and the other were equally willing to do, or how they planned to retaliate to the actions of the other if it couldn't be squashed, you just knew it was going to be a very dark day. Early to mid 2005 Tower Street Adult Correctional Centre was going through its moments, and especially on Building I had my fair share of arguments, even one or two physical altercations with some youths who were associates of mine and we'd fallen out. In one case, one of my cellmates and I had problems but neither of us was willing to move, so tension in our cell was high daily. Why I was being so stubborn only God knows, realistically I was on a different journey with the things I was doing and the level of consciousness I was seeing and portraying amongst my peers, even other inmates said to me and expected me to move out but I wouldn't. Why my heart had hardened so badly, truly, only God knows. I made stupid excuses supporting why I wouldn't move, looking back on it there was a lesson to be learnt. Because of tension in the cell and the anger boiling up in me, it caused me to disrespect a friend of mine who located in another cell further down the block, which I admit I was wrong about. I had left my cell and had gone to visit Buju, whilst I was reasoning with the Kirkist, another mutual friend of ours from across the waters over Portmore had come to his cell. The inmate from Portmore located a few cells away from Buju. Maybe because he saw us both reasoning he thought he'd come over, which wouldn't be strange really; all three of us were good friends. I had brushed him off because I didn't want to really speak with anyone but Buju at that time, and it caused us to argue because he felt disrespected. One thing led to another and he drew for a stick, so I drew for half a brick from Buju's cell. The Kirkist stopped it before it could escalate by standing between us. I walked off to my cell *blinded* by my *action* thinking he disrespected me. It's only when in my cell and I played the whole thing back in my mind, and believe me I replayed it over and over again, because for some reason I still didn't want to take responsibility for starting it. Anger can really blind the truth. The youth from Portmore had walked past my cell with bloodshot eyes, face serious and vex, whether he wanted to continue, to see if I said anything, or just was genuinely passing, it caused me to shake my head in disappointment. He was a youth who'd always shown me genuine respect and love from the day he came into Building, both him and his friend who were jointly sentenced for a murder. The crazy thing about it is, we'd talk and laugh a lot before this happened. In fact, when we had our altercation, his chargie didn't even get involved, as normal he hailed me the following day when he went to empty his piss-bottle. The inmate who I had an altercation with looked at me and nodded his head, that made me feel like shit, that moment I knew I had to move cells. The environment was toxic it was affecting my mind and ability to control self. I had learnt a valuable lesson from it, and false pride was still an issue that I had to deal with. Besides false pride, I had anger issues, which I knew, but it was more problematic than I believed. I'd restrained myself many times, but I wasn't removing the frustration from previous situations. Like the childhood anger, I was carrying shit all over again just for different reasons now, and who knows if it was even connected to my youth still. All I knew was, I had serious issues to deal with and it wouldn't be easy.

I'd jumped ship and located across from Max, things were good for the short time I was in my new location; however, tension throughout the prison and on the block was high. One day I had gone in my cell and had started to read some Hebrew, which was something I did a lot when I wasn't at the gym. Trouble seemed to keep its distance when I was focused and level headed. It was when I strayed that it quickly found its way, not that other inmates couldn't drag me into problems, but I was more likely to avoid trouble if I was active. As my mother would say, 'The Devil finds work for idle hands.' It was lockdown time; I had my water already and wasn't worrying about eating off the tray so my head wasn't coming out of my books for love nor money. I was fully focused and getting on with it. I can never forget that lockdown, I remember warders coming on the block and my cellmate saying to me, "Search!" That got my attention; I looked up even though I had nothing to hide but money. I watched as loads of warders walked past our cell, then I began hearing cells fly open and then I saw a foreigner walking fast with his possessions, then I saw more foreigners and wondered what was going on. Inmates asked them what was going on and the foreigners said they were getting transferred because their lives were in danger. According to the warders, an escape attempt had happened around the front, a shootout between prisoners and warders had taken place on the prison grounds and lives were lost. Warders heard that British foreigners were going to be attacked; they were going to be used as a tool to get attention from the outside world.

When I think about it, unlike Spanish Town prison, I don't recall seeing any American inmates in GP. In St Catherine Adult Correctional Centre, you could find all foreign nationalities there, but not GP. Thinking about it, I only remember seeing British inmates within the walls of Tower Street Adult Correctional Centre, it's like the only foreigners housed at General Penitentiary at that time, were those who lived in the country of the Queen of England.

I wasn't worried one bit about the allegation and situation regarding the safety of foreign inmates even though I could be grouped in that bracket. Truly, what did get me thinking was the fact that other foreigners were leaving and I was more concerned that the warders had walked past my cell and started to let out other British inmates but not me. I asked them more than once "What about me, am I not going?" But none of them responded. Inmates started to shout out on my behalf, "He's a foreigner too, he's an English man; he's not a Jamaican, they must take him too!" It's like they didn't want to take me and then the reality hit me that every English is leaving, for some reason I saw aeroplanes in my head, and the thought of them getting sent back to the United Kingdom on early release for fear of their lives and I'm not, I went from calm to crazy in milliseconds. Kicking the grille telling warders I'm a foreigner and to let me out, all I could picture in my mind was a plane taking off from the airport and me being left behind. It was a blue suit, and green suit that knew me well that said let him out. What really angered me was that a lot of warders knew me, not just by face but name also, those who knew me as Hebrew knew I was a foreigner so why they were acting like they didn't know only God knows. Instantly I was clam again and grabbed my things, which took time as I had accumulated so many belongings by the numerous visits from abroad and local connects; a warder had to help me carry them.

As they chained Building doors and we walked towards the front there was a mad sigh of relief. As much as I was used to General Penitentiary, I was glad to get out of the madness that was bubbling up. At the front while waiting for the truck to export us, which wasn't to the airport as I'd hoped and thought might be the sign of early release, instead it was to Horizon Adult Remand Centre on Spanish Town Road. Even then, I wondered if they really believed English inmates were going to be killed or harmed then which prison on the island was really safe. So that thought of early deportation remained with me until we arrived at Horizon.

We were located in the new section of Horizon; everyone wondered what the next move would be. Some including me hoped for an early release because there was no place for English inmates to hide in the Jamaican prison system if the order was from the top sent down. I wasn't fearful for my life, I knew a lot of people, not to mention the right people too, but I was definitely excited by the thought of getting out. Questions arose regarding the other British inmates that were in Spanish Town prison; even I was caught in the conversation still hoping this was a sign of early deportation. For a minute, I was all excited and really wanting to believe I was going back to the UK early, providing the threats and allegation were as serious as they said they were. Deep down I really wished they were, the UK was going to see me a year and mash earlier. I was feeling good about early release and hoping it was so. We had no phones, no outside communication. No one had been visited, for we had just reached Horizon Adult Remand Centre and therefore anyone who was supposed to get a visit the following day wouldn't, as family members would only find out when they arrived at the prison and they were told. I just couldn't picture the staff at General Penitentiary calling and contacting family members whose information was taken during normal visits. That definitely would be down to the British High Commission, and they would most probably only contact family members abroad, only they or whosoever's contact information they had or were given would receive updates. Our minds were working overtime especially mine. All my curiosity and thoughts ended when across on the other side we heard some noise, inmates shouting and talking. Then I saw Buck-Wheel, the big man from Homestead known as Rat and others and asked them why they were there. It was only a grille, long vertical bars that separated us the foreigners from the Jamaicans so communication was easy, in fact, we were able to spud fist and shake hands, that's how close we were.

Once they'd told us why they were there my heart sank. I just knew we weren't getting on a plane back to the UK, such wishful thinking disappeared suddenly. They were accused of wanting to kill foreign inmates, we all laughed. It was one big joke. They had not been charged with anything to do with the attempted escape but were supposed to have said they were going to take revenge for the inmate who had been killed in the shootout and would take revenge using foreigners as bait. Yet warders located them so close to us, as I stated we could touch hands, exchange gifts and on a serious note, they could have killed anyone if they wanted to once an individual approached the grille. It was straight bullshit. The warders were up to some sort of game, whether they made up the rules or it was those in higher authority orchestrating how it should roll out, whatever they were playing only made sense to them. As for us, all who were locked up behind the walls of confinement, both Jamaican and English inmates were as confused as hell. Nevertheless, it got me out of GP, and really, tension in General Penitentiary at that time was high, the whole situation was total madness.

To add insult to the confusion, after some time staying in Horizon, they transferred all of us, both Jamaican and British inmates to Spanish Town Adult Correctional Centre and located us all on the same block, South Block.

Chapter 43:
South Block

Here I was, back where I began spending my time behind bars, only this time I wasn't out on Grass locating at GB3 but over on South Block. I would go out to Grass occasionally to visit friends over New Hall or GB, but I spent most of my time on South Block. South Block, unlike the rest of the prison was like a prison to itself, in the sense that if war broke out in the general prison, South Block was always less affected. It was only when the whole prison had strikes or a total prison search was taking place, South Block felt it too. Apart from that, South Block stood alone due to where it was situated. South Block had its own little rules and regulations and honestly, war on South Block was never like anywhere else. I'd say it's the way order was set. Plus, with Buck-Wheel and others back on the block, it definitely was going to run how it should if it wasn't running correctly while he was away. Things were guaranteed to fall back into place and that meant a quiet life, well, more peaceful than anywhere else in the prison, that's for sure.

I hardly felt tempted to go out to Grass, I mean I was leaving soon and to be honest the thought of love was on my mind. With South Block running so calmly, the odd little arguments but nothing too serious, I had no reason to want to venture out and put myself into the unknown regularly. When I did see my people out on the Grass it was nothing but respect as always, they understood and felt no way about it.

With less tension in my surroundings, I'd begun writing poems in my hammock and at break. I really poured my emotions into each one, sharing my innermost thoughts regarding past relationships, seeing my errors and the errors of partners, looking at how we could have resolved the issues in our relationships, if we didn't have our own issues affecting our ability to see clearly. Using my pen, I'd write out my thoughts in a more positive way, placing a positive spin on each situation. At times, I'd freeze during a poem, really ask myself questions and then express my emotions putting pen to paper.

After gathering months of poems, I'd share them with one or two female warders and a few ladies on the phone. Nothing beats a woman's view. Touched by my words, they gave positive feedback and knew I was on the right track to self-discovery and clarity. Expressing my thoughts on various aspects of my life via poetry, writing and studying as well as exercising, was definitely building my character, building me for the better too.

In the yard, I'd exercise while most people played ball. Many times, I was asked to play ball, as a foreigner, being English and kind of strong in structure, they told me I could be a good footballer, they weren't wrong. I was pretty okay at football but I was also reluctant to get involved in team sports, body weight training and practising Thai Boxing was more my thing, doing me. Under the hut where I trained led me to catch the attention of a few inmates, one from Holland a kick boxer and the other who I found out to be connected to my people, was a well-respected man from Kingston, known as Sala-Sala. On many occasions, we trained together Sala-Sala and I, but then I did a lot of training by myself. People throughout my sentence knew I liked to be alone and gave me that space to be me, while showing respect at the same time.

Rules had changed somewhat and inmates were allowed to legally have small TV's in their cells. However, way before this new rule came in, some inmates had big screens, some could just about fit in their cells, but then they had a lot of power and connections on road and in prison too. I'd asked my people on road for a TV and they'd brought me a small portable TV and DVD player. Under lock, my cellmates and I would watch movies; mostly they'd be staring at the screen while I was caught up in my studies and writings. But it was definitely a beautiful way to chill when I wanted to.

I was on South Block no longer than six to seven months when I heard a warder call my name as he approached me. I was told to gather my belongings and come to the front; he said I was being transferred to Tamarind Farm Correctional Centre. I had heard about Tamarind and Richmond Farm -both open prisons- and since my return to St Catherine Adult Correctional Centre, I knew of other foreigners who luckily had been transferred to Tamarind Farm. But I thought, due to the nature of my charge I would never see these places, yet I was wrong. Happily, I turned and headed straight for my cell and began to pack. Inmates helped me carry my bags to the front. I couldn't believe it, I was heading to open prison, I was so looking forward to it.

Chapter 44:
Tamarind Farm

I was indirectly tested within the few days of arriving at this open prison; that was to be expected. To many, I was an unfamiliar face. Inmates who never really got themselves in any trouble or were never around serious inmates in Spanish Town or GP were those who ended up in these open prisons. Inmates who received short sentences and were on super good behaviour in the maximum-security prisons or were on less serious offences usually found themselves in Tamarind Farm Correctional Centre. Some inmates had never even been to the maximum-security prisons due to their length of sentence or the nature of their crime. So a lot of them wouldn't have known me. Plus, I didn't know everyone in the maximum-security prisons anyway, and these inmates were definitely not in my circle. An inmate tried to demand to watch my TV, I confronted the inmate and disciplined him verbally, and that was that. There was never a repeat of anything like that afterwards throughout the rest of my sentence.

It's funny how names and titles can change people's perception of someone. I never really understood the respect in it. To me it was false, but in truth I didn't care, as long as people let me be me, I was good. A few inmates located in other dorms who had known of me and knew me by face in Spanish Town, made people aware of who I was, my capabilities, my links and the crime I was sentenced for. Like any place, I would have proven myself if need be. There was no way I was going to be bullied or disrespected by inmates who I never saw on the circuit of real prison thugs. It wasn't even a pride thing, it was more based on the fact that we were in an open prison away from the madness that took place in the maximum-security prisons, and the thought that *now* these individuals wanted to act gangster, pissed me right off. I saw it as the oppressed playing the oppressor and was willing to reverse the cycle. Not that there were many in our dorm that acted up, but the ones who did, even if they had been to the main prisons, they were nobodies. Some were sentenced to serve months and therefore escaped Spanish Town and Tower Street Adult Correctional Centre, to act tough now was a joke. But fortunately for me I didn't need to flip the script, respect was given throughout the facility, even the odd warder who had been transferred and knew me showed respect, personally my time in Tamarind Farm was peaceful, very peaceful.

I did get myself into situations but they were never because of me. It was more to prevent problems and circumstances from arising; I was more of a peacemaker in the process and known for it too. But then I wouldn't allow myself to get involved in every situation. Over the span of half a year, which I did in Tamarind Farm, the odds were always weighted. I was comfortable and glad to be there. I wasn't looking to do anything or put myself in a situation where I got shipped back to maximum-security, the fresh air, trees and spacious environment was too beautiful to go back to living like sardines in a can. I was no longer in the presence of the sound of constant padlocks banging when inmates wanted to get warders' attention or when a hit song came on and everyone wanted to salute, banging their padlocks against the rusty metal grille doors. Truly, at times it was great energy saluting a song, I participated many times, but no way did I miss it, maximum-security prison wasn't for me, Tamarind Farm had far too much nature to see. The thought of urinating in a bottle and doing a number two squatting over a plastic bag lined with newspaper just wasn't exciting. I was now using a toilet, still squatting when doing it, but didn't have to limit my water intake due to fear of my two-litre bottle overflowing and then having to make another piss-bottle. I hated having to carry out *one*, much less two. I was now showering in the dorm when I wanted to at any time of night or day, and the access to food from the kitchen to cook was never so easy. I wasn't going back to Spanish Town or any main prison for anyone.

Adding to the benefits of being in this open prison, I now had longer visiting time and could see my visitors face to face as we sat on a long bench opposite one another and spoke surrounded by cool breeze in the heat of the midday sun. I felt like I was in paradise compared to where I'd come from. The thought of those few minutes in a nasty box separated by a dirty plastic glass at Spanish Town was a thing of the past. Happy is an understatement, I was more than glad that was over; there was no exchange for the comfort I was introduced to. Hence, I couldn't comprehend the desire to act bad in a place like this. Of course, I recognised that those few inmates had personal issues, we all have, but I didn't want to and was unwilling to take on whatever bothered them. The most important thing to me was they kept it to themselves and tormented themselves with it, which they did. One of the little troublemakers was transferred after having a petty argument with an inmate over something that didn't really need to draw so much attention; all mouth and no action, too much bark and no bite. The level of verbal engagement caused the warders to get involved. He was unnecessarily loud and what made it worse, in the presence of warders, he began talking about killing the inmate. Seriously, I thought, who was he trying to impress. With so much time and opportunity available to carry out such an act before warders arrived, and then when they came the inmate starts talking about committing murder and saying, "Watch when warders leave!" I felt it was kind of hilarious. It was quite a comedy show, no award or medal to obtain, but great acting nevertheless. It did reward him with a one-way ticket back to maximum prison where I guarantee he would most definitely quiet his arse right the fuck down and reflect on his actions. I knew when he did look at his environment and began to reflect, he'd regret leaving the perks that came with being in Tamarind Farm. The other inmate just calmed the hell down and turned out to be a really cool guy.

Tamarind Farm for me was really a place where I could further enhance my journey of self-discovery. The air felt different from behind the walls of Spanish Town and GP, and the tension was never so thick nor the energy so negative. The open space gave a physical feeling of freedom. Although I knew I was in prison and still restricted regarding movement, dormitories reminded me of school trips, it just didn't feel as hellish in comparison to where I was coming from. The spaciousness and distance between each dorm and the little area I had already scoped out where I would meditate alone brought a good feeling. I was now really able to get time alone while overlooking nature too. I was looking forward to investing time in my feelings, thoughts and emotions, reflecting and envisioning life.

Chapter 45:
Love & Emotions

I had asked Jan to bring me some more writing books, I was feeling emotional but in a good way. Just under half a year left in prison and I was so looking forward to know what life had in store for me regarding love and happiness. No matter what anyone says or how hard they act within the walls of confinement, everyone desires to be loved on the outside and wants or wishes that a woman would visit them. No matter how many family members come and visit, no doubt it's truly appreciated, but believe me, deep down every inmate yearns for a woman to be connected with, whether it's via phone or in person, that female energy is craved for. Nothing comforts a man's heart like the voice of a woman telling him to take care, or I miss you. Such stimulating words behind bars brings more than comfort, in fact some men can get too overjoyed and go crazy, literally crazy because of their love for a woman. I'd heard and seen this personally whilst incarcerated, inmates attempt suicide because they longed for and desired to be with their loved one. Such emotions are truly deep, if they are healthy, well that's another question. To go as far as to take one's own life, unable to contain whatever the feeling they felt, says something was lacking at some point in their life. I'm no expert to comment on such behaviour, such thoughts have never crossed my mind, but I'm sure there are numerous social factors to be considered. During my remand period, I'd lost the love of my life, my children's mother, but such thoughts weren't even comprehensible. I wasn't wired like that, but then I'm sure one of those prisoners that considered committing suicide over their loved one wouldn't consider hurting innocent people for fun, he may consider my childhood actions as crazy, not righted and poorly wired. The point I'm making is everyone has his or her own battles to fight. We just need to dig deep and find that inner strength to accomplish whatever needs to be accomplished, so the brighter side of life can shine before one's face. The pursuit of happiness awaits. They say God doesn't give a man more than he can take, well going by everything I've been through since I was born, God knows I can take a lot. I may not have always dealt with my issues and emotions the correct way, but I was born a fighter and a lover, so I thank all the women that supported me and showed me love whilst I was incarcerated.

Female support behind bars was a necessity and lucky for me I had the most beautiful woman checking me. Odd times, other women would visit too and a few amazing women calling me on regular bases kept me feeling good. Conversations at times I must admit would play with my head; my lower head would hurt me too. There were times when I couldn't write my emotions down, I had to give attention to my lower head and help him out, there was no woman to do it for me. This was the reality of my situation; I was behind bars being entertained by the outside world; a bit of an illusion, in fact a massive illusion that had played on my mind for years. But what could I do, there is no comfort like the comfort of a woman's voice and steamy conversations to make me feel alive. It came with a price, one that can cause a man to over think, to react or act. That depended on the mindset I was in, and the level of stimulation felt, most times, I'd turn to my books and read or write some Hebrew, or read the Bible afterwards. I guess as time drew near, it became more realistic and the emotions felt more intense. I'd begun writing my emotions down in the form of a book and not just poetry. A whole love scene played out in my mind. Using experiences from my past, writing desires of happiness accompanied by struggles, teamwork and partnership, my first romance novel was written. It had taken me just four months to complete an extensive romance novel, my first book. By the time I was leaving Tamarind Farm, I exited the prison with hundreds of poems and a romance novel. My intention was to compile the poems into a few books along with the romance novel and publish them, which I did. Years later, I had reformatted my poetry books into one big book titled 'Healthy Love' and the romance novel I

312

called it 'Compatible minds.' A proud moment was seeing my books available on Amazon, whilst reflecting back to a troubled time, productively, I had made the best out of a bad situation.

Chapter 46:
Bullying & Karma

Personally, I had no issues with inmates, in fact Tamarind Farm Correctional Centre was smooth sailing for myself, not that I can say the same for other English inmates. During the second to third month of my arrival to the open prison, I could see a little rivalry taking place and tension was building up between a few Jamaican and English inmates. Fights and arguments were breaking out throughout dorms and some individuals were getting bullied during shut down times. The cause was none other than jealousy and red eye. Foreign inmates, especially English, whether or not their families or connects on the outside made sure they were alright, they had Prisoners Abroad income via the British High Commission to always look forwards to. I did not agree with it, no, not at all, but I understood where the jealousy came from. Some inmates knew they were never getting visits, the thought of seeing someone who's not from your island live a better life than oneself can have an effect on the psyche, nevertheless, this is all weakness and lack of responsibility for one's own actions. No one but oneself had caused one's incarceration; and no one, whether on the outside or behind bars is obligated to attend to one's needs. This is one of the contributory factors making so many youths go crazy, commit suicide and bow to man; it's the lack of self-will and determination. Extra food and smoke is luxury, not a necessity, yet inmates felt that they had the right to demand what wasn't their own. Maybe if it was the odd one off here and there, it might have been excusable, but constant arguments, the odd fights and everything stemming from some money conversation, was nothing but shear bullying and extortion. In Spanish Town prison I knew certain inmates had never extorted anyone, in fact they kept their heads down, never intermingled with certain crowds and ran their time quietly, yet now here they were playing the gangster. Knowing there was no risk of I myself being drawn into any problems, I told inmates I would hold their money and give them whenever they needed. Some English inmates, like I myself, had no problems regarding their money, no one thought to demand money from them, others weren't so lucky. The syndicate of bullies knew I was holding money for some British prisoners, plus I'd spoken with a few of the main Jamaican inmates who led this parade of bullying and foolishness, after inmates who were under their wings had problems with an English youth who did Wing Chun. I must say, he stood his ground well against a group of them whilst under lock. I had spoken with the main leader about his actions in Spanish Town and his actions here in Tamarind Farm, and the benefits of being here, advising him not to jeopardise it and get sent back to mainstream prison. We also discussed karma and explained when a cat is placed in a corner it's forced to attack. I told him to stop pushing and bullying certain foreigners because they're not fighting back. At the same time, I asked him how comes no one was demanding from myself and a few others who I noticed they were not troubling. He made no comment, and then made some excuse about other English inmates showing off, which wasn't true. By this time, a few of his friends had come over. During the discussion, I told them I'd learnt the hard way, and who don't hear will feel, and before I left the prison, karma had reached the two main Jamaican Inmates.

Even after our discussion, the odd fight broke out in the dining hall with the same guys and an English youth from W10 who had got the better of them. That didn't even last thirty seconds; a couple of English inmates including myself were on our toes quick. They wanted no retaliation. I remained a peacemaker, but took this one a bit personal; as he was someone I had known. We all witnessed their karma and stood there watching. They had bullied another Jamaican inmate who some would consider slow mentally but he not only looked strong, but also turned out to be as strong as a gorilla. He had punched them up severely, dashing them around like ragdolls. Bullying definitely carries karma; a wrongdoing overall is a transformation of negative energy.

I have done many wrongs as a youth and even in my adulthood. I thank God my karma hasn't destroyed the lives of my family, children and close relatives, even though it has affected specific members especially my children. Absent fatherhood from childhood is never easy to deal with, my three eldest children had to deal with it from when they were small due to my incarceration and poor life choices. I thank the Greatest, throughout trials and tribulations that my children faced they turned out good and are on the right path. The streets have taken many friends, close relatives and associates from me, but that's a part of their own acceptance and interaction with street life, nothing to do with my karma. The universe can repay our debts in very strange and indirect ways, sometimes too direct and painful. Individuals have lost family members, loved ones born disabled, sickness, a child grown with mental issues, family members or siblings getting raped or molested. The hood has many stories; karma is something not to play with. Sometimes when we think we get away with things the burden is placed on others we love. It's insane how even the innocent can pay for our sins, but this is the way of the world. Universal law, bonds and ties, true repentance is key.

Regarding myself, it always seemed that I personally took the beatings for my wrongs and I thank God for that, because it made me the man I am today. Indirectly my family and children, especially my big children have been affected by my past life, causing them to experience issues of their very own. It's something I cannot undo for it has already been done, but what I can do and chose to, is change me to aid them to heal. For every action, there is a reaction and a cause and affect not always manifesting when one desires. An unsettled soul as a youth I was, bouncing from place to place mentally, putting myself through drama after drama and never ever really taking the time to check myself. So I was bringing more problems and emotional discomfort to myself, but was I to understand the spiritual relation between cause and effect, the karma that kept coming and coming? No one had taught me ancestral teachings about energy; neither did I really care to know, because that's where my mind was. Born in a system that kept me reflecting on the sparkle of the outside world and not the internal flame, the brightness that's lit within, I was lost like so many others to the illusion that comes with great consequences. Without truly knowing what karma was from a young age, it led me never to bully people again. Now, I'm not saying after that specific experience I didn't ever rob, steal or even attack someone who didn't really deserve it, I'd be lying to myself if I said I didn't, but I will say I never ever bullied anyone again. Street life on the other hand is a dog eat dog world. Manufactured chaos where everyone wants a taste of the bone and truly, there is no real master on the road to control the hunger and thirst of any individual, every so-called or self-proclaimed street soldier anywhere, in any community has his day. No one really wants or deserves this lifestyle, but this is the reward of living in the world of make believe, street life is a man created cesspool of karma in itself. Artificially formulated and structured by man for destruction, and the results and repercussions are real, all too real. My life on the streets from my childhood through to adulthood was undoubtedly witnessed by the universe, nothing went unnoticed and a lot of unprovoked actions based on pain, anger and lack of self-love manifested. The universe also witnessed how misguided I was and could feel my emptiness and pain. Man is an instrument of creation, a disciplinary tool unto himself and his kind. Nations and people have always been used to reward men for their deeds, this action dates back long before my arrival to this realm and will be used until the total shift has taken place. Life is simple; the Most High created the universe to be in perfect harmony, when shifted out of equilibrium it will react to realign itself to restore a steady plane. Our environment is called destruction by design; man's superego manipulating the very understanding of the laws of nature, trap setting I call it, reaping havoc in our communities.

Not understanding the Divine Law as a youth, we bullied and forced individuals to do and commit acts that weren't in their thought pattern. Back then, terms like, 'You're going out there' or 'Man's sending you out for me' were used. Looking back, I know it was wrong to force someone else to commit an act that kept oneself out of trouble, whilst putting their life in danger, but misplaced pride and lack of self-love can make the worst of actions seem ok. However, nothing is hidden from the universe and I was definitely going to find out about karma and the repercussions of one's actions. Today I thank the Most High for the lesson learnt; it could have been worse.

I don't even member if I had even reached my teens when a friend from South Kilburn and I took a youth out to do something illegal for us. He was someone I'd made do wrongs for me on numerous occasions. It was a smart way of not getting into trouble myself I thought. He wasn't the only one, and I believe the constant bullying, manipulation and abuse for him was enough and maybe it was for the others too, but he was the tool the universe was going to use to give me a lesson. Because when he did what he did, I stopped mistreating everyone and never bullied again. In fact, I began to hate bullies myself. From nowhere he had pulled out a bat, whether it was a rounders or small baseball bat was irrelevant, my nose bridge had been severely broken, one hit across my face, perfect timing I didn't even see it coming. Knocking me out in the process, this surprise hit came from nowhere, I least expected it, especially from him. The funny thing about it, he was a youth who would hide every time he saw me, but this time he made it too easy for me to catch him when I chased him. In my greed and twisted frame of mind, all I could see was money and not that he was lay waiting for one of my friends or me, but then I believe the underlying issue was more than just the money, because that was never my drive as a youth. The money was definitely a factor, but not the *key factor* for my behaviour. Bullying gave me a false sense of control and power, where mine had been stripped from me within the home. The abused becoming the abuser, mimicking my stepfather's ways relieved my pain in a weird and unproductive way. I guess the universe understood that too, nevertheless a broken nose was a small price to pay. This was my karma for bullying and a lesson well learnt.

Chapter 47:
Receiving End

S eeing inmates acting up all the time over the years and thinking about road situations and my childhood errors, even the thought of adults out there in the world, for many who were troubled like me, during the moment of anger, inflicting pain on others felt good. Some may even try justifying it, not understanding why they feel so good, as if they really don't care about another person's emotion, or the consequences of their actions. Not everyone will admit it, or even understand the adrenaline rush they get, but there's a feel-good factor about releasing anger, even though no one ever really wants to be on the receiving end. Trauma may enter one way and leave or display in another, this is a reality and society has created a very vicious cycle. It doesn't take a genius to work this out; just looking at the reactions of individuals during their violent outburst paints a picture of what is going on in their mind. A moment of chaos can seem like such a release to the aggressor, while the mind of someone passing by or the receiver of pain gasps in terror. Most of these actions can be filtered down to one's life experiences and needs, whether lack of emotional or psychological needs, or just one's physical greed, it all boils down to the image of an illusion triggering from one person to another. Has society failed us, indeed it has, and purposely does, let's be clear; society is in total chaos; teaching about rules and regulations, while painting a picture of lawlessness. We are grown in a society wherein hardship for the majority is an everyday part of life, emotions are numbed and pain is forever before our eyes. As generations continue to unfold, the image of illusions worsens, expanding the realm of confusion blurring the lines of right and wrong. Again, emotions are numbed, pain and sorrow are forever before our eyes, affecting the way we see life. With all respect to whatever good is taught in the home, society offers something else, and even that filters into the home creating dysfunctional families, subliminally or consciously. Social distractions and technological dysfunctions are on the warpath. Is there really any way of protecting our young if they see dysfunction in the home, desire to watch, play or seek after these outlets of mass destruction and confusion offered by society. There are so many things to factor into why people find themselves aggressive, angry and short tempered. Issuers of pain, whether psychologically or physically, yet hating to receive, though we constantly do. The whole setup is a destructive cycle in itself. People need to change the way we think, society will never help us to do this, it must come from within. Yet it isn't easy for one to disconnect from this mindset, when social media and our environment plays a key role.

Prison blessed me with the time to reflect on my issues, to overcome them wasn't ever going to be an easy task when I really analysed myself. What I was now glad for was that I had come to the realisation of my errors, and only by acknowledging they existed was there any chance I could address them. Many of us front, portray, clothe ourselves with this false shield of protection believing we're helping our emotions, really believing we're in control, but in truth, we're feeding into our very own hurt or past trauma and not dealing with the situation. Yet we expect our youth to understand the errors of *their* ways when many adults haven't even dealt with their own. The receiving effect is something no one can escape in society. We all receive in some way a level of pain and trauma. Whether it's directly or indirectly, many times our false protective mechanism, some may call it ego, or lack of insight to the depth of our problem, has us saying we don't care, or just running from the reality which then permits us to continue inflicting pain on others, and so therefore it comes back to us. The never-ending receiving cycle; we have to protect our youths. As a child, no one protected me, at least not in the way I needed, but then everyone was caught up in his or her own deception, so who really could have. No two troubles are the same, but every trouble has a reflection, which manifests differently depending on how one looks into the mirror. I had expressed my anger in many ways, swore I didn't care, just as I saw adults say they didn't care about things, loved ones, partners, hiding behind their egos, pride, fear and false shields to protect their emotions, of course it trickles down the generational line. Then I saw the same false notions on TV and via music. I learnt to protect my illusions too and issue pain, releasing anger because I was on the receiving end and in so doing sometimes acted as if I didn't care, even if it was during that moment of time only. Trained to be numbed and disconnected from feeling truly alive.

Nobody really wants to be on the receiving end of any form of pain, and we only give it to protect ourselves in this false shield of comfort. Society has us all messed up. Addressing this mindset from personal experience, I'm sure many can relate when I say I've uttered and thought the words 'I don't care' a million times. I don't care what happens to me, I don't care what happens to you, I don't care if I died, if you die, I don't care if I go jail. I think most youths both street and non-street, even adults, not to leave them out, because this behaviour is generational, they can definitely relate to these words. But the truth is we do, we care a whole lot. The truth is we hate to be on the receiving end, and therefore issue out pain via anger and not really think of the consequences. Years of training and society have numbed our sense of reality and life, removed far from our true purpose of why we are here.

Of course, we care, but we are conditioned to act and respond out of fear and other low vibrations that keep this cycle spinning.

If we as humans really didn't care, some couples would never make it, some friendships wouldn't see the light of day, jobs and careers would be affected, this is just on a physical level. If I really didn't care what happened to me as a youth if I went to jail or died, why then did I run from the police, or during any moment I thought my life was going to be taken why not stand there and let the outcome be? Of course, I cared, and so do these youths who are also caught up in their emotions, tied to an illusion of expressions connected to anger and other feelings stemming from being a receiver of some sort of trauma. Pain for some, like myself may be that deep it's mutated and binds to their DNA. The point I'm making here is, we've all got work to do on ourselves. We need to stop giving to stop receiving and vice versa, learn how to positively channel when one receives to enable oneself not to give back negativity, which is harder than it sounds.

Chapter 48:
Freedom Street

I couldn't believe I was heading home. Almost eight years had come and gone, seven years and ten months to be precise. I was incarcerated from 1998 to 2006; no longer counting days, I was counting hours and minutes. I was so excited yet humbled, thoughtful and extremely thankful. I had not only survived the Jamaican prison system, but was leaving there mentally in a better frame of mind than that when I'd entered. Over the years, I had witnessed the impact of the system, and how it affected some inmates causing them to act out of character, even going crazy, and I mean *literally* crazy. During my last few months in Tamarind Farm, news came to me that a close friend from a ghetto in Kingston attempted to take his life in General Penitentiary, and ended up in the hospital wing under watch. This individual in my eyes was solid as a rock; a real warrior on the road, but circumstances out of his control had affected his mental wellbeing and caused him not to want to live anymore. He wasn't the first inmate that I knew to feel or even attempt the act of committing suicide, but because of our affiliation, it hurt me. Not to compare our strengths but to count my blessings is the grounds upon which the basis of this acknowledgement is made. He had come to prison and seen me in GP. I was incarcerated before him, and to know I went through so much and not only did the Most High protect my life and allow me to find the God in me, but also helped me to manifest talents and nurture skills that were dormant within, for . that I am grateful. I had seen strength in me like never before, overcoming sorrow and hurt from not only my surroundings, but also my youth, accepting responsibility where I played my role or could have done differently. Would I be here mentally thinking like this if I were still on road, I questioned myself; as I sat waiting for the warders to do their search of my belongings and for my paperwork to exit the prison. The unknown is what it was and I couldn't dwell there stuck in the unknown. Would I have found myself, lost myself further, been incarcerated in the UK or even dead, none of it mattered. It's easy to live in the past so I can walk with blame, or think to the future so I don't have to worry about my current situation, but the truth of the matter was where I stood. Before me was only a gate between freedom and incarceration and I was walking out of the gate a better person than when I had entered, nothing more nothing less. I had served time for my crime and concluded that always facing and battling with self is the greatest war that exists, everything else is based on an illusion.

Looking back on inmates as I stood by the car that was to take me to the airport, I didn't see prisoners incarcerated in the system, I saw men who were prisoners to their own selves. Held captives by their own mindset, their own frustrations, anger, pain and sorrows, stemming from their youth or adulthood, all relating to experiences in life, then I asked myself, I wonder how many of them really knew and understood it too.

Chapter 49:
Unpredictable Future

From the moment I stepped off the plane at Heathrow airport, I experienced my first challenge with the outside world. The airport staff questioned me about my entry documents, in calm but eager manner I explained my situation and the excitement that awaited me at the arrivals. My passport expired whilst I was incarcerated. I had the option of getting a new one issued the embassy explained, but I had no desire to stay another day on the island of the sun, so I opted for a letter of citizenship instead of a passport. This choice and emotion weren't based on anger or any negative vibe, it was all about returning to see my two beautiful children who had also been serving time on the outside, they also needed to be set free, to begin their own healing process, readjust their own lives and grow. Throughout my flight, all I could think about was seeing my son and daughter who I knew would be there at the airport. If at any time in my life I really had to show determination now was the time, the time to really live the truth I had begun to find. To seek the peace I sort and found, which was accompanied by pain that had awoken a sleeping man and given hope to a lost child.

Life wasn't easy; nothing on the outside was the same, not that I expected it to be. I had opportunity after opportunity since my release to get my hands dirty but I refused. I was determined never to put my children or myself through similar circumstances if I could avoid it. Since my release I have also reunited with my big son in Jamaica who I am totally proud of, his mother and I are not the best of friends but we do have a respectable relationship today, which is so important in my eyes, I love my son, I love all my children. The Most High has blessed me with four beautiful little daughters since I've been free and I am truly thankful. I get to experience with them the priceless gift called time, which I was unable to do with their elder siblings, due to my actions. You can never get back what you missed, but you can begin to enjoy what you have now, and so I do, I enjoy every minute I get with my children.

Many trials, tests and tribulations from the moment I stepped back into the UK have presented themselves but I was determined to walk after a new life. In fact, so determined, for the first few years I kept away from my old neighbourhood, places and people I hung with, as I gathered strength on the path I was now walking. It wasn't easy, mentally, physically nor financially but with every obstacle I overcame I became stronger within, to the point that when I did see old associates, they would tell me positive things they see about me, and that too reinforced my vigour.

During those early years of tests, I had gone from Minnie's couch to attaining a one bedroom flat in Harrow where I would lay low. The following year I went to college and obtained an Access to Sports Science graduating with the highest marks in the class, not bad for someone who got booted out of four high schools and never graduated school at all, much less leave with a GCSE. While in the process of doing my Access to Sports Science, I achieved other sports related qualifications and a fitness instructor certificate, something about which to feel proud. For a time I worked at numerous gyms, and stopped after my first year of Higher Education to focus on university where I graduated with a bachelor's degree in Sports Rehabilitation in 2011. Faced with numerous trials and problems during university including the loss of an unborn child during exam time, my head was all over the place, but I kept pushing. Some of my problems I could have avoided, nevertheless acceptance of responsibility on my part willed me on.

Faced with death twice via motorbike accidents, one of which caused me back problems, the other damage to my leg, shoulder and elbow upon which I needed an operation, none of this stopped me. In fact, it fuelled me and became the catalyst for me to type out the poems and romance novel that I wrote in prison. In addition, to write my first street novel titled *'I'm a Gun'*, which is a metaphorically written crime novel based on the violent streets of London, telling crime from a gun's perspective. The book was well received and at a later date I went on to make a documentary based on the same title.

In 2012, after both motorbike accidents my focus changed, even though I still worked within the fitness and health industry, the passionate desire for history and culture, that which aided my transformation called out to me from deep within and I answered willingly and joyfully. From the moment I answered, I haven't looked back and decided to make that long desirable trip to the Holy Land, which I was dreaming about during the days I was incarcerated, hoping and aiming to show the indigenous people of the land. On my various trips over the years to the Holy Land and other parts of North East Africa, such as Morocco, Egypt and Jordan, I have documented many things and have made numerous documentaries, including hard hitting visuals about the streets of Chicago and its relation to the violence in the UK, a topic which sits close to my heart, due to my very own experience of trauma and antisocial behaviour as a youth. I also had the opportunity of interviewing Chicago's very own congressman, Danny Davis. All of which are up on my YouTube Channel and website for free.

Coming from a very colourful background, I have been able to share my experiences and helped many aid themselves on their own journey. Not always an easy path, but it is one in which I find great pleasure. Today I revisit my love and passion for music, adding it to my ventures. Who knows what tomorrow will bring for me. Brother Malcolm said "Tomorrow belongs to those who plan for it today," on that note I desire to create and leave my legacy, at the same time enjoy the fruit of my labour, being a living legend.

As I seek to help others, I help myself. Through all that I do and share with the world, I am also feeding my inner being. I am grateful for all my experiences, even though I wouldn't wish them on my worst enemy. There is so much to my life, things that I would never unveil but fight in secret. Occurrences that have taken place hidden from man but not the Creator, regarding them as well as other issues of my youth I still face challenges today, and even maybe tomorrow. But the more I overcome, the greater I feel and such feeling can never be measured.

What is written for my path, the universe will unveil one day at a time, patience alone will aid me on my journey. For myself, only God knows what tomorrow brings.

If one is never taught to look within then we will go even faster in the wrong direction to achieve what we think we need, when in all reality one only needs to step back and take a moment to reflect from within.

Stephen Graham

Look out for this title

ONENESS

Redemption from Religious, Ancestral
& Psychological Trauma

STEPHEN
GRAHAM

Visit: stephengrahamprojects.com

Printed in Great Britain
by Amazon

80775240R00189